D1126013

BROWNING'S BEGINNINGS

The Northwestern University
Research Grants Committee
and the Andrew W. Mellon Foundation
have provided partial support
for the publication of this book.
The University of Minnesota Press
gratefully acknowledges
this assistance.

BROWNING'S BEGINNINGS

The Art of Disclosure

Herbert F. Tucker Jr.

UNIVERSITY OF MINNESOTA PRESS

Minneapolis

Herbert F. Tucker, Jr.
is assistant professor of English at
Northwestern University

Copyright © 1980 by the University of Minnesota.
All rights reserved.
Published by the University of Minnesota Press,
2037 University Avenue Southeast,
Minneapolis, Minnesota 55414

Library of Congress Cataloging in Publication Data

Tucker, Herbert F
    Browning's beginnings.

    Bibliography: p.
    Includes index.
    1. Browning, Robert, 1812-1889 — Criticism and
interpretation. I. Title.
PR4238.T8   821'.8   80-17727
ISBN 0-8166-0946-2

The University of Minnesota
is an equal-opportunity
educator and employer.

For Betsy, who makes the time

01039

01329

ACKNOWLEDGMENTS

One of the gratifying things about giving thanks, Fra Lippo Lippi suggests, is that it lets us find ourselves:

> *and you'll find the soul you have missed,*
> *Within yourself, when you return him thanks.*
> *"Rub all out!" Well, well, there's my life, in short,*
> *And so the thing has gone on ever since.*

I am glad to be able to thank a group of scholars and friends whose interest in this book has often kept me from rubbing all out, and whose generous advice has let the thing go on in better shape than it would otherwise have had.

It began as a doctoral dissertation written at Yale University under the direction of Leslie Brisman, and I cannot very well imagine what would have become of it without his tact and care. My reading of Browning takes its romantic origin in his, and I confess myself happily secondary to his example. The readers of the dissertation were Michael G. Cooke, A. Dwight Culler, and J. Hillis Miller, all of whom offered detailed responses from which I hope the book has profited.

In revision I have gratefully taken cues from a number of friends: Paul Breslin, Martin Brody, Mary Foote, Gerald Graff, Frank McConnell, Timothy Peltason, Fred Pfeil, Daniel Silver, Amy Spitzer, and Thomas Volet were kind enough to comment on all or part of the manuscript in various drafts. I owe special thanks to Susan Hawk Brisman, who provided a timely opportunity, and some timelier encouragement, for second thoughts about Shelley and Browning. My longest-standing debt is to William H. Pritchard: he not only taught me to read poetry closely, but later even furnished a place in which to write intermediate drafts of some of the close readings in this book.

W. David Shaw and Michael Hancher, who read the manuscript for the University of Minnesota Press, made valuable suggestions for the final revision. The editorial pains taken by Lindsay Waters and Marcia Bottoms have made it a pleasure to work with the Press. Kathleen

Beckerman, Estelle Frye, and Marjorie Weiner all assisted in the final typing of the manuscript.

A welcome subvention from the University Grants Committee of Northwestern University is helping to fund publication. And here at last I may give overdue thanks to the Danforth Foundation and the Mrs. Giles Whiting Foundation for grants that underwrote the writing of the dissertation.

My introduction incorporates in somewhat revised form an essay previously published in the fall 1976 issue of *Studies in Browning and His Circle*. A condensed version of the fifth chapter appears in *Critical Inquiry* for winter 1980. I thank the editors of both journals for their support.

A NOTE ON TEXTS

The Complete Works of Robert Browning with Variant Readings and Annotations, ed. Roma A. King, Jr., et al. (Athens, Ohio: Ohio University Press, 1969–1973), is cited for all of Browning's works (1833–1846) that have been published in that edition to date. Variant readings for these works, except where otherwise noted, are drawn from the Ohio edition, which is cited throughout as *Complete Works.* For Browning's subsequent works, beginning with *A Soul's Tragedy* (1846), the text cited is *The Works of Robert Browning,* ed. F. G. Kenyon (London: Smith, Elder, 1912). Except where otherwise noted, variant readings for *Men and Women* (1855) are drawn from Paul Turner's reprint of the original edition (London: Oxford University Press, 1972). Citations of Browning's *Essay on Shelley* (1852) are from *The Complete Poetic and Dramatic Works of Robert Browning,* ed. Horace E. Scudder (Boston and New York: Houghton Mifflin, 1895), which is cited throughout as *CPDW.*

TABLE OF CONTENTS

BROWNING'S BEGINNINGS

BROWNING AND THE FUTURE

*I am somewhat restive and averse to all prepared festivities:
the unforeseen is the dramatically excellent.*

Browning to Isa Blagden (1866)[1]

Browning wrote the poetry of the future, in at least two senses. The first sense is historical and has to do with his place in the literary canon as an influence on future poets. Within the Victorian era itself, Browning was an important precursor both of poets such as Rossetti and Swinburne, who confessed their admiration for his work, and of poets such as Hardy, Hopkins, and Yeats, who explicitly resisted him. In addition, Browning is generally acknowledged to be the Victorian poet who has exerted the greatest influence on poetry written in English during the present century. His concerns and sympathies were unquestionably in the mainstream of British romanticism, and his work has played a major part in determining new directions for romanticism during the last hundred years. He at once extended the technical resources of the romantic tradition in poetry, and broadened its topical range to embrace the extraordinary romance of fancy and fact in the rich particularity of ordinary living—if not quite a new project for romantic poetry, a project Browning managed to rejuvenate by approaching it in novel ways.

As a craftsman, Browning evolved an unmistakable style that has left its mark in one form or another on the work of most subsequent poets. He brought fresh prosodic roughness to nineteenth-century poetry, and he infused into its diction and syntax a colloquial vigor that often distressed his contemporaries but has prospered in an era pledged to wring the neck of rhetoric. Such technical innovations as these, moreover, bespeak Browning's special care for the coarse, grotesquely "unpoetical," bodily life of this world and of its common men and women. Thanks in part to his example, poets since Browning

3

have accorded unprecedented dignity to the mundane; they have paid more scrupulous attention than ever before to everyday life, the detailed complexity of which they have, in many respects, learned from him to appreciate as a subject for serious poetry and to incarnate in poetic form. Browning's influential techniques and attitudes combine in his chief legacy to modernist and contemporary poets, the dramatic monologue—a genre that he may not have invented but that he certainly made his own as a supple instrument for probing human motives and relations. Browning's pioneering development of the dramatic monologue did much to keep poetry alive in a time of rapid change and schism, a time that seems to resemble the present more closely the further it recedes into the past. Many of the major poems of Frost, Pound, and Eliot (to mention only the most prominent twentieth-century heirs) may be regarded as dramatic monologues continuing a tradition that Browning began.

This book has little to say about Browning's poetry of the future in this historical sense, which in any case might more accurately be termed "the future of Browning's poetry." It is concerned instead with Browning as poet of the future proper, the future as an appetite, a feeling, and a love that governs his writing above and beyond any given historical circumstances, whether those of his own period or of the lavishly imagined periods in which he set his diverse dramatis personae. Addicted to anticipation, Browning was a perpetual and knowing beginner. He kept beginning, both in the course of his innovative career and, as the following pages more specifically aim to show, in the course of any one of his distinctively nervous poems. His works not only initiated new movements in poetry; they took as their theme the difficulties and rewards of initiation itself, the issues confronting the man or woman—or poet—who would make a new beginning that keeps the future open. To study Browning's beginnings, then, is to define both a primary body of poetry for local analysis and a larger critical thesis to which analysis may refer. This book concentrates on the poet's comparatively neglected early poems and plays; and it seeks to identify in those works and in representative dramatic poems from his middle years a defense of anticipation, sustained through his elaboration of thematic and stylistic motives that inform his entire oeuvre.

Browning's defense of anticipation has a moral component and an aesthetic one, and the two components are intimately related. It is too well known to need substantiation here that as a moralist Browning champions the imperfect as the definitive note of the human condition: a promissory note, as it were, furnishing an earnest of future work and progress.[2] For Browning, if not indeed for everyone, the sense of the future entails the sting of unrest in the present. In

Browning's temporal economy the anticipation of something yet to be is no mere compensation for present dissatisfaction; his thirst for the future is so strong that the apparent compensation in effect prepays and insures the loss. The imperative of expectation demands that the present always be found wanting. If there is to be something to look forward to—and for Browning there must be that at all costs—then there must be something missing now. That is why Browning persistently explodes as illusory or cruel, as instinctively *wrong*, whatever presents itself as completion, triumph, or stability in the stories he tells or in the consciousnesses he imagines. His goals, once attained, are invariably disappointing and are often ruined by the very act of attainment, so that they become in turn conditions of imperfection furnishing grounds for renewed desire and progress. The thoroughly provisional value of a Browningesque goal consists not in the gratifying sense of possibility fulfilled, but in the more purposeful fulfillment that Browning discovers in the sense of possibility itself.

A central argument of this book is that Browning's moral doctrine of incompleteness finds a clear aesthetic analogue in his poetics. From the formal effects of its largest structures to the minutiae of its verbal style, Browning's is an art of disclosure, an art that resists its own finalities. He typically prolongs the curious action of his longer poems and his plays through strategies that defer and thus continually anticipate what another author might make the narrative or dramatic climax. Often at the end of these works the expected deed remains uncommitted, the complex issue unresolved, so as to suggest a residue of action exceeding the formal and temporal limits of the plot. In Browning's lyric poems, likewise, the traditional weight of closure feels less like exhaustive aplomb than like a force temporarily compressing a spring that remains tensed for further speech. Such tension may be located in Browning's reader as well as in his speaker, and it is essential to an understanding of Browning's dramatic irony to see irony as a way of composing a question for the reader's benefit without resolving it. Those occasions where a poem does snap shut, where action or speech does appear to have played itself out satisfactorily, are usually also those occasions where Browning's irony emerges at its strongest. Browning forges poetic forms that dramatize the relationship of accomplishment to desire, of heritage to initiative, and of present to future. Far from eschewing the closural resources of traditional poetic form, he uses those resources for the purpose of calling attention to closure in order to question its validity and worth.

Validity and worth to whom? To any and all who seek, the Browningesque moralist would answer; and the cultural historian would add, to a Victorian reading public whose faith in traditional religious and social compacts, and in the stability and inherent fitness

5

of things, was subjected over the course of the poet's career to increasingly rude shocks that sent readers for explanatory solace, among other places, to meetings of the Browning Society. Both responses are appropriate; yet, without dishonoring either of them, it should be possible to suggest another response that is more pertinent to the proper business of the literary critic. The principal beneficiary of Browning's moral and aesthetic philosophy of incompleteness may have been Robert Browning—not as a man of his era, but as a poet, especially a poet writing in what was to him inevitably a late romantic era. His intricate preservation of the future helped preserve his own future as a practicing poet; not least among its many uses, Browning's defense of anticipation offered a means of self-defense against that familiar hobgoblin of the poetic latecomer, the threat that there may be nothing left to say.

It is a moot point whether Browning wrote open-ended poems because as a moralist he wanted to affirm human possibilities or whether he adopted a philosophy of possibility because he wanted to keep writing poems. Although from time to time it may be convenient to invoke one alternative or the other, to decide this question either way would be a naive pretense, untrue to the interpenetration of moral and aesthetic impulses within Browning (as within any poet worth study) and untrue to the task of explicating the relations of form and content which remains, amid all debate, at the heart of the critical enterprise. To exalt either form or content, either morals or aesthetics, at the expense of the other would be particularly naive in view of recent developments in critical theory and practice. Three contemporary critics deserve special mention here, because their original and exemplary attention to the relations of literary form and content has advanced the general understanding of poetry, and because their strikingly different perspectives on issues of poetic timing converge in a richly complementary way for the study of Browning's beginnings.

Barbara Herrnstein Smith's *Poetic Closure* rapidly transcends an apparently formalist bias, as the best formalist criticism always does, and rises to challenging speculation about the stop-and-go of poetry, about the play of expectation, satisfaction, and surprise as they are orchestrated by the craft of poets and apprehended in the experience of readers.[3] Although her concern with "strong" or "successful" closure leads her to omit much consideration of nineteenth-century poetry (and to overlook Browning almost entirely), Smith repairs the omission in a final discussion of the anticlosural tendency of poetry since the romantic period, which she interprets as a formal change of fashion evincing a cultural change of heart. The manifestations of such an anticlosural tendency in Browning's verse constitute the subject of the discussions of poetic form in the present study. Its concerns

6

are in effect Smith's concerns turned inside out; and in examining Browning's literary art, despite some obvious differences in sympathy, this book silently adopts many of the assumptions and methods capably articulated in hers.

A critic much more directly in sympathy with Browning's romanticism is Harold Bloom, whose theories of poetic influence and revisionism have appeared over the past decade in a series of books flanking *The Anxiety of Influence*.[4] Bloom's "antithetical" criticism seems indeed antithetical to Smith's, and in many respects the two critics do move in contrary directions. Of Smith's readerly patience and responsiveness to the nuances of poetic form there is almost nothing in Bloom's recent criticism. At his quintessential and persuasive best, he succeeds instead in the unlikely project of approaching a poem not from the standpoint of its reader, but from the reimagined standpoint of the poet who wrote it. Smith's "weak" closure is precisely what Bloom deems "strong." The prospective imperfection with which Browning's poems typically end represents for Bloom the ultimate poetic strength; the "transumption" whereby a poet overcomes his belatedness is not a closural failure but an assertion of the power of origination. Bloom has shown how his ideas might bear on Browning with provocative discussions of several of the dramatic monologues; and, insofar as the present study provides an account of Browning's imagination, of the spirit behind the poetic form, it is an attempt to follow Bloom's lead.

Despite pervasive differences in approach and emphasis, Smith and Bloom share a certain common ground on which the critic of Browning's poetry may stand. Each of them refreshes a reader's conviction that a state of mind implies a way of stating, and vice versa: that any aesthetic, deeply considered, will disclose a moral position, and that no morality is without its aesthetic side. Bloom revives the traditional idea of poetic "argument": the term lets him treat at once the structure of a poem and the dynamics that generate it, whether the dynamics of a speaker's internal quarrels or of a poet's disagreements with tradition. Smith similarly aims to embrace the structural and semantic features of poetry in a single view: her analyses of what makes a poem stop elicit observations about what makes a poem go, and in these observations her criticism frequently approximates a sense of "argument" like Bloom's. Both critics are exceptionally sensitive to allied formal and thematic forces that make for extension or termination in poetry. More often than not they each attend to forces of quite different kinds; one would not consult Smith on rhetorical tropes, for instance, or Bloom on prosody. But the two critics concur in fostering a temporal reading—a reading that, mindful that poetry is a temporal medium, keeps watch over the course of a given poem in time.

In this they concur as well with Browning, who in the *Essay on Shelley* (1852) praised his influential forerunner for contriving "an embodiment of verse more closely answering to and indicative of the process of the informing spirit . . . than can be attributed to any other writer whose record is among us."[5] Particularly when confronting Shelley, Browning had reason to be aware of the connections between reading and writing; here he acknowledges the complementary priorities of the two activities. Verse *answers* to spirit: like Bloom, Browning urges a reader to reimagine the moment of composition, when the informing spirit precedes the embodying form. But verse also *indicates* spirit: like Smith, Browning recognizes that, in the experience of reading, it is form that has the prior claim. Finally, both content and form, the informing spirit and the answering embodiment of verse, exist for Browning in *process*. The endeavor to appreciate the sort of poetry Browning admired in Shelley, and for his own part went on to write, has repeatedly to contend with the processionality of such poetry, the pulse of its life in time. Smith and Bloom offer mutually illuminating methods for reading such poetry and for thinking with respect and precision about the temporal issues it raises.

Exploration of the temporal issues of Browning's romanticism can find further aid (aid more distant but potentially wider in scope) in the school of "deconstructionist" criticism headed by Jacques Derrida. Derrida's *L'écriture et la différence* and *De la grammatologie* outline a thoroughgoing semiotics in which all experience is textual and is constituted in the play of an anarchic and atelic tissue of signs.[6] According to the rhetorical conversions of Derridian analysis, every signifier points to a signified that deconstruction reveals to be yet another signifier. All text thus proves to be commentary, and every center the margin of an absence; in Derrida's favored temporal terms, every origin bears traces disputing its originality, and the venerable mystique of origins consequently migrates to the trace itself. That such ideas are fruitful for the study of nineteenth-century literature should cause no surprise; for all his modernity, Derrida writes in a nineteenth-century philosophical tradition, as a disciple of Hegel and Nietzsche. His thinking about the originary nature of the trace, for example, can illuminate the hermeneutics of Christian apologists in England from Coleridge onward as they responded to the challenge of the Higher Criticism, the Continental deconstruction of its day. It can also illuminate the interpretive dilemmas and opportunities that greet Browning's characters as they strive to decipher the signs of religion, art, and love.

Of particular help in the study of Browning is Derrida's term *différance*, a coinage that puns on the French verb meaning both "differ" and "defer," to describe the process of representation whereby lan-

8

guage displaces and postpones indefinitely the verities it ostensibly signifies. The rhetorical troping of figurative language represents the absent object by re-presenting it, making it present in a different way. In such a process, which is essential to poetic language itself, Browning finds one of his surest defenses against the semantic or metaphysical foreclosure of meaning. Moreover, the analysis of Browningesque psychology in the following chapters proposes another turn of meaning's press and screw by working an auxiliary pun on "defer." Browning's characters tend to place themselves in secondary or deferential postures; by deferring to their ideals or to each other, they defer to the future and thus heighten the climate of anticipation in which Browning's poetry thrives. Juxtaposing the senses of temporal deferral and emotional deference not only can show how the oddities of Browning's characters have a place in his poetry of the future, it can give to the formidably dispassionate tone of much deconstructionist theory a welcome human resonance. Deconstructionist criticism has generally slighted character analysis, probably because the notion of "character," with its assumptions about the coherence and continuity of the self, is among the fictions of integrity that it is the avowed business of deconstruction to put (and often enough to leave) in question. Here, at least with regard to Browning, deconstruction's gain may be literary criticism's loss. Browning certainly believed in the self, and for that very reason he was able to prize the diversity of its habits. His work begins with the self—albeit the self thoroughly nested in the mediations of "a most clear idea of consciousness / Of self" (*Pauline* [1833], 269-70)—and it would be a strange book, on this of all poets, that disregarded his imaginative construction of compellingly self-conscious personalities. The present study has frequent recourse to the procedures and lexicon of Derrida, in the hope that, without discarding "character" as a workable category, a deconstruction of Browning's characters may suggest how and why the poet constructed them in the first place.

STYLE: PUTTING THE INFINITE WITHIN THE FINITE

In Shelley's poetry, and by implication in his own, Browning values poetic forms that answer closely to "the process of the informing spirit." When that process intends an attack on the closural constraints of form, as it does with Browning, the problem of style is apt to arise with particular insistence. Since its first publication, Browning's poetry has aroused charges of stylistic obscurity. Even at present, in a time that has weathered and for that matter canonized the difficulties of modernist poetry, Browning's early works retain their notoriety. Though many of the poet's better-known monologues are scarcely less "obscure" than the early works, the charge of obscurity is in some measure justified; and it will be helpful to address it here, first in general terms and then by seeing how on one occasion Browning addressed it himself. Browning's obscurity proceeds from a principled evasiveness that is utterly in keeping with his attitudes toward form and with his governing orientation towards the future. He makes his style slippery with the consistent purpose of avoiding any structural or semantic enclosure that would dim the sense of the future with which he identifies his poetic mission.

Radically introductory, or (as it sometimes seems) acutely claustrophobic, Browning's art of disclosure posits a fundamental kinship between the act of initiation that his poetry variously describes and the act of writing that begins or sustains a poem. The sense of inauguration holds immense significance for Browning, for a number of interdependent reasons that were suggested above. It is the burden of his discontinuous style to enforce this sense of inauguration by inaugurating its reader. A reader soon learns that in Browning's text any turn of phrase may signal a turn away from what has come before, a fresh departure asserting the poet's right to begin afresh and demanding a correspondingly fresh orientation in the reader. Swinburne may have had such tactics in mind when with eminent practicality he advised readers to meet Browning punctually in "the freshest, clearest, most active mood of the mind in its brightest and keenest hours of work."[7] The metrical bumps and semantic twists of Browning's pied style express, and labor to create in his reader, the poet's faith that the range of human possibilities knows no ultimate bound and that the properly human attitude is therefore one of anticipation. Hence the genuine difficulty of Browning's style, and hence its rationale.

Browning thought his poetry provided its own best rationale, and for a major nineteenth-century poet he was uncommonly chary of explaining it in other terms. He abstained from paraphrase and theoretical discussion of his poetry with a reluctance—or was it confidence?—that is matched only by Tennyson's, and that may indeed surpass Tennyson's when one considers that Browning remained a comparatively misunderstood and unsupported writer from the 1830s well into the 1860s. The lights shed on his own work by his prefaces and notes, and by his prose essays on Chatterton and Shelley, are sidelights at best; and in an enormous volume of literary correspondence with his associates, his friends, and even his wife-to-be, one finds fitful gleams but nothing approaching a coherent explication of his practice.

Perhaps the most illuminating gleam anywhere in Browning's prose was struck by a letter John Ruskin sent him on 2 December 1855 after a late night spent puzzling over the recently published *Men and Women* with D. G. Rossetti, who was already one of the few ardent Browningites. Ruskin's letter focuses on the lyric "Popularity"; after firing dozens of queries and complaints about the poem's meaning and manner of proceeding, Ruskin comes up at last with an image no reader of Browning is liable to forget:

> Your Ellipses are quite Unconscionable: before one can get through ten lines, one has to patch you up in twenty places, wrong or right, and if one hasn't much stuff of one's own to spare to patch with! You are worse than the worst Alpine Glacier I ever crossed. Bright, & deep enough truly, but so full of Clefts that half the journey has to be done with ladder & hatchet. However, I have found some great things in you already, and I think you must be a wonderful mine, when I have real time & strength to set to work properly. [8]

In its intelligence, persistence, and mingled attraction and resistance to the poem in question, Ruskin's letter entitles him to stand in for any first reader of Browning. Browning's beginning readers need every ladder and hatchet at their disposal, as they negotiate a stylistic terrain continually requiring "stuff of one's own" and prompting them to ask with more or less perplexity the question that concludes another poem from *Men and Women*, "Master Hugues of Saxe-Gotha": "Do I carry the moon in my pocket?"

Not just the beginner, but any reader of Browning whatsoever may profit from the reply he sent Ruskin some days later:

> We don't read poetry the same way, by the same law; it is too clear. I cannot begin writing poetry till my imaginary reader has conceded licences to me which you demur at altogether. I *know* that I don't make out my conception by my language, all poetry being a putting the infinite within the finite. You would have me paint it all plain out, which can't be; but by various artifices I try to make shift with touches and bits of outlines which *succeed* if they bear the conception from me to you. You ought, I think, to keep pace with the thought tripping from ledge to ledge of my "glaciers," as you call them; not stand poking your alpenstock into the holes, and demonstrating that no foot could have stood there;—suppose it sprang over there? [9]

"All poetry being a putting the infinite within the finite." One seizes on this absolute phrase as the nearest thing in Browning to a commitment that might serve as the foundation for a general poetics. But the phrase is forbiddingly abstract in itself, and it will be best understood after a consideration of its context. The purpose of Browning's response to Ruskin is to defend stylistic obscurity as a means to spirited illumination. It should be noted that, while Ruskin's letter compares Browning to a craggy glacier, Browning takes the glacier to stand not for himself, but for his poems. He silently revises Ruskin's image in order to distinguish himself and his "conception" from the work that is its trace. This revision allows him to relocate meaning not *in* the poem, as an object one stands and pokes at, but *through* the poem, as a method or series of signs that one actively traverses. Only in springing from sign to sign does a reader recover the poet's "conception"; only in granting a wide poetic "licence" does a reader fulfill the "law" of Browingesque reading. Browning's imaginary reader must also be a highly imaginative one, whose pursuit of meaning retraces and in effect recreates the poet's prior pursuit, of which the poem itself is a various and artful record. Browning's letter offers an intriguing parallel with a passage from *Sordello* (1840), which describes Sordello's poetic improvisation in similar terms of "keeping pace":

> On flew the song, a giddy race,
> After the flying story; word made leap
> Out word, rhyme—rhyme; the lay could barely keep
> Pace with the action visibly rushing past.

(II.84-87)

The resemblance is striking between the poet's activity here and the reader's in Browning's letter. Not only does the poet pursue his flying story and record it in language, but as he listens to his words and rhymes they beget fresh words and rhymes. The poet becomes his own first reader, with an exemplary, secondary creativity that anticipates Browning's recommendation to Ruskin, and also anticipates the acts of reading that begin poems as different as "By the Fire-side" (1855) and *The Ring and the Book* (1868-1869), in which deep calls to deep through a readerly re-vision of the signs of the past.

The recreative leap that Browning's "various artifices" compel his reader to share receives figuration throughout his career in the image of the walk or ride: the tour through the landscape with Pauline, the gallop from Ghent to Aix, the rides of Childe Roland and of the lovers in "The Last Ride Together," the grammarians's funeral procession, Thamuris marching, Pheidippides racing, the walk with Gerard de Lairesse and the march of Charles Avison in the late *Parleyings*. These and other excursions are filled with the processional music—whether jaunty swing or struggling tread—that the ear remembers Browning by. They may also serve as reminders of a semantic counterpart to Browning's versification: meaning for Browning is always processional, current, eventual. Meaning occurs *by the way*, not because it is only incidental to Browning's work, but because it is an incident, some-

12

thing that happens in poetic time. The Browningesque pursuit of meaning draws his reader out, and the root sense of "education" as a drawing out chimes appropriately with a passage later in the letter to Ruskin in which the poet says of his poetry that "it is all teaching." Browning aims to move his reader, with works whose meaning is in their motion. That is why, paradoxically, his poetry is at any given moment so intensely tactile and vivid—so much "upon us," as Henry James finely described it—and at the same time so mobile in its preoccupation with the future.[10] Browning's poetry *succeeds*, in the term his letter underscores, through succession, as an art purposefully bound to time.

This paradox of an art that is at once intimately present and compellingly anticipatory answers to the paradox in Browning's definition of poetry as "a putting the infinite within the finite." Perhaps any proposition will be paradoxical that asserts a relationship between the infinite and the finite, the boundless and the discrete; and Browning's word "putting" heightens the paradox and pushes it towards nonsense by inviting Ruskin to imagine the impossible task of containing what by definition cannot be contained. In order to redeem the sense of Browning's definition, it is necessary to discard the ludicrous spatial metaphor and to reconceive his suggestion in temporal terms. That, after all, is what Browning's entire letter encourages Ruskin to do: to reconceive poetic meaning as a process instead of an entity and to take the gaps in Browning's poem, the very obstacles to understanding that Ruskin's letter complains about, as occasions for "tripping from ledge to ledge." Furthermore, time, not space, is the dominant mode of poetry, particularly poetry written in the tradition of evangelical and romantic iconoclasm from which Browning came even more decidedly than did Ruskin.

For both writers a commanding figure in that tradition was Wordsworth, who found a reprieve from the tyranny of the eye by attending to the ear and its music of humanity. Browning meant to repudiate Wordsworth in "The Lost Leader" of 1845, and a year later he wrote to Elizabeth Barrett that "I could not get up enthusiasm enough to cross the room if at the other end of it all Wordsworth, Coleridge & Southey were condensed into the little China bottle yonder."[11] But Browning could not have followed his chosen master Shelley as long as he did without perceiving Wordsworth's importance, and the "Prologue" to *Asolando* (1889), Browning's last volume, begins by picking a quarrel with the "Intimations Ode" that the poet resolves in quite Wordsworthian terms, preferring "the purged ear" over "the eye late dazed." In any case, it is not as a source for Browning's letter but as an illustration of its ideas about

13

the "infinite" that the following passage is offered from Wordsworth's discussion of imagination in *The Prelude*:

> Our destiny, our being's heart and home,
> Is with infinitude, and only there.
> With hope it is, hope that can never die,
> Effort, and expectation, and desire,
> And something evermore about to be.

(VI.604-8)

Wordsworth's lines enact precisely the revision of "infinitude" from
a spatial to a temporal concept that is required by Browning's letter
to Ruskin. At first apparently a place out "there," a center or goal,
"infinitude" enters into apposition with "hope" and thus becomes a
condition of mind: that mental state of "effort, and expectation, and
desire" in which goals are glimpsed and striven for—and in which,
incidentally, readers seek for fulfillment as they grapple with texts.
It is not with a sense of spatial transcendence or immanence but with
a sense of temporal imminence, of "something evermore about to
be," that greatness makes abode for Wordsworth. And there it also
abides for Browning, whose "infinite" describes not some eternal
realm above mutability, but the conviction of endlessness or processionality to which the careful imperfections of his art of disclosure
give poetic currency. "Putting the infinite within the finite" is the
task of the poet who plays his terminations against a faith that
knows no term: "Here were the end, had anything an end" (*The
Ring and the Book*, XII.1). Browning's "infinite" and his "finite"
need each other for mutual definition. Intimations of endlessness
support his intellectual skepticism about the finality of any argumen-
tative or formal conclusion that pretends to be more than a way of
putting it. Conversely, the Browningesque sense of an ending as a
threshold or frontier lends affective force to his thought of infinity
and preserves it from the stasis of abstraction.

Infinity, endlessness, incompleteness, unfulfillment, imperfection:
the words are unwieldy in their accumulated cancellations, but they
suggest a cardinal principle for Browning's poetry of the future.
Browning habitually affirms his positives, as these words do, by
negating the corresponding negatives; this habit, like much else in his
work, is due to a marked preference for transition and movement in
all things. Whatever the personal or political creeds of the man, the
poet in Browning cares as little for untrammeled liberty as for perfect bondage; and when his work presents such conditions it does so
with satiric intent. Browning's evident distaste for confinement
emerges, for example, in the image of distilled Essence-of-Lake-Poet
quoted above from his letter to Elizabeth Barrett and in the similar

14

image from "Popularity," in which "the extract, flasked and fine /
And saleable at last" (56-57), represents the stoppered wares of imitative, creatively stopped poets. Such gestures are to be expected of
an anticlosural poet; but as the next pages will suggest, Browning has
a comparable distaste for sheer freedom, which in its purity is a condition as static as its opposite. What interests Browning's imagination
is rather the transition to or from such conditions: the break into the
open or the trick of self-containment that marks so many of his
characters. Browning's is less an art of openness (like Whitman's,
perhaps, or that of some of Whitman's heirs) than an art of opening—
again, an art of disclosure.

By putting the infinite within the finite through the use of a style
that acknowledges its own insufficiency, Browning styles himself a
romantic poet in full pursuit of the sublime. Wordsworth identifies
poetic sublimity or "greatness" with the "strength / Of usurpation"
(*Prelude*, VI.599-600), and at its moments of greatness the protestant poetry of Browning also involves a "usurpation" or transgression
of given limits. Outburst and invasion are the definitive events of the
Browningesque sublime, and its characteristic images are the break
and the crossing. Sublimity for Browning entails not the traditional
sending up, but a sending out or a sending across. As with the images
of walking and riding discussed above, his poetry is most often horizontal in thrust, and it intensifies at moments when the negotiation
of a frontier marks a new beginning.[12] Meaning breaks into the lives
of his characters, as it breaks out of the phenomena in his world.
In " 'Transcendentalism: A Poem in Twelve Books' " (1855), "in
there breaks the sudden rose herself, / Over us, under, round us every
side, / . . . / Pouring heaven into this shut house of life" (40-45).
As Bishop Blougram tells the skeptical Gigadibs,

> *Just when we are safest, there's a sunset-touch,*
> *A fancy from a flower-bell, some one's death,*
> *A chorus ending from Euripides,—*
> *And that's enough for fifty hopes and fears*
> *As old and new at once as nature's self,*
> *To rap and knock and enter in our soul.*

("Bishop Blougram's Apology" [1855], 182-87)

Browningesque apprehensions of the future, the realm of hope and
fear alike, pour over the threshold of the soul at the point of risk
where old and new change places, where a terminal limit—a sunset,
a death, the ending of a chorus—becomes a beginning.

The foregoing remarks suffer from the abstraction that bedevils
summary introduction, and perhaps they too amply illustrate in
critical terms, and in a negative way, the worth of Browning's focus

15

on the concrete. Browning is a dramatic poet, and even the most delicately framed general discussion of his leading ideas will be of little help without consideration of the startling ways in which he can dramatize those ideas in verse. The rest of this book will make amends by adhering closely to the texts it studies, in the belief that Browning's writing—even when it is most "obscure," and often especially then—repays the most deliberate attention its readers can muster. The following analysis of a difficult but revealing passage from the elaborate close of *Sordello* is offered both as a secondary, more "dramatic" introduction to this book and as a sample of the analyses to come.

BROWNING, EGLAMOR, AND CLOSURE
IN *SORDELLO*

The sixth and final book of *Sordello* is filled with endings.[13] The first half of the book traces in detail the movement of Sordello's last thoughts; from the contemplation of a sunset panorama, Sordello passes through a retrospect of his past actions to an intense philosophical consideration of the proper ends of life itself. In closing with these ultimate issues, he meets his own end and dies. After an attempt at summing up his hero's career, Browning puts the finishing touches to his account of the Guelf and Ghibbelin wars, including a description of the last years of the warrior Salinguerra. Having thus disposed of his principal actors, Browning is left alone to confront an urgent question that has never been far from the narrative surface of this concluding book: the question of poetic closure.

In the course of the poem Browning has frequently reminded his audience that they are hearing not only the story of the poet Sordello, but Sordello's story *told* by the poet Browning (I.1,34,444,604; III.1023; VI.886). As a way of bringing his storytelling to an end, Browning turns for a final theme to storytelling itself. Such reflexive turns are common enough among sophisticated storytellers; Browning's manner of turning here, however, is so deeply characteristic of his procedure not only in *Sordello*, but throughout his poetry, that it merits a long and careful look. In confronting poetic closure, Browning breaks his uneasy solitude and recalls the spirit of Eglamor, a minor but dedicated poet of Mantua, who has died heartbroken at his defeat by Sordello in the poetic contest that opens Book II.

And Naddo gone, all's gone; not Eglamor!
Believe, I knew the face I waited for,
A guest my spirit of the golden courts!
Oh strange to see how, despite ill-reports,

16

Disuse, some wear of years, that face retained
Its joyous look of love! Suns waxed and waned,
And still my spirit held an upward flight,
Spiral on spiral, gyres of life and light
More and more gorgeous—ever that face there
The last admitted! crossed, too, with some care
As perfect triumph were not sure for all,
But, on a few, enduring damp must fall,
—A transient struggle, haply a painful sense
Of the inferior nature's clinging—whence
Slight starting tears easily wiped away,
Fine jealousies soon stifled in the play
Of irrepressible admiration—not
Aspiring, all considered, to their lot
Who ever, just as they prepare ascend
Spiral on spiral, wish thee well, impend
Thy frank delight at their exclusive track,
That upturned fervid face and hair put back!
    Is there no more to say?

(VI.797-819)[14]

The abrupt reappearance of Eglamor here is doubly significant. First, Eglamor embodies the spirit of closure itself; he is the formalist poet who has permanently, "safely," tamed and "fixed" the "power" of poetry in "bonds of rhyme," "In rhyme, the beautiful, forever!" (II.204-10). His is a decorous poetry of beginnings, middles, and ends, quite in keeping with the humility of his belief that "Man shrinks to naught / If matched with symbols of immensity" (VI.2-3). Eglamor's work consists in the patient "arrangement" of his materials (II.218), with the turning of finished verses:

        for he believed
Himself achieving all to be achieved
By singer—in such songs you find alone
Completeness, judge the song and singer one,
And either purpose answered, his in it
Or its in him.

(III.617-22)

Eglamor is naively devoted to a poetics of complete correspondence between fixed form and fixed meaning. This devotion has a psychological parallel: he completely identifies his own worth or "purpose," his personal meaning, with that of his formally faultless works. When in the contest at Mantua the song improvised by Sordello shows the limitations of such a purely formalist achievement, Eglamor finds his

17

purpose exhausted and decorously dies. Browning implies through his Eglamor's career that in the enclosure of meaning lurks death; that any perfectly, beautifully elaborated form may be a menacing form of death. As Browning approaches the completion of *Sordello*, the little death that is poetic closure, his claustrophobic worries are significantly represented in the return of his own fictive formalist.

Yet Eglamor's very fictiveness gives to his presence here a second significance. "And Naddo gone, all's gone; not Eglamor!" Naddo is the spirit of criticism, a literary Great Cham of Mantua, who has dispensed cautionary advice to both Eglamor and Sordello about building on the natural, general truths of "the human heart" (II.788): " 'Beware,' he said, / 'Of setting up conceits in nature's stead!' " (II.11-12).[15] At the close of Book V, Browning has granted immortality to Naddo's tireless labors: "Gone they are— / Palma, Taurello; Eglamor anon, / Ecelin,—only Naddo's never gone!" (V.1010-12). But in the passage from Book VI that grant is specifically revoked; it is Naddo who departs, while Eglamor remains. For Browning to dismiss Naddo and summon Eglamor is to upset a reader's commonsense expectations of narrative consistency and of the coherent "completeness" that such consistency would support. By reversing the apparently final facts of Book V, Browning insists upon their unnatural fictiveness and so maintains the first fact of his own creative authority.

With the summoning of Eglamor, Browning begins one of the least Eglamoresque passages of the poem. He interrupts the continuity of his storytelling to contradict himself; he finds his way not in obeying formal limits, but in transgressing them. The next word in the passage, "believe," seems both to acknowledge the contradiction in Eglamor's return and to justify it as a break in continuity that will let the poem continue. The word recalls Browning's originating injunctions to "believe," from the opening verse paragraph of the poem and from his many subsequent, prospective reminders that the reader who *will*, may hear Sordello's story told. In the line immediately preceding this passage, Browning has challenged his audience to "choose" between the importance of a recently exhumed Ghibellin skeleton and of modern techniques for silk fabrication (VI.790-96). The juxtaposition of these two items of "news" is Browning's oblique way of modulating between a corpus of historical material and a present process of remaking, between the story of Sordello and the story of the storyteller. In turning to the audience and having them "choose" which news is really new or "believe" in his right to revise his own story, Browning implicates the audience in the renewing of his narrative.

In the very act of welcoming Eglamor, the spirit of closure,

18

Browning finds a way of asserting his willingness to start all over again. The first lines of the passage are already busy anticipating and answering the question posed in the last: "Is there no more to say?" This is a question of the utmost importance, here and throughout Browning's work; his perennial answer is a resounding no. His poetry is shot through with the conviction that there is and must be more to say; that poetry must make provision for its own growth; that a poem pretends to enclose fullness of meaning only at its peril. The difficulty of this passage proceeds from Browning's attempt to come to terms with the necessity of formal closure without sacrificing the openness of meaning that may make future beginnings possible. Its difficulty is Browning's genuine, necessary difficulty in avoiding terminal origins, ways of opening that in fact lead to enclosures plausibly disguised.

Such an enclosure attends the opening gambit of the first line, if it is taken as sufficient in itself, rather than as an introduction of what follows. The simple reversal of the fates of Naddo and Eglamor offers itself too palpably to encapsulated interpretations like this one: "Eglamor at least fulfilled his nature to the extent of his capacities. His ability to love enabled him to act out his identity."[16] Even minor poetry like Eglamor's, one might say in the same vein, is better than Naddo's meddling criticism and Sordello's utter paralysis. But in saying so, one would be both premature and uninteresting. There must be more to say; this first line, Browning's break with his earlier narrative, should be read less as a statement of meaning than as a declaration of independence from conventional expectations, an expression of his governing intention to keep things open. This line is less about Naddo and Eglamor, that is, than about Browning's *Sordello*; an important part of its message is that a reader should pay attention and wait for what is to come.

It is interesting that in the following lines Browning takes upon himself attitudes (exemplary for his readers) of attention and surprise:

> *Believe, I knew the face I waited for,*
> *A guest my spirit of the golden courts!*
> *Oh strange to see how, despite ill-reports,*
> *Disuse, some wear of years, that face retained*
> *Its joyous look of love!*

A beginning may be recognized as a beginning because it disrupts continuity; it breaks with what has come before. Browning's opening tactic has been an instance of such a break. But it has been too pure an instance to stand alone: its simple reversal invites too comfortable a reading. In these lines Browning moves to a second tactic for banishing closure: he reaches out beyond the confines of the present to grasp at a future in which anticipation will be adequately realized. In the golden courts of poetry, the imaginative realms of gold where a poet can travel with the ease and freedom of a guest, where promises are fulfilled and correspondences complete, Browning says, "I knew the face I waited for." This confident assertion about the power of poetry seems as readily and insipidly "meaningful" as the opening gambit until it is qualified by what follows. The word "strange" introduces a disturbing difference that estranges promise from fulfillment, as it opens a temporal ambiguity between the verbs "knew" and "waited." Which comes first, knowing or waiting? Is Browning saying that he knew all along the face he was waiting for? If so, it is difficult to explain what he should find "strange" in the actual sight of "that face" as a face *retaining* its old, recognizably joyous look of love. If the knowing is prior, one must suppose that what Browning knew was that Eglamor's face would be different from what Browning had once known it to be. This would be a complicated way of "knowing" something or someone but, nevertheless, a way quite characteristic of Browning's poetry—a way, in fact, of which the reversal of the fates of Naddo and Eglamor has just reminded his reader.

Or does the waiting come first? Is Browning saying that he knew what he had been waiting for only after it had come to pass? That, after a wait long enough to include "ill-reports" and "some wear of years," his patience was rewarded with the sudden vision of a well-known face, "strange" because uncannily familiar? The ambiguity in Browning's "knew" and "waited" is that which is implicit in any recognition: it is an ambiguity that emerges from the gap between expectation and event. In the course of these lines, Browning's reader rediscovers that gap and learns to expect a surprising meaning that will differ from what has been anticipated. Whether the knowing or the waiting comes first, the action of this passage disperses the simple sense of a graspable future from which it has seemed to begin. The passage reposes instead in the one proposition about the future that supports both sides of its ambiguity: that the future will come in another form, and with another meaning, than can now be imagined.

The reversals and ambiguities of this passage thus enforce a paradox of reading: a lesson in the expectation of surprise, it consigns Browning's reader to a suspenseful limbo or "mean-time" in which the gratifications of narrative and semantic closure are deferred to the future. In writing so ambiguously about an imaginary encounter with his own creation, Browning also gives expression to a related paradox of writing. No poet invites inspection of the scene of his writing more urgently than does Browning in *Sordello*, where the

20

writer's primary domain is persistently depicted as the uncertain, unchartable future of what he is engaged in writing. Foremost among the talents that may gain him admittance to the golden courts is the talent of patiently waiting to recognize that which is in a sense already his but which he cannot yet know. In awaiting the face of Eglamor, a face that exists only in the text of his own poem, Browning figures his own situation as a poet. He waits to read what is utterly unknown to him and yet intimately familiar: what he himself will write. It is significant that Browning renders this situation as a fruitful suspension between past and future knowing, between memory and recognition. He waits to recall Eglamor's "face," to reimagine a "figure" that is also a purely fictive "figure" of speech. What Browning remembers will give him the future of this passage, and the lines he goes on to write will delineate a face that from its origin is already a figurative representation—asserted, as it were, in the face of an initial absence where "all's gone."

Earlier in the poem Browning has described Eglamor in a similar attitude of anticipation, "uncertain at the shrine / He knelt before, till, soothed by many a rite, / The power responded" (II.202-4). The poet is in attendance upon his own imaginative "power," a power that at the very moment of creation he imagines as external, as different from himself. To be sure, Eglamor attempts to enclose the meaning yielded by that power as soon and as completely as possible, while Browning seeks other "rites" or tactics that may keep meaning free. But for both poets, poetry depends upon the establishment of an original difference; they carefully place themselves at a remove from, and in a secondary position to, the inscrutable power by which they hope to speak. They deliberately differ from themselves and defer to the future that is their yet unwritten poetry. This displacement or postponement, this difference, this patient uncertainty at the shrine, is what enables them to write. Instead of irritably reaching after conclusive meaning, as Sordello has done throughout his career, Eglamor and Browning choose a secondary stance; in deferring to the future, they preserve an opening in which meaning may grow.[17]

If such a stance were in itself sufficient to banish closure, there would be no distinguishing Eglamor's way of meaning from Browning's, and the passage from Book VI might end with Browning's second tactic, the espousal of a wise passiveness. But Eglamor, for all his secondariness, is not patient enough; he so cultivates his art as to bring poetic meaning to a poor and early harvest. Browning's description in Book II suggests a reason why; for Eglamor, poetry is a "temple-worship" whose "ceremony" withdraws the "veil" hiding "the holy place" (II.197-200). Although Eglamor is deferential, he

21

envisions the power to which he defers as fundamentally static, and the ritual distance he maintains between the power and himself is as ceremonially fixed as are the conventional meanings of his verses. He conforms to the orthodoxy of "Naddo's notion" of imaginative inspiration (II.196): the patiently generated poetry that Eglamor writes is in an important sense already prescribed by convention. Thus "cloistered up," "a poor gnome," he keeps meaning close-nipped (II.215). Despite some "uncertainty," Eglamor's imagination remains quite firmly grounded, enshrined, and limited.

Browning's third tactical movement away from closure is an attempt to escape such groundedness. He turns from the face of Eglamor and gloriously scorns the ground itself in a grand proclamation of imaginative autonomy:

> Suns waxed and waned,
> And still my spirit held an upward flight,
> Spiral on spiral, gyres of life and light
> More and more gorgeous—ever that face there
> The last admitted!

Once again, what has looked like the desired opening turns into a trap. Browning's spirit frees itself from the solar cycle and its "wear of years" and soars with independent strength and mobility—into the enclosures of its own brightness, its own repetitively cycling spirals. The assonant and alliterative movement of Browning's verses enacts this captivating repetition. The long vowels of "spiral on spiral" extend their lineage through "gyres of life and light"; in the next line the alternative vowel sound "or" is no less tenacious and the alliterating l's become m's to no avail—the pattern of repetition repeats itself. Trapped in repetition, the poet can find "more to say" only by saying more of the same thing, even of the same sound. The word "still" often serves Browning as a mild pun linking temporal continuity and spatial fixity, and so it serves him proleptically here. In his zeal to achieve emancipation from all hindrances, Browning only imprisons himself in the "stillness" of unhindered continuity. His sheer soaring is a disastrous failure, bringing him to an impasse as threatening as those he has aspired to escape.

The return of Eglamor to interrupt the fourth of these lines betokens Browning's recognition of a threat of self-enclosure; assonance and alliteration belong, after all, among Eglamor's formalist tricks of "arrangement." As Browning recognizes in the surface of his own verses the familiar face of Eglamor, he checks himself and begins again. He initiates a fourth tactic, a brilliantly successful one for this passage and one that in various manifestations quickens much of Browning's finest work: a tactical and syntactical play between two

22

distinct but mutually dependent "spirits." When the phrase "ever that face there / The last admitted" interrupts and refreshes the repetitive poetic line, it performs stylistically the liberation from enclosing sameness that Eglamor's presence offers to the passage as a whole. A willfully self-revising poet, Browning is forever asking his reader to reconsider the beginnings of his poems or passages in view of what follows. Here the word "ever" dramatically opens the temporal frame of his encounter with Eglamor. Retroactively it gives to Browning's verbs the force not of the stable past tense, but of the imperfect, a tense that it is anything but frivolous to connect with the poet's philosophy of the imperfect.

The energies of vital process and anticipation that have given that philosophy its strong appeal to generations of readers now begin to charge these lines, which from this point are governed grammatically by absolute and participial constructions. In the absence of an anchoring main verb, the temporal design of the passage becomes slippery in the extreme, as ends start to leapfrog with beginnings. If Eglamor's face is *ever* the last admitted, then the renewing freshness it brings to Browning's soaring must itself be renewable. Browning's attitude of wise attentiveness ("I knew the face I waited for") is thus transformed into an active pursuit, its endlessness guaranteed by the imperfection of his knowing. He awaits Eglamor by chasing after him, and at the end of the chase he confronts not an enclosure, but a saving interruption, an opportunity to begin again. Even as he comes "last," Eglamor ever initiates a fresh pursuit. Here Browning discovers the groundless play he has been seeking and discovers it in the strangest way imaginable: in the regenerative entrance of his own spirit of closure.

The invocation of Eglamor lets Browning differ from himself in a new way. Eglamor has written his poetry by establishing a fixed difference between his formal talents as a writer and his own well-grounded "power" of imagination; his poems have exhibited the weakness of a timid orthodoxy. In this passage Browning establishes a stronger, groundless, and elastic difference of his own. He doubles himself into two spirits or poetical characters: "Eglamor," the Browning that must end *Sordello;* and the "I" of the passage, the Browning that must keep writing. Neither of these spirits subsumes the other. That is what makes their play in this passage possible, and their play, in one form or another, is what makes possible the disclosure of Browningesque meaning in general. The mutual distinctness of the two spirits is ensured by the fact that they can encounter each other — or, to adopt Browning's more difficult but accurate imperfect, by the fact that they can ever keep encountering each other. The more distinctly they can recognize each other as *other,* the more clearly they will assert their radical difference. Hence the increasing particularity

23

of the facial imagery as the passage unfolds from "the face," to "that face," to "that face there," to "That upturned fervid face and hair put back."

Browning finds his opening in doubling and so differing from himself. This wise duplicity is figured in the sustained grammatical ambiguity of the lines that follow:

> And still my spirit held an upward flight,
> Spiral on spiral, gyres of life and light
> More and more gorgeous—ever that face there
> The last admitted! crossed, too, with some care
> As perfect triumph were not sure for all,
> But, on a few, enduring damp must fall,
> —A transient struggle, haply a painful sense
> Of the inferior nature's clinging—whence
> Slight starting tears easily wiped away,
> Fine jealousies soon stifled in the play
> Of irrepressible admiration.

Grammatical reference itself is stifled in the irrepressibly free play of these lines. One begins by assuming that they describe Eglamor. As his face is "admitted," so is it "crossed" with anxiety lest "perfect triumph" be only for those to whom he is "inferior." Nevertheless, his capacity for "admiration," his secondariness, is so great that it overpowers the initially painful conviction of inferiority.

While such a reading of these lines is consistent with itself, it is consistent at the cost of overlooking their context. The encounter with Eglamor's face comes at the end of Browning's "upward flight," so that, if one must choose, Browning himself is plausibly the lower or "inferior" spirit of the two. Punctuation is so flexible in *Sordello* that the dash in the seventh line above may introduce Browning's self-portrait, with a diffident but explicit confession of his inferiority.[18] Eglamor's "care" may then be rather for the tardy Browning than for himself. Or indeed, yet another possibility is that the entire passage beginning with "crossed" may describe Browning, that in admitting Eglamor, he admits to struggling doubts about his own abilities. Stranger things have happened with syntax in this poem, and Browning's gorgeous gyres have just been interrupted or "crossed" by the face of his perfectionist double—an interruption in which Browning has conceded that single-minded aspiration towards the permanence of "perfect triumph" has a way of turning into the uglier permanence of "enduring damp." This last possibility awakens an ambiguity latent in the first lines of the passage: the "ill-reports,/Disuse, some wear of years" may suggest the plight of the ambitious but largely unnoticed Robert Browning of the 1830s; that may be why Eglamor's

24

welcoming "look of love" comes as such a glad but strange surprise.

However one sorts out their ambiguities, a responsible reading of these lines will recognize two related principles that are central to Browning's work. The first is that a play of difference between two or more perspectives, or persons, or parts of a single person, may constitute the richest ground for a writer who would preserve meaning from enclosure. At its best such play will be a matter of syntax as well as theme, as in these lines whose relentless ambiguity keeps one from paraphrasing or otherwise exporting their meaning. Instead, one begins to observe, for instance, that the "admission" of the fourth line must be a mutual process. Either spirit, Browning or Eglamor, admits the other in a face-to-face recognition that is both a confession of failure and a restorative, "joyous look of love." This look plays between them in either direction and so confirms a dynamic relation that depends on their difference. Each spirit respects or defers to the otherness of the other, and in this gesture of deference each inherits a significant strength.

This strength, the strength of secondariness, is the second central principle reinforcing these lines. The evolving willingness of the inferior spirit, of Browning or Eglamor, to be inferior and to release the springs of "irrepressible admiration" is what makes that spirit so interesting. (The *Oxford English Dictionary* suggests that the word "interest" comes into English as a substantive use of the Latin verb *interest*, "it makes a difference.") In secondariness, and not in the unchanging condition of "perfect triumph," one finds the contradictory variety of human experience: "care" and "struggle," a "painful" power of beginning ("slight starting tears"), and a later power of change, of "stifling" what has already begun for the sake of something newer and better ("irrepressible admiration"). Here in secondariness one finds the changing lineaments of the human face, the self-renewing play of failure and recovery that furnishes the drama of Browning's poetry.[19] A dramatic lyric, a drama proper, or a dramatically discontinuous poem like *Sordello* may find an originating motive and a sustaining interest in the infinitely various play of human inadequacies, defenses, and partial recuperations. It is Browning's wonderfully humanist hypothesis that all men and women are artists, secondary to what they would ultimately make of themselves and of each other, living and speaking in a region of energetic difference between reach and grasp, between their desire and its articulation. This difference creates and maintains a temporal reserve in which they, and Browning with them, may have their say.

Deferring to the object it admires, the secondary spirit in its imperfection triumphs over the spirit assured of "perfect triumph." Browning registers the limitation of such perfect assurance most tellingly in these lines by leaving the prior spirit featureless. It remains, like other sublime objects in his poetry, an undifferentiated postulate that exists for the sake of the changing attitudes that may be adopted toward it. In the lines that end the passage, Browning sustains the preceding ambiguity and complicates it by calling the prior, "perfect" spirit into play. He writes of the secondary spirit as

not
Aspiring, all considered, to their lot
Who ever, just as they prepare ascend
Spiral on spiral, wish thee well, impend
Thy frank delight at their exclusive track
That upturned fervid face and hair put back!

This last line is both the most concretely descriptive and the most tantalizingly ambiguous of the entire passage. The emotional tension within the line, between the "fervid" expectancy of the upturned face and the careful restraint of "hair put back," expresses a more pervasive tension of reference. Is the face to be read as an image of the secondary spirit's "frank delight" or of what causes the delight, the countenance of the prior, superior soarer? Either reading seems arbitrarily exclusive and reductive of the play between prior and secondary, superior and inferior, out of which the entire passage is written.

Browning might have written "thy face" or "their face" had he intended to authorize either reading; instead, he insists upon the ambiguously demonstrative "that." The passage frustrates any attempt to determine just who the owner of the face may be—and that is its significance and success. Browning proposes not an identity, but a mutual dependence between what is prior and what is secondary. In choosing, "all considered," not to aspire, the deferential secondary spirit gains a certain ascendancy over the spirit it chooses to watch ascend. In the groundless atmosphere of these skiey lines, it is the secondary spirit that defines "ascent" in the first place by declining to aspire and so constituting a point of departure whereby ascent may be measured. The soarer paradoxically depends upon the watcher: it is meaningless to be prior without first having something to be prior to. The prior spirit acknowledges this dependence in its preparatory turn to "wish thee well." Browning's surprising shift here to the second person can hardly be accidental; it is a deft grammatical enactment of the mutuality in play that underlies the passage. The "I" of the passage has learned to say "thou," to recognize in an other the necessary counterpart that gives it meaning. It has learned, too, that in saying "thou" it may interrupt its own aspiring "spiral on spiral" in favor of a more genuinely liberating difference. It acknow-

26

ledges the paradox that secondariness is inherent in its aspiration to priority. This acknowledgement is what entitles the prior spirit to a face and earns for the prior spirit the right to figure in the play of Browning's ambiguous concluding image. The spirit exchanges its blank, impassive assurance of "perfect triumph" for the possibility of differentiation; "That upturned fervid face and hair put back" are human features that may emerge with the spirit's acceptance of secondariness and imperfection.

Nothing is resolved in this last line; it deepens the ambiguity and sharpens the paradox of the entire passage it concludes. That mystifyingly frank face is neither prior nor secondary; nor is it both at once. Nor is it Eglamor's; nor is it Browning's. Its identity is withheld with a stubbornness remarkable even in Browning, and even in *Sordello*. The skeptical Browning treats the human face perhaps more reverently than any other image in his poetry, and it seems to be used here to represent something of profound importance. One might venture most safely, looking back to "the play / Of irrepressible admiration" the face expresses, to suggest that what the image represents is Browning's frank delight in representation itself, in the play of figurative difference. With its internal play between fervor and restraint, the face is an image of the individuating, imperfect uncertainty that keeps meaning free, the originating wrinkle in the mind to which Browning so often returns to renew his poetic impulse.[20] Browning envisages neither the spirit that says stop nor the spirit that says go because his sense of "going" (whether poetic, readerly, or broadly human) requires patience of a special sort. Looking back further to the face's "joyous look of love," one may finally recall that patience itself is a manifestation of love—love that is enacted, like Browning's nimbly extended figure of speech, in the willingness of different spirits to defer, through each other, to their future.

Encounters between poets occur frequently in Browning's early work, especially at the beginnings and endings of poems, where they strike prospective notes of dedication or renewal. Browning goes on to finish *Sordello* with the picture of "A child barefoot and rosy," running "up and up" a hill by Asolo and singing a snatch of poetry by Sordello, "Some unintelligible words to beat / The lark, God's poet" (VI.856-66). Early in Book I, Browning more pointedly uses the pure-faced "spirit" of Shelley in order to define his own position as a different poet: "this is no place for thee!" (I.60-64). As will be seen in the next chapter, *Pauline* is a poem that not only invokes Shelley near its beginning and at its close in a remarkable play of deference and triumph, but also evokes Shelley in a series of subtler encounters. In Part II of *Paracelsus* (1835), the poet Aprile greets

Paracelsus as his double, with a song about the renewing difference between aspiration and attainment that underlies poetic tradition. Paracelsus himself, a displaced if not an actual poet, locates such a renewing difference in scientific tradition when he undergoes a hallucinatory encounter "face to face" with his predecessor Galen (*Paracelsus*, V.182). Browning's plotting protagonists in dramas like *Strafford* (1837) and *King Victor and King Charles* (1842) draw power from confrontations with figures, or figureheads, of political authority. Their dramatic confrontations foreshadow the play between provisional figuration and authoritative meaning that lies at the heart of the dramatic lyrics; there Browning's speakers, frustrated poets all, differ with themselves as they encounter the inadequacies of their own figures of speech.

In each of these strange meetings a secondary figure comes to terms with a prior one and emerges with a distinguishing, sometimes chastening difference. But in none of Browning's many encounters is the stylistic play more exhilaratingly free than in his own encounter with Eglamor at the close of *Sordello*. (Its only real rival in syntactic and figural complexity is the "lyric Love" invocation that closes Book I of *The Ring and the Book*, a baffling passage associating poetic regeneration with human weakness through vertical and facial imagery remarkably like that in which Browning conceives his meeting with Eglamor.) It may be because Browning's encounter with Eglamor is so clearly his own, so archetypally internal, that the passage enjoys so special a freedom: the distinguishing difference that it establishes is *the* difference from himself that lets the poet write. He discovers the possibility of writing an ending that eludes orthodox closure by embracing closure as its subject. The meaning of such an ending is that meaning itself is endless, that no comprehensive cognitive statement will suffice, precisely because it would deny the possibility of fresh re-cognitions. Browning's formal task, as he wrote to Ruskin, is putting the infinite within the finite." His poetry discharges this task by using form to call attention to the gap between formal finitude and the endlessness of meaning. It is a task that can never be performed by packing meaning into an enclosed and unifying symbolic pattern—not only because such a pattern is in Browning's view unavailable to the poet writing in and of the modern condition, but because even if it were available it would rob the poet's formal task of its greatest value, its status as a problem to which he can always return. Closural unification is Eglamor's work, and it is to Eglamor that Browning turns in order to forestall a reader's formalist impulse to identify form with meaning too quickly, to "judge the song and singer one." One of the things *Sordello* most surely means is that poetic form, if simply trusted, is always treacher-

28

ous, "the vehicle / Never sufficient" (V.653-54). The formal resources of poetry must be extended, fractured, and recreated in "true works" (III.622). A poem that is thus "true" will perforce make the process of recreation one of its subjects, and so will alert its reader to a significant difference between song and singer.[21]

Only through form, however, can a poet achieve freedom from the tyranny of form in order to assert such a difference. As Browning finds in the passage from Book VI, for a poet to neglect form completely, in the interest of immediate "life and light," is to become its prey—is to become as uninteresting as Eglamor, who contents himself with the limitations of formal orthodoxy. In summoning an Eglamor from within himself, Browning serves a complex need to avoid the contrary pitfalls of neglect of form and absorption in it. He rejects a simple formalism; if he can *meet* Eglamor, then he cannot *be* Eglamor but must be a different sort of poet, a poet with more to say. Yet he must not deny Eglamor altogether; for if he does that, he will lose the difference upon which his poetry depends. He can reject Eglamor only if he has an Eglamor to reject, just as he can subvert conventional form only by intimately acknowledging the restraints of its conventions.

Browning's summons to his ghostly creation is thus an invocation as well as an exorcism. For the spirit of closure that Eglamor embodies is something like Browning's muse; and in welcoming its return, Browning confirms his difference from it, a vital difference that lets him reopen meaning and lets his "true works" continue. After this dazzling passage, the continuation of *Sordello* for another seventy lines may be taken as Browning's recognition that the question of closure remains an open question.[22] Browning carried on a lifelong affair with the fatal, frightening, yet necessary muse of closure. The following chapters propose to describe episodes in this affair, while exploring some of the strategies of difference and disclosure that make it possible, and that motivate the extraordinary poems that are its record.

29

CHAPTER ONE

RENEWED BY CHANGE:
PAULINE

Genius almost invariably begins to develop itself
by imitation. It has, in the short-sightedness
of infancy, faith in the world: and its object is
to compete with, or prove superior to, the world's
already recognised idols, at their own performances
and by their own methods. This done, there grows
up a faith in itself: and, no longer taking the
performance or method of another for granted, it
supersedes these by processes of its own. It creates,
and imitates no longer. Seeing cause for faith in
something external and better, and having attained
to a moral end and aim, it next discovers in itself
the only remaining antagonist worthy of its ambition,
and in the subduing what at first had seemed its most
enviable powers, arrives at the more or less complete
fulfilment of its earthly mission.

Browning's *Essay on Chatterton* (1842)[1]

When in *Sordello* Browning approaches closure by embracing a poet of his own creation, he confirms a habit at least as old as his first published work, *Pauline* (1833). The closing words of that poem, "Love me and wish me well," are addressed not to Pauline, but to the "Sun-treader"—Browning's hyperbolical name for his acknowledged master Shelley. The hyperbole expresses an exaggerated reverence whereby, as W. C. DeVane observes, Browning "at once repudiates and yet follows adoringly his master."[2] DeVane's phrasing indicates a paradox of secondariness, a paradox of which *Pauline* is Browning's initial exploration: Browning follows his Shelley in ways that make the activity of following an activity of the first importance. Even where readers of *Pauline* have regarded Browning's idolizing hyperbole as a device rather than a gush, they have tended to censure him for it: "Browning appeases his Shelleyan impulses by worshipping them as something ethereal, distant and unattainable; he elevates the subjective quester, and abases himself, in order to impugn the possibility of emulation."[3] What such criticism leaves unsaid is that Browning impugns the possibility of emulation in order to raise a new and distinctive poetic voice.

The problem of finding a distinctive voice is *the* problem for a beginning poet of any ambition, and Browning's ambition was immense. The truly initial gesture of such a forward youth must be made in a work that bears his own mark, through a willed engagement with, and disengagement from, his literary past. Chronologically, *Pauline* is not Browning's first poem; two poems survive from his teens, "The First-Born of Egypt" and "The Dance of Death," both of them pastiches in the visionary manner of Coleridge and Byron that fail to transcend imitative mannerism. The failure of these adolescent pieces illuminates the original success of *Pauline*, a poem that deserves its place at the beginning of the oeuvre of a major poet because it knows itself to be "first" in a more important sense than the chronological. Although Browning's juvenilia, beside the patently chaotic *Pauline*, manifest a degree of authoritative composure and firmness of structure, their authority is borrowed and they stand so firmly because they stand on ground other poets have already secured. Precociously accomplished, they remain the work of an adolescent apprenticed to the past.

With *Pauline*, Browning took the first step of poetic maturity by returning to the adolescence that the composure of his juvenilia had masked and by finding there a new principle of form — indeed, a new attitude toward form itself. Instead of concealing adolescence, he now dramatizes it, overtly in a Latin epigraph from Cornelius Agrippa declaring that "I wrote this work when I was less than a youth [*minor quam adolescens*] " and implicitly in the rush and tumble of its hectic imagery and convoluted narrative. While no one has ever wished the poem longer, and while the more formally sophisticated works that followed from Browning's pen pay ampler rewards to the patient reader, *Pauline* first sounds a note of discomposure, indeterminacy, "adolescence," that will play its part in all of his richest music. One use of the term "adolescence" is to protect its user against the turmoil of a time whose very vitality is often an embarrassment, a time, as the conjectural etymology in the *Oxford English Dictionary* suggests, during which one undergoes "alteration," or even "adulteration," while moving towards a time of adulthood that

31

is yet to be. In *Pauline*, Browning abandons adult securities and goes into the dark to embrace the vitality of adolescence: he takes his stand not within the protective enclosure of an established poetic form, but on the energetic and perforce formless potential that such an uneasy time of alteration offers. Browning first experienced the poetry of adolescence in its full force in 1826 with his reading of Shelley, which followed his less wittingly adolescent efforts and may have influenced his decision to burn them. By the time of *Pauline: A Fragment of a Confession*, he had learned to write more capably, consciously adolescent poetry and made the Shelleyan mode his own in a complex drama casting the figure of Shelley in a decidedly supporting role.

PAST PRESENCE

Pauline holds Shelley in a reverence that enshrines and in effect immobilizes him as its created object. It turns Shelley into a static figure distantly sanctifying an immediate, imperfect, and vitally interesting process of present change and hope for the future. Consider the tactics of Browning's concluding valediction:

> Sun-treader, I believe in God and truth
> And love; and as one just escaped from death
> Would bind himself in bands of friends to feel
> He lives indeed, so, I would lean on thee!
> Thou must be ever with me, most in gloom
> If such must come, but chiefly when I die,
> For I seem, dying, as one going in the dark
> To fight a giant: but live thou for ever,
> And be to all what thou hast been to me!

(1020-28)

Here a calculating eclecticism on Browning's part aligns the atheistical Shelley not only with truth and love and friends, but also with God. Theological objection to the sacrilege in such an outrageous alignment is less to the point than is critical alertness to the consequences of the outrage for the hapless figure of Shelley. For if Browning is bound to Shelley in these lines, so is Shelley no less bound to Browning. Shelley is bound, moreover, in such a way that the loving, trusting escapee Browning may lean on him, as from the superior position of one who, conscious of his own comparative liveliness, feels "He lives indeed."[4]

"I would lean on thee." Browning turns his dependency to advantage, with a peculiar reversal that anticipates the ambiguous play of

32

attitudes between Browning and Eglamor at the close of *Sordello.*
This reversal is as odd as it is characteristic of the placing of Shelley
throughout *Pauline.* When in this passage Browning says, "Thou must
be ever with me" and "live thou for ever," he recommits his master
to the artifice of eternity to which he has been carefully exalted
since the earlier invocation, "Sun-treader, life and light be thine for
ever!" (151). It is in the light of such alien, perpetual brilliance that
the more substantial Browning may cast his varying shadows. Indeed,
as he speaks these lines of farewell, Browning wastes no time in extri-
cating himself from the gyres of life and light and heading for "the
dark," where abide exciting giants of the shadowy race that furnishes
the meat and drink of this "fragment of a confession." While it is
true that Shelley ranks among those precursors "whom trustingly /
We sent before into time's yawning gulf / To face what dread may
lurk in darkness there" (548-50), he has clearly emerged long since as
a thing enskied and sainted in the perfection of his quest. The interesting and suspenseful role, Childe Roland's role as active quester,
Browning arrogates to himself. It is intriguing that in 1888 he should
have altered the mild "and" of line 1027 to a sharper "but." Since
the devious assertion of Browning's difference depends upon Shelley's
immutability, it is difficult to say which conjunction makes the more
telling gesture of humble repudiation.

By praising Shelley's steadfastness, Browning sets up a standard
against which his own fallings off exhibit a distinct vitality. "And be
to all what thou hast been to me!" Through this line, as throughout
the poem, Browning removes Shelley from the realm of temporal
process. Shelley's future and past are to be one and the same, while
Browning's perfect tense ("what thou hast been to me") indicates
within the follower a significant difference between past and present
moments and a further potential for momentous change. Likewise,
when Browning says to the Sun-treader, "The air seems bright with
thy past presence yet" (161), the temporal oxymoron of a "past
presence" fuses tenses in order to play Shelley's permanence against
Browning's persistence in mutability. Shelley remains motionless in
order that Browning may move. It is, appropriately, through a consideration of Browning's motives in *Pauline,* of how and why he
moves as he does within and between its often discontinuous verse
paragraphs, that the significance of the poem may emerge.[5]

> But thou art still for me as thou hast been
> When I have stood with thee.

> (162-63)

> But thou art still for me who have adored
> Tho' single, panting but to hear thy name

33

Which I believed a spell to me alone,
Scarce deeming thou wast as a star to men!

(168-71)

And I, perchance, half feel a strange regret
That I am not what I have been to thee.

(191-92)

The movement of these excerpts from a single verse paragraph rehearses the repudiating or differentiating movement of the paragraph that ends the poem. The word "still" slides from its adverbial sense of continuity towards its adjectival sense of immobility, as the more accomplished passage from *Sordello* makes it do within the space of a few lines. Already in this first poem, however, Browning has hardly to do more than mention his ambivalence, the estranging partiality of his "regret," to still the Sun-treader in his tracks. Near the end of *Pauline*, Browning again speaks of himself as "a soul half saved" (990) and "as one half afraid / To make his riches definite" (998-99) —in short, as the speaker of a fragment, who by avoiding definition makes his deficit his treasure and keeps the future open.

In the second paragraph of his early address to the Sun-treader, Browning appropriates even those spiritual prerogatives that ought rightfully to belong to his dead predecessor, even if nothing else does.

And if thou livest, if thou lovest, spirit!
Remember me who set this final seal
To wandering thought—that one so pure as thou
Could never die. Remember me who flung
All honour from my soul.

(206-10)

Remember me who praise thee e'en with tears,
For never more shall I walk calm with thee.

(219-20)

"Remember me." A reader does not need to think of *Hamlet* to find these temporal reversals dramatic. The fathering spirit of Shelley is commanded to remember his descendant—that is, *if* that spirit lives at all. At the same time, the continuance of Shelley's "life" is made to depend upon an ideal of his purity that is finally sealed up in the mind of the descendant whom he is commanded to remember. Even when Shelley is later credited with power to effect change, it is in winning men "back to peace" (409). This is a specifically restorative kind of change to which Browning gives lip service in *Pauline* but no convincing force. However Shelley's pacifying power may work for

34

others, it will be ineffectual for Browning: "For never more shall I walk calm with thee."

> *And now when all thy proud renown is out,*
> *I am a watcher whose eyes have grown dim*
> *With looking for some star which breaks on him*
> *Altered and worn and weak and full of tears.*

(226-29)

Here the spiritual descendant casts himself in an attractive attitude of anticipation, an attitude leading to an "alteration" that gives him an interesting difference. An altered watcher, he looks forward to the outbreak of Shelley, the unalterable, distant, and completely renowned star—whom he has just fixed in an attitude of retrospective remembering.

There is a sense in which this last image of Browning's does to Shelley what Shelley had done to Keats at the end of *Adonais*:

> *I am borne darkly, fearfully, afar;*
> *Whilst, burning through the inmost veil of Heaven,*
> *The soul of Adonais, like a star,*
> *Beacons from the abode where the Eternal are.*

(492-95)

Browning's stylistic disclaimer, "Yet I aim not even to catch a tone / Of harmonies he called profusely up" (216-17), is clearly disingenuous. *Pauline* is full of echoing Shelleyan harmonies, but those harmonies are consistently used to affirm a difference: in this case, the difference between being borne darkly, fearfully afar, and patiently waiting, full of tears. In both passages the living poet defines himself with respect to his dead and starry predecessor; both passages handsomely celebrate the advantages of assuming such a respectfully secondary position. But Browning has learned the lesson of secondariness well enough to beat Shelley at his own game. Of course Browning is literally secondary in following the example of Shelley's famous elegy and likening a dead poet to a beckoning star. What is more significant is that Browning's version of the likeness makes Shelley's, by comparison, appear the least bit hasty in its grasp of "the Eternal"—as if the earlier poet has intemperately squandered reserves of anticipation and change, which the later poet's more modest claim lets him treasure up, "looking for some star which breaks on him / Altered and worn and weak and full of tears." Browning's image grows strong in its weakness by exploiting possibilities of interruption and of renewing alteration. He discovers a poetry both "weak and full," a poetry as embarrassingly but vitally "adoles-

35

cent" as that of Shelley himself, the past master of perpetual adolescence.

In *Pauline* the master Shelley is repudiated through Browning's secondariness to the master's voice. In an extended image immediately following that of the altered, dim-eyed watcher, Browning seems to acknowledge the repudiation while setting his confession in a significantly secondary season:

> *Autumn has come like spring returned to us,*
> *Won from her girlishness; like one returned*
> *A friend that was a lover, nor forgets*
> *The first warm love, but full of sober thoughts*
> *Of fading years; whose soft mouth quivers yet*
> *With the old smile, but yet so changed and still!*
>
> (230-35)

As in *Paracelsus* and *Sordello*, a return is an opportunity less for reunion than for noting a change; the seasonal change noted in these lines figures Browning's difference from Shelley. Like the no longer girlish "friend that was a lover," in this poem Browning turns upon his Shelley an "old smile" at the memory of "fading years." That the old smile is "yet so changed" indicates in the woman, as in Browning, a discrepancy between past and present selves that holds forth a promise of future change. Her "stillness"—like that of Browning, the altered star-seeker—"quivers" with that promise. The constancy of her faded lover, in contrast, corresponds to Shelley's constancy throughout *Pauline*; he is imprisoned in the bonds of sameness, in the "sober thoughts" of a memory that does not forget. In fact, it is only as the object of a thought, or of a smile, that the faded lover exists in these lines at all. Like Browning's Shelley, he is gently objectified and distanced.

Browning thus distinguishes himself from Shelley even as he apologizes for doing so. The distinction is more cruelly deepened, however, by autumn's coming "like spring returned": Shelley's *Adonais* and "Ode to the West Wind" had so unambiguously prophesied that it would happen the other way round. "Grief made the young Spring wild," in *Adonais*, "and she threw down / Her kindling buds, as if she Autumn were, / Or they dead leaves" (136-38). Shelley's pathetic fallacy figures the universal lament at Keats's death as an exchange of early force for late. But the image from *Pauline* stations Browning, as it were, on the receiving end of this exchange; he stands as a belated or autumnal poet winning his way back into figurative earliness by reviving the "dead leaves" of his predecessor and correcting the killing tendency of "girlish" youth to fancy itself prematurely weary of the world. Similarly, Shelley's "Ode to the West Wind" predicts not

36

the springlike autumn of *Pauline*, but the return at winter's end of autumnal life in the forms of spring, the return of "wingèd seeds" in "sweet buds" feeding in air (7-11) and of "withered leaves" in "a new birth" (64). Shelley entreats the autumnal west wind to blow "The trumpet of a prophecy" anticipating "Spring" (69-70)—spring that will sound a trumpet of her own: "Thine azure sister of the Spring shall blow / Her clarion o'er the dreaming earth" (9-10). In the seasoning of *Pauline*, however, the anticipated clarion of Shelley's spring has been muted into a recollected breath: "Thou wilt remember one warm morn when winter / Crept aged from the earth, and spring's first breath / Blew soft from the moist hills" (55-57). The "first breath" of spring, like the "first warm love" from an outlived time of girlishness, survives only to commemorate an intervening change. As Browning less subtly and graciously puts it later in the poem,

> *The vaunted influence poets have o'er men!*
> *'Tis a fine thing that one weak as myself*
> *Should sit in his lone room, knowing the words*
> *He utters in his solitude shall move*
> *Men like a swift wind.*

> (530-34)

In each of these cases, the object of Shelley's eager anticipation has become for Browning a thing of the past, if not downright passé.[6]

Poetic allusion is a form of commemoration that, like other forms, is subject to subversive manipulation on the part of the rememberer. The dizzying speed with which temporal focus in *Pauline* shifts back and forth, between the present and various pasts, keeps quite fresh in a reader's mind the tyranny of a memory that "forgets not, not a shred of life forgets," yet also calls "The dark past up to quell it regally" (288-90). Browning's tendentious recreation of Shelley as a fixture of memory illustrates the politics of poetic allusion: he remembers lines from Shelley's works at moments in this work when his theme is the pastness of the past. When Browning takes up his complementary theme, the promise of what is yet to come, he carefully alludes not to Shelley but to himself.

As if to place his difference from Shelley beyond all doubt, near the end of the poem Browning represents his hopes for the future by expecting the Shelleyan advent of spring:

> *So, when spring comes*
> *With sunshine back again like an old smile,*
> *And the fresh waters and awakened birds*
> *And budding woods await us, I shall be*
> *Prepared, and we will question life once more,*

37

Till its old sense shall come renewed by change,
Like some clear thought which harsh words veiled before.

(971-77)

Browning makes the Shelleyan advent his own in the simile of the "old smile"—an allusion to the half-regretful "old smile" at Shelley's expense from line 235, in which Browning's womanly autumn has soberly, memorably repudiated her former lover. The strength of her secondariness has been more chillingly prefigured in a yet earlier feminine smile, the "grin" with which Browning's young witch views the "perishing" of her captive god (112-19).[7] Browning's smiling simile for the coming of spring, by alluding to earlier imagery from Browning's own poem, celebrates his strategic victory over a deified and captivated Shelley. Furthermore, it anticipates a transfiguration that will prepare Browning, as a mutable poet, to write future poems. He will refresh, awaken, and reveal the "old sense" of earlier "words" by uttering his own distinctive word, "renewed by change." Line 976 originally read, "And all old loves shall come to us—but changed"; Browning's addition in 1888 of the phrases "old sense" and "renewed by change" brings out—and, at the end of his career, resumes—the revisionary intention latent here and throughout his text of 1833. It seems especially appropriate that Browning should assert his difference with a smile, a significant opening in a face or "figure." One of the ways in which Browning differs from his Shelley in *Pauline* is by making openings in Shelley's figures of speech, finding significance in possibilities that Shelley has hurried past.[8]

It is impossible to tell whether Browning's strategic humility arises from a need to come to terms as a young poet with so proud a pathbreaker as Shelley or whether Browning's early fascination with the power of secondariness simply meets in Shelley a worthy and convenient antagonist. In either case, the fascination of *Pauline* is that Browning embraces the fact of his literary secondariness as a means of self-assertion. The most impressive gesture of repudiation in the poem affirms a relation of attentive dependency in place of Shelleyan resourceful autonomy. Browning invites Pauline to join him in an imaginative flight to "A home for us, out of the world, in thought" (730). The flight leads, at noon, to a central account of imaginative sources, which makes unmistakable allusion to Shelley's *Alastor*.

This is the very heart of the woods all round
Mountain like heaped above us; yet even here
One pond of water gleams; far off the river
Sweeps like a sea, barred out from land; but one—
One thin clear sheet has overleaped and wound
Into this silent depth, which gained, it lies

38

Still, as but let by sufferance; the trees bend
O'er it as wild men watch a sleeping girl,
And through their roots long creeping plants out-stretch
Their twined hair, steeped and sparkling; farther on,
Tall rushes and thick flag-knots have combined
To narrow it; so, at length a silver thread,
It winds, all noiselessly through the deep wood
Till thro' a cleft-way, thro' the moss and stone,
It joins its parent-river with a shout.

(766-80)

Shelley's Poet in *Alastor* (457-84) comes, also at noon, to a "still fountain" or "well, / Dark, gleaming," "silent," with "secret springs," whose waters he follows from their source to the scene of his eventual death. This gleaming source wells up first in the passage from *Pauline* as the "one pond." But Browning immediately puts in question the independence of his pond, its status as a source. In the same line that introduces this image of origination, Browning turns away to a thought of the invisible, distant river. He learns to reinterpret the apparently original pond as in fact derivative: it is "one thin clear sheet" that, while it has "overleaped" its bounds and serpentined its way into the woods, nevertheless proceeds from the "parent-river." There it "lies / Still, as but let by sufferance." Browning's oddly legalistic phrase "let by sufferance" suggests a temporary delay or respite and judges the moment of illusory autonomy by placing it in an expanded temporal context. Only apparently a pond with springs of its own, in time the sheet of water finds the "cleft-way" and confesses its continuity with the great prior river.[9]

The double repetition of the word "one" in Browning's passage calls attention to the paradox of his deferential secondariness. The word insists both upon a unity of process, a gentle flow that keeps the sheet "clear" and frees it from stagnant stillness, and upon the uniqueness of the highly particularized channel through which the flow proceeds. What makes this sheet of water unique is that, like the sheet of poetry that Browning is writing, it acknowledges its derivation from a parent. The moment of acknowledgment is the moment at which the "silent," "noiseless" sheet gains a voice: "It joins its parent-river with a shout."[10] As usual in Browning's poetry, the moment of acknowledged derivation provides a more memorable occasion for poetic voice than the moment of apparent priority. Quite early in the poem, Browning says, "I ne'er sung / But as one entering bright halls where all / Will rise and shout for him" (77-79). The problem with this naive fiction of heroic presence, as with the "golden courts" from the end of *Sordello*, is that it unwittingly gives voice away. In the exclamatory mode of Browning's imitative juvenilia

39

someone else—Coleridge, perhaps, or Byron—is doing the shouting "for him." With *Pauline* he learns to shout for himself by engaging and not just parroting his master's voice.

Browning's voice comes into its own through a complex gesture of deference that differentiates him from the Shelley of *Alastor*. Shelley sees his pond as a source, a self-generating fountain. Browning introduces his pond as if it were a source like Shelley's, but he defers any assertion about its originality; he takes the time to revise his pond, to see it anew as a dependent. If Browning's revision went no further, it would be interesting but not compelling. It would be a too nearly prim critique of a Shelley too simplistically decked out as a Satanic overleaper; that is, it would too nearly and weakly repeat the position taken by Shelley himself in the preface to *Alastor:* "The Poet's self-centred seclusion was avenged by the furies of an irresistible passion pursuing him to speedy ruin." Browning's concern in *Pauline,* however, is less to question Shelley's account of imagination than to explore secondary resources of his own, which are valuable to him in part because of their difference from Shelley's.[11]

Accordingly, his revision of Shelley does go further; he strengthens it by putting the valuable difference between his poetry and that of his predecessor into a complex allusion. Once more he plays against his allusion to Shelley an allusion to an earlier passage from *Pauline*. What prompts Browning to revise his pond is a thought, in the third line of the passage, of the distant "parent-river," which he likens to the sea: it "Sweeps like a sea, barred out from land." This simile recalls the early invocation, in which Browning represents the Sun-treader as an irrepressible "great river," which he goes on to liken to the sea: "for it does ever spread / Like a sea's arm as it goes rolling on, / Being the pulse of some great country" (180-89). Browning makes Shelley's pond his own, revising it by showing that it derives from an anterior source—which turns out to be the hyperbolically oceanic Shelley.[12] A sophisticated strategy of repudiation by deification lets Browning make a necessary, distinguishing break by keeping his glorious predecessor "far off" and so "barred out."

A WAKING POINT

Browning's elaborate deference to Shelley is a single, consistent manifestation of the temporal deferment that is a larger subject of *Pauline*. The title page bears the first two lines of Marot's poem "On Himself," which the Ohio edition translates in its entirety:

> *I am no longer that which I was,*
> *Nor will I ever know how to be so again;*

40

> *My beautiful springtime and my summer*
> *Have gone out the window.*
> *Love, thou hast been my master,*
> *I have served thee above all the gods.*
> *O if I could be born a second time*
> *How much better would I serve thee!*[13]

The pastness and absence of spring and summer, the posture of humility before an exalted yet loving master, and the hope of a fresh birth that will make new service possible, are thematically central in *Pauline.* Possibly, Browning keeps his quotation from Marot fragmentary in order to defer those themes for his own treatment. It is more likely, however, that he means his epigraph to emphasize the intermediacy of his position in the poem it precedes. He suspends himself between a past that cannot be restored and an indeterminate future. No longer that which he has been and never to be so again, like the womanly autumn of lines 230-35 the Browning of *Pauline* remembers his past as a way of registering his separation from it, in order to expect something new and different in the future. In writing a first poem that transforms an initial sense of loss into a source of renewal, he outlines a pattern characteristic of his entire poetic career. Writing in a curiously empty present, Browning postpones fulfillment to the future and so replenishes the present with the energies of anticipation that make reading *Pauline* so inspiriting, and so exhausting.

The yearning in Marot's poem for a return to original relations is an impulse towards continuity, in the wake of which Browning's deeper sense of discontinuity makes itself felt. He would "seek/ Again" the altars of nature (23-24); he would "be young again" (127); he "would give up all to be but where I was" and "to sit/Once more" with those he has deserted (82-87). But this impulse towards continuity repeatedly checks itself, as Browning disrupts the even current of his verse:

> *Sad confession first,*
> *Remorse and pardon and old claims renewed,*
> *Ere I can be—as I shall be no more.*

(25-27)

Browning's style throughout *Pauline,* now headlong and now choppy, moves "Rudely, the verse being as the mood it paints" (259). One cause of this moody rudeness is that Browning listens to himself with what John Stuart Mill identified in his marginal commentary as "intense and morbid self-consciousness," and Pauline in her note as "ce retour soudain sur soi-même" (this sudden return upon himself).[14] Pauline's phrasing is the more valuable of the two, not only because it suggests how Browning's self-criticism had preempted the criticism

41

of Mill (to which Browning scholars have now perhaps paid enough attention), but also because it directs readers to the relationship between psychic and stylistic events. Browning's sudden, analytic returns upon himself often expose his desire to return to a former state as the desire to acquiesce in a consoling but ultimately undesirable repetition. In this passage it is as if sudden awareness of the undesirability of repetition in the prosodically retarded "old claims renewed" convinces Browning, in the middle of the next line, to reinterpret the phrase. That self-contradictory line rejects the possibility of any simply repentant return and retroactively glosses the phrase "old claims renewed": not "old claims reiterated" but "old claims made new." Browning's impulse towards continuity lays bare a gap between past and future selves that gives him the room he needs in order to make a new beginning.

In another expression of this impulse, Browning embodies the threat of repetitive sameness in an alliterative near-tautology only to dash out of its enclosure with a significant change of mind:

> I would lose
> All this gay mastery of mind, to sit
> Once more with them, trusting in truth and love
> And with an aim—not being what I am.

(85-88)

"Trusting in truth," Browning's movement in these lines suggests, is too much the same as being what one is. It is as uninteresting to practice as it is to say; its circuit is boring, unplayful, and short. With interruptions like the one in this last line, Browning prepares to open the circle into a warmer, ampler embrace of "God and truth/And love" (1020-21), and Pauline and the Sun-treader, with which the poem may come to its prospective close. Browning interrupts himself in line 88 with a reminder that he is too interesting for the tautological circuit: being what he is, he cannot resume former aims. The argument of *Pauline* is that this discrepancy, the difference between "am" and "aim," is a blessing in disguise. His strength is the negative capability "to trust / All feelings equally, to hear all sides" (597-98), despite his momentary "envy" of the soul that "Turns its whole energies to some one end,/To elevate an aim, pursue success/However mean!" (605-7)—and already here Browning's last two words, with a "sudden return upon himself," demean the aims of the not so enviably single-minded. By the end of the poem, Browning's aim is to be what he is not, to rejoice in "going in the dark" and confronting what he has not yet known.[15]

The apparently frustrating discontinuity revealed by each attempt to complete a return opens to Browning the chance of reorigination

42

for which he finds such a variety of images. Riverbanks "lie quivering / In light as some thing lieth half of life / Before God's foot, waiting a wondrous change" (183-85)—and so does the poet, whose well-preserved deficiency ("half of life") is at least as important as the God who stands by to make it up. Browning occupies, and clearly plans on continuing to occupy, that indeterminate breaking point in time when he claims to "have lived all life / When it is most alive, where strangest fate / New-shapes it past surmise" (703-5). When he tells Pauline in the lines discussed above that "we will question life once more, / Till its old sense shall come renewed by change" (975-76), he bypasses the entrapping repetition of "old claims renewed" in favor of an interrogative mode that promises to renew the familiar by changing it. Here "once more" refers to the one redemptive repetition in all of Browning's poetry, the ever-different repetition of re-origination, and to the one saving tautology whereby the act of renewal is itself a self-renewing act. Browning will never yield for an instant in maintaining the significance of renewal, and his later poetry will be a search after new forms and postures in which he may maintain it.

Since Browning chooses to rest where life is most alive, in his "principle of restlessness" (277), he also chooses to make his poem a discontinuous fragment.[16] As with his allusions to Shelley, he persistently defines the discontinuity of his own work against imbedded images of perfection, assurance, and triumph. A more perfect work than *Pauline*, even one as highly charged with anticipation as Browning's beloved painting of "Andromeda," approaches closure too nearly for comfort:

> *And she is with me: years roll, I shall change,*
> *But change can touch her not—so beautiful*
> *With her fixed eyes, earnest and still, and hair*
> *Lifted and spread by the salt-sweeping breeze,*
> *And one red beam, all the storm leaves in heaven,*
> *Resting upon her eyes and hair, such hair,*
> *As she awaits the snake on the wet beach*
> *By the dark rock and the white wave just breaking*
> *At her feet; quite naked and alone; a thing*
> *I doubt not, nor fear for, secure some god*
> *To save will come in thunder from the stars.*
> *Let it pass! Soul requires another change.*

(657-68)

Andromeda occupies a position similar to that in which Browning is busy fixing Shelley. Despite the "wave just breaking," the expected snake, and the god coming to save in thunder, her position is too "still" and "secure" to be of abiding interest. "I shall change, / But change can touch her not." Browning distinguishes himself from Andromeda by placing her, like his Shelley, in a changeless region inaccessible to "doubt" or "fear." These definitively human emotions, rich manifestations of secondariness, require play in Browning's poetry, and he turns away from Andromeda to assert the needs of a changeable humanity. He dismisses her and her scenic tableau, first as a "thing" and finally as an "it": "Let it pass! Soul requires another change." The figure that replaces her is the significantly human and literally dramatic figure of the actor Edmund Kean, one "sunk by error to men's sympathy, / And in the wane of life, yet only so / As to call up their fears" (670-72).[17]

Browning so tidily disposes of his Andromeda because her picture of the future is so tidily perfect. She is insufficiently secondary; because she knows too much, she leaves too little room for renewing surprise. As Browning seems to have realized in 1888 when altering the line that dismisses her, the original reading, "I will call another change," is in a sense too original. It diminishes the force of the secondariness that Browning adopts throughout *Pauline*, a force to which the "Andromeda" passage has just finely borne witness; it displays directly an authorial initiative that Browning has elsewhere been careful to subdue. The poem depends for its effects upon Browning's assumption of a less authoritative voice than is claimed by such an "I." His more passive revision, "Soul requires another change," disclaims such authority and distances him from the awaited agency of renewal.

Another revision in the lines succeeding those on Andromeda lays additional stress on the dangers of assuming authority too explicitly:

> and there shall come
> A time requiring youth's best energies;
> And lo, I fling age, sorrow, sickness off,
> And rise triumphant, triumph through decay.
>
> And thus it is that I supply the chasm
> 'Twixt what I am and all I fain would be.
>
> (672-77)

In earlier versions line 675 reads, "And I rise triumphing over my decay." In Browning's poetry, present triumph almost always has to submit to time's revenges. His wiser repetition of "triumph" suggests, as do the repetitive spirals forming part of his encounter with Eglamor at the end of *Sordello*, that a fulfilled present may stultify poetic utterance by leaving a poet with nothing more to say. The prepositional change from "over my decay" to "through decay" hints at a

central truth for Browning in and after *Pauline*: that he will find
something more to say through returning to his imperfections, that
he will achieve an enduring because renewable success by virtue of
his vices. In either version the lines after the gap on Browning's page
deny that the assertion of independent triumph will suffice. They
testify to the presence of a "chasm" between realization and desire
through which such mere assertion sends hollow reverberations,
dramatically appealing but no longer credibly authoritative.

A similar gap follows a similarly planned failure of originative
assertion during Browning's internal inventory early in the poem.
One of his "powers" appears to constitute an autonomous resourcefulness:

> *an imagination which*
> *Has been a very angel, coming not*
> *In fitful visions but beside me ever*
> *And never failing me; so, though my mind*
> *Forgets not, not a shred of life forgets,*
> *Yet I can take a secret pride in calling*
> *The dark past up to quell it regally.*

> *A mind like this must dissipate itself.*

(284-91)

Grand assertion brings Browning's verse paragraph to a full stop, and
after pausing between paragraphs, he makes a new beginning by un-
dermining what he has just built. The poem may continue only if the
victories of "never failing" imagination over the "dark past" of memory are less regally and unequivocally won. This angel of imagination
offers healing gifts that Browning is not sure he wants to accept right
away, gifts of continuity and perpetuity like those of Shelley or of
Andromeda—both of whom, like the angel, Browning describes as
"beside" or "with" him in the very passages in which they are repudiated (1024, 657). Browning's project of self-definition through
self-abasement finds expression in a poetic technique of bas-relief,
in which "beside" means "contrasting" and "with" means "against."
Like a premature Perseus, the imagination "springs up to save"
Browning too assuredly and too soon (281). Browning goes Andromeda one better: he wisely and thriftily saves imagination from itself
by rejecting its guardianship as inadequate in its very wholeness.

The gap between Browning's paragraphs at lines 290-91 expresses
a characteristic hesitation about the imagination's regality, and the
lines that follow make a decisive break with what has come before.
Through this break enters the Browningesque "yearning after God":

> *But I have always had one lode-star; now,*

45

> *As I look back, I see that I have halted*
> *Or hastened as I looked towards that star—*
> *A need, a trust, a yearning after God.*
>
> (292-95)

The repeatedly frustrated impulse towards continuity becomes a yearning after God, which may suffice precisely because of the impossibility of its ever reaching consummation. The roomy, open future that Browning promises to himself elsewhere through idolizing such intermediate figures as Pauline, Andromeda, and Shelley, is ultimately guaranteed by his deferring to the ultimate figure, God. "I saw God everywhere," Browning says, "I felt / His presence, never acted from myself, / Still trusted in a hand to lead me through / All danger" (302-8). It is remarkable how in these two paragraphs Browning transfers into God's safer keeping the attributes of the "never failing" imagination from lines 284-87. He deposes the regal imagination in favor of a more distant and alien monarch to whom he may be more confidently secondary. God receives the dread attributes of stillness and eternity; in later poems such as *Sordello*, *Pippa Passes*, and the "Epilogue" to *Dramatis Personae*, Browning will be more guarded in speaking of the attribute of "presence."

Even in *Pauline*, however, it is the remoteness of God that finally matters. The climactic turn to God late in the poem hinges upon a claustrophobia that anticipates the later Browning's courting of absence and importuning of alcoves (see "Love in a Life" [1855], 16). The sustained imaginative flight with Pauline "out of the world, in thought," collapses when Browning's spirit wanders into Wordsworthian "little smoking cots" and "hedgerows." As in "Tintern Abbey," the word "hedgerows" is significantly repeated:

> *Hedgerows for me—those living hedgerows where*
> *The bushes close and clasp above and keep*
> *Thought in—I am concentrated—I feel;*
> *But my soul saddens when it looks beyond:*
> *I cannot be immortal, taste all joy.*
>
> *O God, where do they tend—these struggling aims?*
>
> (806-11)

No matter how lovingly or imaginatively recast, the flight into nature always lands Browning before long in constraining hedgerows; and, to twist the lines from Wordsworth to which Browning is alluding, *he* runs wild. This passage is especially helpful to a reading of *Pauline* that takes deferential secondariness as its subject, because the passage shows just what kind of secondariness the poet does not seek.

46

Browning denies himself presence and fulfillment for the sake of the immortalizing look beyond at the invisible "parent-river" or at Shelley or, ultimately, at God. But these clasping, closing bushes propose themselves as sufficient ends in themselves. They impose an enclosing repetition quite as threatening as the earlier, discredited assertions of imaginative priority or security. Browning's is an elaborately willed secondariness in which he chooses to deprive himself of autonomy, but not to be deprived of it by nature, by his predecessors, or by anything else.[18] In Browning's remarkable analysis of genius from the *Essay on Chatterton*, quoted as the epigraph to this chapter, the creative soul has emerged from apprenticeship when it "discovers in itself the only remaining antagonist worthy of its ambition." Accordingly, Browning ingeniously founds his first poem upon a deliberate deference, a willing away of the will, not upon a seizure or rapture that is initially imposed from without. *Pauline* begins and ends in the imperative mood (1, 1031), and the turn away from choking presence in this passage is, for all Browning's humble secondariness, just as imperative.

Earlier in the poem Browning's confession that a mind like his "must dissipate itself" has prepared the way for his meaningful yearning after God, and a similar preparation undergirds this passage. His confession that he "cannot be immortal, taste all joy" evokes across the gap between paragraphs the figure of God, Browning's guarantor of the future and stay against mortality: "O God, where do they tend—these struggling aims?" This question may be read as an explicitly theological version of the question from late in *Sordello*, "Is there no more to say?" It is a question that underlies gaps and interruptions throughout Browning's poetry, and here it is brought to bear on two related forms of closure. Pauline's critical footnote to this line suggests the relevance of the question to poetic closure by pointing to the difference between artistic conception and execution, and by intimating how that difference may be exploited in the creative "struggling aims" of a soul willing to ascend the Browningesque ladder of plateaus.[19] As usual in Browning, poetic closure adumbrates the darker closure of man's mortality, the subject of the lines immediately following:

> What would I have? What is this "sleep" which seems
> To bound all? can there be a "waking" point
> Of crowning life? The soul would never rule;
> It would be first in all things, it would have
> Its utmost pleasure filled, but, that complete,
> Commanding, for commanding, sickens it.
> The last point I can trace is—rest beneath

47

> *Some better essence than itself, in weakness;*
> *This is "myself," not what I think should be:*
> *And what is that I hunger for but God?*

(812-21)

Browning's prospective look beyond turns the priority of the soul that "would be first in all things" into secondariness, "beneath/Some better essence than itself." With the break in line 818, Browning reinterprets his "last point" not as an ending, but as a beginning, a first point. The will to be in second place lets him elude the seeming bonds of mortal closure and gives him the waking point he wants to look forward to. His confession of weakness preserves a gap in which the yearning "hunger" of the concluding line may be regenerated. [20]

FOUL FORMS

Pauline would end here if Browning's "rest" meant anything but his energetic discipline of restlessness. It is in order to have somewhere to go that he chooses to defer fulfillment and assumes a secondary stance to begin with. By the end of the poem, it comes as a significant joke that its penultimate paragraph should repeat a line verbatim and that the line should express a "perfect" fulfillment: "No less I make an end in perfect joy" (994,1007). By protesting too much, Browning here parodies any cadenza that is not also an overture. As the poem moves towards its open, decidedly imperfect ending, among the things it foresees are its successors, *Paracelsus* and *Sordello*, in a dense passage of fragmentary mythopoeia:

> *There were bright troops of undiscovered suns,*
> *Each equal in their radiant course; there were*
> *Clusters of far fair isles which ocean kept*
> *For his own joy, and his waves broke on them*
> *Without a choice; and there was a dim crowd*
> *Of visions, each a part of some grand whole:*
> *And one star left his peers and came with peace*
> *Upon a storm, and all eyes pined for him;*
> *And one isle harboured a sea-beaten ship,*
> *And the crew wandered in its bowers and plucked*
> *Its fruits and gave up all their hopes of home;*
> *And one dream came to a pale poet's sleep,*
> *And he said, "I am singled out by God,*
> *No sin must touch me."*

(911-24)

Here are three myths of election and failure, which may most use-
fully be read in overlapping conjunction with each other; as on a pa-
limpsest, they trace the pattern of deferred regeneration that informs
Pauline. All three myths posit an initial state of sameness and integrity, a state of innocence prior to choice. The drama of each myth
begins with an act of differentiation: "one star," "one isle," "one
dream" separates itself from the initial whole. Each of these differ-
entiations then leads to a falling off, and what has once been "bright"
or "fair" or "grand" becomes a cause for pining or despair or anxiety.

It is at the moment of painful complication that each myth becomes interesting, and it is also at that moment that each drops out
of the poem. Their incompleteness may be the most important fact
about these myths; "things half-lived" (167), their actions are unresolved so as to extend their meaning beyond the present in which
Browning narrates them and into the future. The most severely truncated of the three myths is the last, that of the poet's election, and it
is difficult not to read the other two myths as less explicit prefigura-
tions of its theme of guilty failure; one presumes that the elected
poet is about to embark, like the errant star and the wandering lotus-
eaters, on a course of grief and guilt. Browning, the self-consciously
guilty poet who has made these myths, breaks off his mythmaking
just as this theme comes to articulation, and he returns to his larger
exploration of guilt, the fragment of a confession that is the poem
proper. He leaves behind him the sketchy but accurate self-portrait
of a poet who engages to redeem a fallen world through wildly hopeful acceptance of human deficiency and guilt, in earnest of a home-
made God displaced into the superlatively dim, far, and undiscovered
future.[21]

A prevenient sense of guilt, of being touched with sin, underlies
this redemptive poetic scheme; and, if the poetry is to go on, then
Browning must not approach redemption too quickly. For him to
bring his fragmentary myths to resolution would run counter to the
characteristic intermediacy of *Pauline.* Even when he resumes one of
his mythic motifs later in the poem, he preserves its valuable tension
by deferring any ultimate resolution. The crew of lotus-eaters give up
"all their hopes of home," and Browning describes the "song" that is
Pauline as one that "shall remain to tell for ever / That when I lost all
hope of such a change, / Suddenly beauty rose on me again" (1004-6).
The comforting completion of a restorative pattern is projected into
the future.

In the meantime, the provisional time of poetic utterance, Browning chooses to live with his guilt. "I stained myself," he tells Pauline,
"But to behold thee purer by my side" (905-6). This expression of
purpose is implicit in the earlier confessions of inferiority to Shelley:

"I to rise and rival him?/Feed his fame rather from my heart's best blood,/Wither unseen that he may flourish still" (557-59); "foul forms/Seek me, which ne'er could fasten on his mind" (213-14). The presence of these foul forms constitutes Browning's difference from Shelley and furnishes Browning with a warrant that his own goal is yet to seek. In this regard the myth of the poet's election from the passage just discussed offers a striking departure from *Prometheus Unbound* (I. 737-51), in which a spirit describes its visit to a dreaming poet who can create "Forms more real than living man,/Nurslings of immortality!" The difference between the two poets is the difference between creative innocence and creative guilt. Where Shelley's poet is already fully empowered to create forms unquestionably fair, Browning's poet, whose creative occasion lies somewhere in the future, associates his dream or partial vision with the foul thought of sin. This mythic alliance of guilt and futurity is not accidental but essential to *Pauline,* in which the persistence of Browning's conviction of guilt and imperfection redeems time by giving him a workable future and redeems the poem by furnishing its distinctive chiaroscuro. Appeals of the guilty imagination sound throughout the poem: Pauline and Browning listen "To the wind murmuring in the damp copse,/Like heavy breathings of some hidden thing/Betrayed by sleep" (66-68); "in the heaven stars steal out one by one/As hunted men steal to their mountain watch" (254-55); "God is gone/And some dark spirit sitteth in his seat" (471-72); Browning even fancies killing Pauline for love's sake (902). To these appeals one responds somewhat as Mill responded to what may be the foulest form of all, Browning's god-seducing, blue-eyed witch of self (112-23): "a curious idealization of self-worship. very fine though." The finesse of the poem arises from the stamina of its foul forms.

Browning acknowledges the persevering appeal of dark truths in his prefatory excerpt from Cornelius Agrippa. There Agrippa contends that the effect of his occult teachings will be beyond even the power of "an Angel from heaven" to allay, much as in lines 284-91 Browning rejects the solacing angel of imagination. Browning husbands his guilt; and, when confronting his own dark truths in the poem proper, he takes care to place them under the regime of a temporal economy. His "craving after knowledge," for instance, takes shape as "The sleepless harpy with just-budding wings." Although it is a "power/Repressed," Browning says, "it lies in me a chained thing, still prompt/To serve me if I loose its slightest bond:/I cannot but be proud of my bright slave" (620-33). Here, as with the blue-eyed witch, the contrast between what is foul, on the one hand, and what is fine or bright or fair, on the other, derives from a precarious balance between repression and growth, oblivion and recovery. It is because the harpy of knowledge is "chained" that it is yet bright and that its wings may keep beginning to bud. Browning will treat more extensively the relations between the repressed and the reclaimed in *Paracelsus*, in which the harpy's "wild eyes" will reappear in a "wild nursling" and a "wildly dancing" witch (*Paracelsus*, II. 222; V.198). Here it is sufficient to note the analogy between Browning's deliberate repression of knowledge and the deferment of meaning that is so characteristic of his poetic practice. As a poet, Browning must exercise his "yet commanding will" (622) by voluntarily forgetting what he knows in such a way that he may rediscover and write it out later on. *Pauline* supplies abundant evidence that much of what Browning knows is unseemly, shameful, and foul; that is why he speaks of it as a "sleepless harpy." But because his guilty craving after knowledge is rich with literary potential, he represents it as "bright," "in its dawn" (623), "with just-budding wings" that promise him a sequel.

A less oblique confession that Browning knows the power of his guilt and its appeal to the most available reader, Pauline, has come earlier in the poem:

> *O dearest, if indeed I tell the past,*
> *May'st thou forget it as a sad sick dream!*
> *Or if it linger—my lost soul too soon*
> *Sinks to itself and whispers we shall be*
> *But closer linked, two creatures whom the earth*
> *Bears singly, with strange feelings unrevealed*
> *Save to each other.*

(243-49)

Browning certainly does not speak to Pauline of his foul forms in order to have them forgotten. Or, if there is to be a forgetting, it will be for the sake of a postponed, "lingering" recollection that may bind him and Pauline, poet and reader, in a shared community of guilt, a shadowy lovers' commerce in the "unrevealed." Browning says to the "troops of shadows" (474) met in the temple of his soul, "I have nursed up energies,/They will prey on me." The shadows answer with suspicious assurance, "Lord, we are here and we will make/Safe way for thee in thine appointed life!" (481-84). If they are right, then there can be no *Pauline*, because the poem feeds on energies nursed up and makes a way for itself by repudiating any way that is "safe" from their ambiguous power.

Harold Bloom identifies in Browning "a fear of forbidden meanings, or in Freudian language precisely a fear of the return-of-the-repressed, even though such a return would cancel out a poem-as-poem, or is it *because* such a return would end poetry as such?"[22] Although the terms at which Bloom sinuously arrives here are help-

51

ful ones, the reading of *Pauline* proposed in this chapter calls for a slight rectification of his line on Browning. Browning does not fear but *loves* the forbidden meanings of his foul forms. He woos them and the answering foul forms of his reader, but he woos with the proviso that the repressed material that they embody not return in its fullness just yet. The passages last quoted express Browning's fear lest even the liberating knowledge that there exists a community of guilt be a conclusive meaning prematurely released and whispered "too soon." In the fragmentary prospectus *Pauline*, as in the no less prospective works of the career that it introduces, Browning consistently postpones such meaning. What he is really fearful about is the treasonous threat of a closure that would deprive him of his poetic birthright, the promise that there will be more to say.

CHAPTER TWO

AUGUST ANTICIPATIONS: *PARACELSUS*

*And surely, when such an Adventurer so perishes in the
Desert, we do not limit his discoveries to the last
authenticated spot of ground he pitched tent upon, dug
intrenchments round, and wrote good tidings home from—
but rather give him the benefit of the very last heap
of ashes we can trace him to have kindled, and call
by his name the extreme point to which we can track
his torn garments and abandoned treasures.*

Browning's Essay on Chatterton (1842)[1]

*An absolute vision is not for this world, but we are
permitted a continual approximation to it, every degree
of which in the individual, provided it exceed the
attainment of the masses, must procure him a clear
advantage. Did the poet ever attain to a higher
platform than where he rested and exhibited a result?
Did he know more than he spoke of?*

Browning's Essay on Shelley (1852)[2]

Browning ends *Pauline* by binding himself in "bands of friends" (*Pauline*, 1022), in a shared community of the guilty. A major difference between *Pauline* and *Paracelsus* (1835) is that the latter work gives to this communal bond a temporal dimension. It extends the burden of guilt backward in time to Paracelsus's predecessors, and forward in time to his successors, through the failure of his limited attainment to match his infinite aspiration. At the point of failure in *Pauline*, "The last point I can trace" (*Pauline*, 818), Browning embraces a wise deference and finds in his guilt a possibility of reorigination; *Paracelsus* records his more radical discovery that at the point

53

of origin itself, at the mainspring of human tradition, there is already a guilty consciousness of failure. Paracelsus is more swift, proud, and impatient than the Browning of *Pauline*. He must fall hard and for a long time before he appreciates the wisdom of choosing second place as the only place from which he or anyone else may begin. The poem is the story of his fortunate fall from isolated self-assertion into an intermediate niche in human time and its renewing traditions.

The wider social and historical resonance of Browning's themes is echoed in his choice of a loosely meditative dramatic form for *Paracelsus*. Although Browning obviously designed it for a mental and not an actual theater—"I have endeavoured to write a poem, not a drama," he insists in his 1835 preface—he does occasionally make telling use of dialogue as a way of unwinding the abrupt inward turns of *Pauline* and weaving them into an equally rough but more objective texture of dramatic interruptions and suppressions. Moreover, the quasi-dramatic format of *Paracelsus* commits Browning to something like a narrative order, its five parts approximating the five acts of a stage play and defining in large structural terms the interplay of beginnings, middles, and ends that is conspicuously absent from the informal *Pauline* but thematically central to both works. Finally, the conventions of dramatic art, rudimentary though they be in this poem, persistently cast Browning's reader as a member of a hypothetical audience; this theatrical sense of community in turn gives particular point to Paracelsus's lengthy endeavor to know his own mind in relation to other minds past, present, and future.

A VOICE FROM WITHIN

In *Paracelsus* Browning argues for a tradition rooted in renewal and recreated at any historical moment by an extension of the legacy of the past, which makes that historical moment an historic one as well. Although his Renaissance protagonist is only intermittently a poet, Browning's main argument receives its most explicit articulation in the terms of poetic tradition:

> [A voice from within.]
> *I hear a voice, perchance I heard*
> *Long ago, but all too low,*
> *So that scarce a care it stirred*
> *If the voice were real or no:*
> *I heard it in my youth when first*
> *The waters of my life outburst:*

But, now their stream ebbs faint, I hear
That voice, still low, but fatal-clear—
As if all poets, God ever meant
Should save the world, and therefore lent
Great gifts to, but who, proud, refused
To do his work, or lightly used
Those gifts, or failed through weak endeavour,
So, mourn cast off by him for ever,—
As if these leaned in airy ring
To take me; this the song they sing.

(II.281-96)

This is indeed, as the stage direction says, "a voice from within." Whether it is "real or no," the voice carries its own authority, reenacting in the present the past confession that it describes. It goes on to repeat the song of an internalized voice, which is itself repeating a song heard long ago. The voice greeting Paracelsus here is the voice of Aprile, a poet who shares a sense of election and guilty failure not only with Paracelsus and with the Browning of *Pauline*, but also with earlier poets. His predecessors' "fatal-clear" admission of guilt has been with Aprile since his initiation—and has arguably constituted that initiation.

Yet we trusted thou shouldst speak
The message which our lips, too weak,
Refused to utter,— shouldst redeem
Our fault: such trust, and all a dream!

(II.311-14)

Must one more recreant to his race
Die with unexerted powers
And join us, leaving as he found
The world, he was to loosen, bound?

(II.319-22)

Browning added all three of these quoted passages in 1849 as if to strengthen the peculiar continuity between the present singer and the past singers of whom he sings. Browning's revisions in 1849 seem to have been directed with particular care towards clarifying the relations between predecessors and successors that are implicit in the original text of 1835.[3] Even in the original text, Aprile's mournful "peers" refer to him as "the last" of their line (II.306-7) and urge him to

Tell us of thy sad undoing

> *Here, where we sit, ever pursuing*
> *Our weary task, ever renewing*
> *Sharp sorrow.*

(II.335-38)

The ambiguous "here" in the second line seems to invite Aprile to join his predecessors on their ground ("where we sit") and at the same time to hint that their ground is already also his (the scene of his "sad undoing"). The effect of this ambiguity is to place both Aprile and the earlier poets at an indeterminate but critical point of commerce between the present generation and the generations of the past. This passage suggests what Browning's 1849 additions reinforce: that, with his awareness of ultimate failure, the poet returns to something profoundly original; that, at the end of his career, the poet rediscovers a primary truth, one that has been present at the outbursting source of his poetic vocation.

Aprile's birth into poetry has been accompanied by challenging intimations that he is doomed to betray his own inspiration. There is a voice within his voice from within, and even in its earliest song it sings of a fall and a failure: "Lost, lost!" (II.297,401). The "message" Aprile's peers have weakly refused to utter matters less than the fact that they have refused to utter it. The message that matters is precisely the message they are once again uttering through Aprile: a message about the necessity of failure passed on from one generation to the next. Aprile renews the sharp sorrow of the song by making it his own, through having lived its truth. As his lips bear witness during Part II to his own "fault," to the gap between his aspirations and attainments as a would-be redeemer of the world, he makes the message of failure new and so attests the continuing validity of its tradition.[4]

Aprile's song invokes tradition as a check against two delusive responses to failure: solipsistic self-exaltation and nihilistic self-exhaustion. Both responses have attracted Paracelsus during the long and desperate soliloquy with which he opens Part II. Aprile breaks in on the soliloquy just as Paracelsus is beginning to enjoy his failure and to assert the unique grandeur of his guilt: "No man could ever offend as I have done . . . " (II.280). As usual throughout the first four parts of the poem, Paracelsus's self-aggrandizing assertion is both right and wrong. Aprile's song corrects the assertion by reinterpreting it through the discipline of tradition; *every* man has so offended, in that every man has offended by failing in his own way. Paracelsus has been tempted to accept a nihilistic reduction of his failure while reading the inscription of an earlier, anonymous "remembrancer." This "remembrancer" has written that the disappointments of experience

56

offer a lifelong proof of the adage that "Time fleets, youth fades, life is an empty dream" (II.41-53). Nihilism holds a powerful appeal for Paracelsus, and he will approach its abyss again in the predominantly retrospective Parts III and IV. But in the meantime Aprile's song counters the power of nihilism; he holds forth a different and more prospective power. For the featureless pattern prescribed by the remembrancer, as for Paracelsus's assertion of a sublimely guilty solitude, Aprile substitutes the evocative personality of a living tradition. It is to such a tradition that Paracelsus will refer his failure in Part V and thereby redeem it.

Aprile's song of failure, despite its apparent gloom, is finally as cheerful as anything in Browning. Putting failure at the origin makes the poet's decision to be a poet a joyful protest, a challenge from within answering the deeply personal challenge of his predecessors' failure. The predecessors, after all, have become predecessors in the first place by undergoing versions of the same experience and being challengers in their own right. That the joy of the challenge should be suppressed in their song is an act of strict kindness—their kindness to their followers or Aprile's sophisticated kindness to himself. They defer to their future by leaving their song incomplete and thus passing on to the successors who create that future the painful but rewarding burden of rediscovery.[5] The song is literally incomplete in the version of 1835, since Aprile breaks it off as he enters the scene in person; Browning's revision in 1849 may reflect an awareness that he had meanwhile taken such devices of interruption to their limit with *Sordello* in 1840.

The kindness of the song is also Browning's kindness to Paracelsus, who has just asked for the chance of renewal that the song covertly offers: "what hinders/Reward from springing out of toil, as changed/As bursts the flower from earth and root and stalk?" (II.275-77). For the time being Paracelsus misunderstands the song, of course, and misses its joy. It is a song meant to be misunderstood. Its joyful truth may be embodied by an Aprile or a Paracelsus, but not known before he gives his mission over to his followers in a climactic recognition of failure that joins him to his predecessors as their "peer." Not even Aprile grasps the full significance of the song until at the moment of his death the "White brows, lit up with glory; poets all!" come to crown him, too, with glory. He regally justifies their choice in the courtesy of his deference to his successor, the nonplussed Paracelsus (II.646-59).

Paracelsus understands more of the song, however, than the ironies of his encounter with Aprile in Part II would indicate. Near the end of Part IV, his friend Festus asks the question Paracelsus has asked in Part II, why Paracelsus will not renew his efforts and so "redeem the past" (IV.430). Paracelsus replies with a song of his own, which, in effect, reductively revises Aprile's song by dwelling only on the pain of its burden of loss: "The sad rhyme of the men who proudly clung / To their first fault, and withered in their pride" (IV.526-27). Browning's 1849 interpolations here parallel those that he made in Aprile's song; they enrich the context in similar ways by invoking the temporality of tradition. Browning gives Paracelsus a new introductory speech:

> *Often at midnight, when most fancies come,*
> *Would some such airy project visit me:*
> *But ever at the end . . . or will you hear*
> *The same thing in a tale, a parable?*

(IV.435-38)

The break in the third line is reminiscent of those through which Browning escapes potential enclosures in *Pauline*. Paracelsus's willingness to extend his fancies in a parable suggests a saving dissatisfaction with the thought of coming too quickly to "the end."

Paracelsus's parable suggests a further dissatisfaction with any simple sense of his own priority:

> *You and I, wandering over the world wide,*
> *Chance to set foot upon a desert coast.*
> *Just as we cry, "No human voice before*
> *Broke the inveterate silence of these rocks!"*
> *— Their querulous echo startles us; we turn:*
> *What ravaged structure still looks o'er the sea?*
> *Some characters remain, too! While we read,*
> *The sharp salt wind, impatient for the last*
> *Of even this record, wistfully comes and goes,*
> *Or sings what we recover, mocking it.*
> *This is the record; and my voice, the wind's.*

(IV.439-49)

These lines rapidly act out the play of assertion, deference, and recovery that is also important to Aprile's song. Paracelsus breaks the silence of the rocks with a cry that claims to be the first of its kind but only provokes a quarrel. His assertion of human priority at once transforms itself into something secondary, a startling echo. In the dreamlike atmosphere of this parable, the echoing voice is then further transformed into an echo of another kind, a "record" of earlier voices charactered amid the rocks. The acoustic force of Paracelsus's initial assertion brings him to a recognition of his secondariness as he "reads" and "recovers" the ravaged characters engraved by his newly found predecessors.

58

As Browning's poetry never wearies of suggesting, the proud imagination of the quester, if the quester is lucky, is subverted by its own authority. The "turn" in the fifth line above, with the return of Paracelsus's echoing voice, figures his turning on himself, his discovery that he is not the first of path-breaking, silence-breaking wanderers. Nor is Browning, who happily acknowledges his secondariness in a Shelleyan allusion of the type that one comes to expect at such moments in his early poems. The Poet of *Alastor* meets his death in a stony nook, where "One step, / One human step alone, has ever broken / The stillness of its solitude" (588-90). That one step is the Poet's own, and his splendid isolation is his doom. But Paracelsus's parable records his realization that he is not thus first or thus alone; perhaps that is why he has invited Festus along for the imaginative ride. In *Paracelsus*, as in *Pauline*, Browning defers to Shelley even while correcting him; more precisely, he defers to Shelley as a way of correcting him. For the fatal dilemma of solipsism imagined in *Alastor*, Browning substitutes a myth offering a way out of solipsism, a way that lies through the lively community of tradition.

This passage represents in miniature the transformation of Paracelsus from an autonomous to a deferential figure, which is the chief action of the poem. By imagining himself as secondary, as a reader finding his place in a tradition, Paracelsus grudgingly points the way to his own eventual recovery. In Part V he will learn to take the world as a grandly optimistic and open text, forever in the process of being written. But in Part IV Paracelsus is divided against his own healing powers. While he profoundly needs to enjoy an open future, he is superficially tormented by an intemperate desire for complete priority, which seems to close the future off. His consequent ambivalence about being either in first or in second place leads him to regard the activity of reading ironically and to identify his voice with that of the erosive, mocking wind, "impatient for the last."

This ambivalence emerges in the parable, where Paracelsus finds in the graven characters a song to the point, a song of impatience, or failed deferment. Despite the advice of their pilot to "avoid," "check," and "restrain" (IV.489-90), a crew of voyagers bring to light their bright statues of "lucid stone," come ashore, and build hollows of rock in which the statues are enshrined (IV.500-505). Such is their "task"; and, unlike the "task" of perpetual pursuit and renewal undertaken by Aprile and his peers (II.337), this one is all too capable of completion. No sooner have the voyagers finished than "happy throngs / Of gentle islanders" arrive by boat, "too late" to inform them that their work has been prematurely done on the wrong island (IV.508-16).

PARACELSUS   *Yet we called out — "Depart!*

59

	Our gifts, once given, must here abide.
	Our work is done; we have no heart
	To mar our work,"—we cried.
FESTUS	In truth?
PARACELSUS	Nay, wait: all this in tracings faint

On rugged stones strewn here and there, but piled
In order once: then follows—mark what follows!
"The sad rhyme of the men who proudly clung
To their first fault, and withered in their pride."

(IV.519-27)

The indispensable Festus interrupts to mar the work that is this parable, and Paracelsus ambiguously insists upon decorous closure by telling him to "wait," to defer his curiosity and mark what follows. One wants an answer to Festus's inserted question, to know whether Paracelsus's telling aligns him with his impatient voyagers or with their deferential pilot; but that is precisely the question Paracelsus's ambivalence toward his quest will not yet let him answer. By formulating the question, however, in the terms of a tradition, he anticipates the answer that will come to him in the evolutionary vision of Part V. Although Paracelsus's present discontent with either closure or postponement will lead him on to the renovating outburst of that final vision, in Part IV he can recollect from the earlier song of Aprile only its superficial message: all questers shall fail.

It is significant that Paracelsus concludes his visionary lecture in Part V with a vision of himself as a predecessor of future questers. "I shall emerge one day," he says (V.903), even though

As yet men cannot do without contempt;
'Tis for their good, and therefore fit awhile
That they reject the weak, and scorn the false,
Rather than praise the strong and true, in me:
But after, they will know me.

(V.895-99)

Paracelsus finally comes to understand the valuable challenge of a failure at the point of origin and to see in his own failure the origination of his successors. But first he must pass through a long-repressed infernal encounter with those exemplars of failure, his scientific predecessors; and, in the condensation of hallucination, he must see himself in them. With mingled resignation and bravado, he declares his independence of tradition: "No, no; I am the first and last, I think" (V.156). Much as a similar assertion has summoned Aprile's song in Part II, Paracelsus's assertion of uniqueness summons the ghosts of his predecessors:

60

> *What had you to do, sage peers?*
> *Here stand my rivals; Latin, Arab, Jew,*
> *Greek, join dead hands against me: all I ask*
> *Is, that the world enrol my name with theirs.*

> (V.160-63)

> *Just think, Aprile, all these leering dotards*
> *Were bent on nothing less than to be crowned*
> *As we! That yellow blear-eyed wretch in chief*
> *To whom the rest cringe low with feigned respect,*
> *Galen of Pergamos and hell—nay speak*
> *The tale, old man! We met there face to face:*
> *I said the crown should fall from thee. Once more*
> *We meet as in that ghastly vestibule:*
> *Look to my brow! Have I redeemed my pledge?*

> (V.177-85)

Paracelsus's very name records a debt to his predecessor Celsus. If he has redeemed the pledge, it is thanks to the challenge he has recognized in the failures of those who have gone before him. Galen's unspoken "tale," one suspects, is as like that of Paracelsus as the phrase "face to face" would imply.[6]

As Paracelsus faces up to tradition, so does Browning. He incorporates into Paracelsus's response to his forerunners a note of his own response to Shelley; the last line quoted above, "Look to my brow! Have I redeemed my pledge?" echoes the "Hymn to Intellectual Beauty" (61-62): "I vowed that I would dedicate my powers / To thee and thine—have I not kept the vow?" As in *Pauline*, Browning echoes Shelley's text to affirm a difference, a difference that humanizes Shelley's metaphysical aspiration, the difference between a private "vow" and a more public "pledge." Whereas Shelley dedicates himself to the service of an "unknown and awful" power and recalls his own dedicated labors by calling "the phantoms of a thousand hours / Each from his voiceless grave" ("Hymn," 40, 64-65), Browning writes of dedication to a power that is no less mysterious in its operation but more readily recognizable in its form. He has Paracelsus confront the phantoms of a past including not only his solitary labors, but the influence of earlier scientists in prompting and attending those labors. Tradition, the empowered past as Browning represents it, is neither unseen nor voiceless, but bears a human face and owns a human voice: Galen's past presence for Paracelsus and Shelley's past presence for Browning.

Browning's allusion to his predecessor underscores the rich analogy in *Paracelsus* between the situations of character and author, of

61

belated scientist and belated poet. Paracelsus at this ultimate stage of his quest sees what Browning sees about the individual's relation to tradition, but Paracelsus still hates it. In his idealistic insistence on personal autonomy, he too closely resembles the Shelley whom Browning would correct. He still feels the past too much as a burden to welcome it as an opportunity and justification for his incomplete but not insignificant work. Hence the febrile rhetoric of these lines, which defends him only temporarily against a dawning realization that the failure of each of the sages constitutes an august anticipation of his own imminent failure. The ultimate stage of Paracelsus's quest for scientific knowledge is but the penultimate stage of the quest for tradition on which Browning has sent him. In the lines that follow, his attitude toward the sages softens and more nearly approximates that of Browning. Paracelsus turns more reverently and receptively to another predecessor, "Persic Zoroaster, lord of stars," an earlier demystifier who, like Paracelsus, has taken on gods and declared them demons.[7] Paracelsus then goes on to effect a silent reconciliation with tradition by observing that "these old renowns," his predecessors, no longer stand on the far side of gloom (V.187-91). There is no need for him to say what has become of them. He has seated them deep inside himself, where his note may hearten the chorus of their challenging voice from within.

OPTIMISM AS REVISION

In *Paracelsus* Browning chose to dwell on the relations between predecessors and successors because he was intimately aware of their importance to his career—and of their importance to the career of any ambitious poet. Moreover, he had already found such relations to provide fertile ground for play in the writing of *Pauline*. In exploring the psychological relation of an individual talent to tradition, Browning was able to explore as well the technical problems of making a beginning and of sustaining an interest: problems that occupied him especially as he worked on *Paracelsus* and on the longer *Sordello*, which was begun over a year before it. The generational gap of poetic tradition, the saving break that characterizes successful relations between predecessors and successors, also characterizes successful relations between the beginnings and endings of individual poems. Like traditions, poems are generated or extended by an originating or reoriginating difference. This difference is a primary concern for Browning's management of narrative in both of his long early works —a concern variously resumed and refined in his dramas and dramatic lyrics. In *Paracelsus* and *Sordello* he sports again and again with premature closures and disclosures and so throws into narrative prominence the dialectic of anticipation and deferment, which is also his psychological theme.

In its "rise and progress" (Browning's 1835 preface), the attitude of Paracelsus toward his predecessors follows a romance movement of digressive return to the point of origin; *Paracelsus* traces this movement in its structure. The difference between the culminating insights of Part V and the initial insights of Part I is often remarkably slender. The following exchange from Part I, for example, articulates Browning's themes of repetition and deferment, failure and renewal, with considerable sophistication:

FESTUS
As strong delusions have prevailed ere now.
Men have set out as gallantly to seek
Their ruin. I have heard of such: yourself
Avow all hitherto have failed and fallen.

MICHAL
Nay, Festus, when but as the pilgrims faint
Through the drear way, do you expect to see
Their city dawn amid the clouds afar?

PARACELSUS
Ay, sounds it not like some old well-known tale?
For me, I estimate their works and them
So rightly, that at times I almost dream
I too have spent a life the sages' way,
And tread once more familiar paths.

(I.584-95)

Paracelsus is to learn that the "old well-known tale" is Zoroaster's, and Galen's, and Aprile's, and his own, and that it is true. The unique sense of election upon which he insists throughout Part I seems to him here, perhaps surprisingly, to be a repetition. But it is "almost" a repetition, the "almost" constituting a difference that separates his aspiration from the attainments of his predecessors on "familiar paths." Paracelsus's "almost" makes room for his own strivings; in turn those strivings by the end of the poem will have made him into a predecessor, a partial attainer, also one of those who "hitherto have failed and fallen."

To study Browning's narrative control in *Paracelsus* is to watch him guarding this "almost" and preserving a gap for the generation of his poem. Michal's speech in the passage quoted above very nearly tells the fortunes that await Aprile and Paracelsus. It closely approximates Paracelsus's later lines (which are in part about her), " 'Tis only when they spring to heaven that angels / Reveal themselves to you" (V.216-17; see also V.121-25 and V.286-91). Further on in Part I, Michal's intuitive grasp of the dangers to Paracelsus of "a complete success" (I.705) so exactly anticipates Browning's argument that it is no wonder Browning hurries her out of the poem and even out of life. At one point he silences her with the dramatic equivalent of techniques practiced in the narrative of *Sordello*:

> MICHAL   *Ask at once, Festus, wherefore he should scorn . . .*
> FESTUS   *Stay, Michal: Aureole, I speak guardedly*
>   *And gravely.*

(I.224-26)

Festus's interruption is a happy intersection of thematic with stylistic issues, as of dramatic with authorial apprehensions. If Festus (or Browning) does not take pains to speak guardedly and gravely, Michal's unstayed intuition may cut the poem short by leaping straight to its major conclusions about the value of the communities and traditions Paracelsus here scorns. The jagged surface of the reckless and bantering *Sordello* will demand that such interruptions be recognized as elaborations of meaning. *Paracelsus*, like almost any other work one cares to mention, moves smoothly in comparison to *Sordello*, and moments like this one obtrude themselves less sharply. It may be that an awareness of disparity between the earlier poem's endorsement of a tradition renewed by change and the comparative stability of its poetic form led Browning to the experimental extremes of its successor.

From the first *Paracelsus* exhibits ironies like those in the passages just quoted. Speakers not only say things that are truer than they can possibly know at the time, they often say them *about* time, the time of the poem. Browning gives himself a severe problem of authorial deferment with the very opening lines. In his first speech Paracelsus tells his friends that the right way of remembering him will be to "forget" his "waywardness," "to dwell / Only on moments such as these" (I.11-14),

>   *as Michal, some months hence,*
> *Will say, "this autumn was a pleasant time,"*
> *For some few sunny days; and overlook*
> *Its bleak wind, hankering after pining leaves.*

(I.16-19)

This is a pleasant articulation of the optimistic perspective traditionally given as the last word on Browning.[8] Before joining tough-minded modern readers in revising that critical tradition, one should observe the close similarity between this passage and the vision of forgiveness with which the poem ends in its grand proclamation that "even hate is but a mask of love's" and its general benediction of all souls, "All with a touch of nobleness, despite / Their error" (V.874-81). The close similarity between Parts I and V of *Paracelsus* makes the problem of revising optimism Browning's problem, too. In fact, it makes it Browning's problem *first*. It invites the critic to let Browning's optimism justify itself and to settle for the humbler task of seeing how he carries out the project he had announced in *Pauline*, the project of renewing an old claim. Browning has begun by giving his Paracelsus an advanced awareness of temporal issues: Paracelsus anticipates memories, recommends lapses of memory, and programs happy returnings "home" (I.6-7). Such sophistication in his protagonist will make Browning's task the difficult one of discrediting an initial optimism without banishing it beyond recovery by Part V.

As Paracelsus already understands in these early lines, optimism involves a kind of "overlooking" or revision, and his notion of just what kind of revision may sustain an abiding optimism is precisely the substance of his difference from Browning at this point. For Paracelsus, "overlook" here means "forget"; by the end of the poem, he will have come to the better understanding that to "overlook" is to survey sunny human possibilities without blinking the equally human frailty and distress that such a survey must include. Browning's task of revising his hero's revisionism is further complicated by a passage at the end of Part I, in which an optimistic Paracelsus predicts that even those "adventitious aims" and common pleasures that his quest pledges him to neglect (I.807),

> *even these will follow with the rest—*
> *As in the steady rolling Mayne, asleep*
> *Yonder, is mixed its mass of schistous ore,*
> *My own affections laid to rest awhile,*
> *Will waken purified, subdued alone*
> *By all I have achieved.*

(I.810-15)

Not only does Paracelsus in his hubris aspire to know "the secret of the world" (I.276), here he verges on the secret of the poem, foreseeing his own recovery through Festus's song of the Mayne, a song of continuity gently broken by subdued beginnings (V.418-46). Paracelsus's quest "to comprehend the works of God" (I.533) bears a curious relation to his apparent comprehension of the works of Robert Browning.

For such precocious comprehension he pays the price of sustaining Browning's irony. Much of what Paracelsus says in Part I is charged with double meaning, as in this last speech the word "rest" is charged. The word occurs twice, and its two senses of "remainder" and "repose" begin to merge. Ordinary aims like those of winning praise and love, Paracelsus says, will follow with the attainment of the "rest," the extraordinary aims of his quest. Praise and love will follow him once he has achieved his "all" and come to a point of rest where nothing remains to be done. His own affections will also be "subdued," made more restful, through the benign neglect entailed by his pursuit of that total achievement. A reader of *Pauline* will suspect that this ideal of restful totality is too securely soothing to be true. There is an impulse in Paracelsus that obscurely suspects it, too, as his next lines suggest:

> Till then—till then . . .
> Ah, the time-wiling loitering of a page
> Through bower and over lawn, till eve shall bring
> The stately lady's presence whom he loves—
> The broken sleep of the fisher whose rough coat
> Enwraps the queenly pearl—these are faint types!
> See, see, they look on me: I triumph now!
>
> (I.815-21)

These lines express the restless impulse in whose energies Paracelsus will finally find a more Browningesque repose than he has just been imagining. The break in the passage—"Till then—till then . . ."— introduces that restless impulse through images of impatient "loitering" and "broken sleep." These images mount to a climax of impatience that collapses the future into the present, as the "then" of line 815 becomes "now" at line 821: "I triumph now!"

Whenever Paracelsus thus aspires in Part I to fix the future, Browning fills his mouth with ambiguous prophecies. "All / Whose innate strength supports them shall succeed / No better than the sages" (I.295-97); "too intimate a tie / Connects me with our God!" (I.359-60). Both of these statements about how Paracelsus will differ from his predecessors are true, and both are true in senses different from those he intends. He intends to say that he will meet the challenge of the sages' failure by virtue of a unique alliance with his God. The poem will end, however, with his recognition that, as a worthy successor to the sages, he has succeeded by failing in his own way, just as they have done. In tying down God, meanwhile, as in tying down the future, he ties himself too intimately. He refuses to defer; he repeatedly insists on change and triumph *now*.

> 'Tis time
> New hopes should animate the world, new light
> Should dawn from new revealings to a race
> Weighed down so long, forgotten so long; thus shall
> The heaven reserved for us at last receive
> Creatures whom no unwonted splendours blind.
>
> (I.372-77)

> *Make no more giants, God,*
> *But elevate the race at once!*

(I.779-80)

In Part V Paracelsus will inherit a future of freer hopes and splendors when he accepts his predecessors in aspiration and failure and when, like the wisely faulty poet in *Pauline*, he breaks the constricting "seal" of completeness from his brow (I.548).

SIGNS: THE ROBE OF TRUTH

The completeness of Paracelsus's plans in Part I receives expression in discrete, pictorial imagery: the similes of "the steady rolling Mayne," for instance, or of "the fisher whose rough coat / Enwraps the queenly pearl." This picture of the future is dramatically broken when in the first sentence of Part II Paracelsus says that the skyline of Constantinople runs "Like a Turk verse along a scimitar" (II.6). For Browning a simile often serves as a form of interpretation in which the vehicle comments upon the tenor it replaces. In Part I Paracelsus's similes are relatively direct and self-contained, but by Part II he has become a more tentative and bewildered interpreter. With the simile of the "Turk verse," he stands at a second remove from his perceptions and likens what he sees to an inscription, a series of signs requiring further interpretation. The experience of failure in the intervening years between Parts I and II has made a difference and has begun to teach Paracelsus his own secondariness. The paradoxical value of this secondariness lies in the fact that no further interpretation is forthcoming; the "Turk verse" remains enigmatic, untranslated, and therefore incomplete. In retrospect, Paracelsus's earlier description of his simpler similes as "faint types" becomes quite accurate. In comparison to the more difficult and genuinely exploratory language of Part II, the similes of the Mayne and the fisher seem as prematurely determined as the triumphantly projected career that they represent. The sense of defeat plaguing Paracelsus in Part II lets the poem open — as his simile opens — and enter on the course towards recovery.

In Part I Festus countered Paracelsus's assertive simile, "I see my way as birds their trackless way" (I.560), by denying its interpretive validity:

> *This would hold*
> *Were it the trackless air, and not a path*
> *Inviting you, distinct with footprints yet*
> *Of many a mighty marcher gone that way.*

(I.567-70)

67

The opening of Part II justifies Festus's emphasis on tradition. Paracelsus has traveled to Constantinople in order to visit the house of a Greek conjuror, who has amassed a library of depositions from earlier questers. Paracelsus pauses to plunder tradition by consulting "the scrawled / Uncouth recordings of the dupes of this / Old archgenethliac" and to add to the prints of other mighty marchers his own "few blurred characters" (II.23-36). As Paracelsus obsessively recurs to scriptorial imagery, it becomes clear that among his new attainments is a rudimentary semiology, which itself betokens his estrangement from the confidence of Part I.

> *Yet God is good: I started sure of that,*
> *And why dispute it now? I'll not believe*
> *But some undoubted warning long ere this*
> *Had reached me: a fire-labarum was not deemed*
> *Too much for the old founder of these walls.*

(II.262-66)

An 1849 revision of the fourth line makes explicit the connection with other inscriptions: "stars would write his will in heaven." The original version, restored in 1863, reinforces the secondariness of reading such inscriptions by placing Paracelsus after Constantine, the earlier reader of signs who gave his name to the city ("In hoc signo vinces"). [9]

Paracelsus finds worthy of belief "the old Greek's prophecy" that "I shall not quit / His chamber till I know what I desire," and he joins to the prophecy a cryptic question of his own, "Was it the light wind sang it o'er the sea?" (II.62-65). Browning added this line in 1849; it serves to confirm previous indications that Paracelsus has become not a voice but an auditor, secondary in spite of himself. The conjuror's "chamber" is a microcosm of the incomprehensibly inscribed universe into which Part II rudely ushers its frustrated hero. The added line about the wind's song suggests that Paracelsus, might he but know it, has already heard what he desires in the fluent nuances of the wind. But Paracelsus may understand the wind's song only by deferring to it and striving to decipher its meaning—that is, by patiently enlarging the chamber of inscription to include such an evidently outdoor phenomenon as a sea breeze. He is far from such patience in Part II; and even in the somewhat better tempered atmosphere of Part IV, when the light wind returns to play over the graven characters of his parable of failure, he will hear in its elusive song not the voice of prophetic promise, but a barren mockery.

Paracelsus's unwilling discovery of his status as a secondary reader or auditor shows how Browning uses the very strength of his protagonist's excessive foreknowledge against him. The champion of "now," Paracelsus wishes in Part I for uniform elevation of his race "at once" (I.780) and in Part II for an apocalyptic reckoning of his personal attainment: "now, let my time be!"; "Now! I can go no farther; well or ill, / 'Tis done" (II.55-57). Part II grants a version of his wish, and the unitary fullness of its presence appalls him. Time itself comes to seem a filled "interspace," and the intervening years seem a gap that is not a gap:

> All is one day, one only step between
> The outset and the end: one tyrant all-
> Absorbing aim fills up the interspace,
> One vast unbroken chain of thought.

(II.151-54)

As in the "hedgerows" of *Pauline* and in Browning's gorgeous "gyres" from *Sordello*, Paracelsus's impatience chains him in the confining monotony of the repeated "one" and in the tyranny of a continuity that fuses even the breaks between poetic lines. [10]

As in *Pauline* and *Sordello*, however, there is freedom in declining instant autonomy. Paracelsus momentarily realizes this freedom in the handsome passage that follows his vision of infernal "oneness." In the course of his quest, as he now remembers it,

> life, death, light and shadow,
> The shows of the world, were bare receptacles
> Or indices of truth to be wrung thence,
> Not ministers of sorrow or delight:
> A wondrous natural robe in which she went.
> For some one truth would dimly beacon me
> From mountains rough with pines, and flit and wink
> O'er dazzling wastes of frozen snow, and tremble
> Into assured light in some branching mine
> Where ripens, swathed in fire, the liquid gold —
> And all the beauty, all the wonder fell
> On either side the truth, as its mere robe;
> I see the robe now — then I saw the form.

(II.156-68)

Paracelsus's distinction between the splendid "form" of truth and "its mere robe" suggests the traditional image of language as the dress of thought, and a linguistic analogy is helpful for an appreciation of these lines. Heretofore, Paracelsus has regarded the phenomena of the natural world as "receptacles" or "indices," the manifest signs of a fugitive latent truth. As he pauses from his quest and reclaims the past in memory, all that remain to him are these signs: mnemonic traces now rich with a "beauty" and "wonder" all their

69

own. He turns aside from the dreary inscriptions of the Greek conjuror's chamber only to become a reader of his own internal inscriptions and to be caught up by the power of secondary revision. Paracelsus has just said that "all life has been forgotten" (II.150); but, as these brilliant lines reveal, it has been not forgotten but imaginatively transformed. He experiences the truth of what he has glibly told Michal in the opening speech of the poem: memory is an agency of representation and speaks a kind of language that can change and renew what he has thought lost.

In confronting apparent failure, Paracelsus succeeds in forging a new, quick voice that outstrips his pictorial imagery from Part I. What makes the passage a tour de force is the thorough ambiguity of its reference. Is the language scientific or figurative? Does it describe outward or inward events? The sources cited in the note Browning appended to the poem make it clear that Paracelsus was, after his fashion, an empiricist and explorer of the natural world. But if the "mountains" and "pines" are real mountains and pines of sixteenth-century Europe, what about the "wink" of truth or the swathing "fire"? If, on the other hand, the "assured light" is figuratively the lamp of scientific knowledge, are the "branches" of the "mine" ramifications that the light reveals for further investigation? Or is Paracelsus, the medical metallurgist who, according to Browning's note, was also "the father of modern chemistry," talking here about an actual mine?[11] The fiery play of this poetry refuses to commit itself to either a geological or a psychological landscape. It is "wondrous natural," both natural and supernatural, and thus utterly characteristic of those moments in this and other poems when Browning's theme is the creative revision of the received past.

For the first time in the poem, Paracelsus enjoys a triumph free from irony, and it is no coincidence that, for the first time in the poem, he is discovering the unexpected. He has begun in Part I by gloriously anticipating acts of memory; now an authentic glory takes him unawares, in a memory that is totally unpredicted, and even unpredictable. So Browning takes revenge upon his precocious protagonist by showing up such precocity in the light of something better. As Paracelsus has said earlier, the special pain of remembering pleasures hitherto unnoticed is something he has not bargained for, something "beyond / The obligation of my strictest vow, / The contemplation of my wildest bond" (II.109-11). He has not foreseen that

> The tract, doomed to perpetual barrenness,
> Would seem one day, remembered as it was,
> Beside the parched sand-waste which now it is,

70

Already strewn with faint blooms, viewless then.

(II.116-19)

Could he have foreseen and forestalled this consequence, however, Paracelsus could never have recalled the wonderful, neglected wayside beauties of his quest. For it is the blinding energy of his repression that has awakened those beauties. "I see the robe now—then I saw the form"; his earlier pursuit of the "form" of truth is what makes its visionary "robe" recoverable now in memory. Aprile will later expose the original desolation at the root of such recovery when he gently hypothesizes that the world itself is a "contrived" show of thought:

> *Some say the earth is even so contrived*
> *That tree and flower, a vesture gay, conceal*
> *A bare and skeleton framework. Had we means*
> *Answering to our mind!*

(II.507-10)

As Aprile understands, to re-cover this barren framework through imaginative perception is to recover the beauty of the earth and make it human. Paracelsus, who has ravaged and uprooted the "shows of the world" for the sake of "truth to be wrung thence," now stands at the brink of seeing himself as the unconscious weaver of the robe of truth—as the contriver of a more imaginative beauty.

Realizing that the pleasure of memory is a compensation that he issues to himself brings Paracelsus small comfort:

> *So much is good, then, in this working sea*
> *Which parts me from that happy strip of land:*
> *But o'er that happy strip a sun shone, too!*
> *And fainter gleams it as the waves grow rough,*
> *And still more faint as the sea widens; last*
> *I sicken on a dead gulf streaked with light*
> *From its own putrefying depths alone.*

(II.170-76)

Paracelsus imagines the energies of his own will first as the vigor of a working sea, then as the slow heat of a stagnant decomposition. "That happy strip of land" that he would set against these consuming energies represents the early time when he ran over "the seven little grassy fields" to tell Festus of his decision to undertake the glorious quest (II.144). Yet, as Paracelsus seems dimly to realize, even the beauty of this early memory derives from the joy of his decision to leave the fields behind; it too lives only in light cast up by his own "putrefying depths." All is subject to Paracelsus's irrepressible

71

will; this is the sense in which "All is alike at length" (II.179)—the sense in which Browning's first poem had declared that "Commanding, for commanding, sickens" the soul (*Pauline*, 817). But between this assertion of sameness and the earlier "All is one day," Paracelsus's surprising memory has denied sameness and found a momentary virtue in the difference between expectation and event.

ONE DISSEVERED WORLD

This difference between expectation and event is precisely the difference between aspiration and attainment; it is what defines failure and initiates regeneration in *Paracelsus* and throughout Browning's works. Aprile's voice from within sings of this difference as a "fault," which successors may strive to redeem. Even before that voice interrupts the opening soliloquy of Part II, Paracelsus anticipates its message and crudely practices its kind deceptions on himself:

> *Even now, why not desire, for mankind's sake,*
> *That if I fail, some fault may be the cause,*
> *That, though I sink, another may succeed?*
> *O God, the despicable heart of us!*
> *Shut out this hideous mockery from my heart!*
>
> (II.198-202)

Paracelsus's defensive denial here protects him from a paralyzing conviction of original fault. He must ultimately recognize his fault and defer to its regenerating power; at this point, however, the furtherance of his quest requires that he exclude any such recognition from consciousness as completely as possible. The likelihood of failure mocks him, and he both acknowledges and defends against its painfulness by calling the likelihood a "mockery"; he has to turn its mockery back upon itself if his quest is to continue.

Such willful forgetting is writ large into the encounter between Paracelsus and Aprile, and it accounts for much of the scene's grim humor.[12] The song of Aprile elicits Paracelsus's scarcely forgotten fears—as it is intended to do. Browning inserted the following lines in 1849 to make the return of Paracelsus's threatening knowledge unmistakable:

> *Art thou the sage I only seemed to be,*
> *Myself of after-time, my very self*
> *With sight a little clearer, strength more firm,*
> *Who robes him in my robe and grasps my crown*
> *For just a fault, a weakness, a neglect?*
>
> (II.347-51)

The apposition of "fault" and "neglect" suggests again what Paracelsus cannot let himself know: that in order to proceed he must err by forgetting the possibility that there exists an original, irreparable fault. When Aprile reveals the cause of his own failure, he uses temporal terms that apply to Paracelsus as well: "I could not curb / My yearnings to possess at once the full / Enjoyment" (II.388-90). Paracelsus errs wildly in construing Aprile's home truth as the raving of "Some moonstruck creature" (II.405). That he errs not only wildly, but willingly, is clear from another 1849 revision that gives him the additional lines "yet he seemed / To echo one foreboding of my heart / So truly that . . . no matter!" (II.407-9). The enormity of the threat that Aprile's knowledge poses to Paracelsus's vestigial optimism is matched only by the enormity of Paracelsus's evasion in calling such significant repressed material "no matter."

The greatest evasion in Part II comes with Paracelsus's climactic and reductive question to Aprile:

> *Are we not halves of one dissevered world,*
> *Whom this strange chance unites once more? Part? never!*
> *Till thou the lover, know; and I, the knower,*
> *Love—until both are saved. Aprile, hear!*
> *We will accept our gains, and use them—now!*

$$(II.634-38)$$

The urgent "now!" (another 1849 addition) repeats the reduction to mere presence that has come at the end of Part I and crystallizes the sad relapse of the whole speech from the fiery heights of Paracelsus's earlier soliloquy. The spatial fixity of the future as it is pictured here prefigures major ironies of Sordello's career: for him as for Paracelsus, such schematic imagining is ample "penance" in itself (II.627, III.588). Rejecting as he must the possibility of failure, Paracelsus snatches up the future rather than deferring to it. He encloses himself in a spatial fiction of complementarity and earns the airtight future he deserves: "I have attained" (II.661). His fear of failure is appeased by such a fiction, because it presents a diminished, determinate goal. But in accepting this goal Paracelsus insults his own insatiable energies; he will obliquely acknowledge the insult with his song of the intemperate voyagers in Part IV. Browning thus lets the intemperate optimism of his protagonist work out its own fitting ruin. Paracelsus locks himself into dualistic misconceptions, which will confine him for the next two parts of the poem within the epigrammatic scope of "mind is nothing but disease, / And natural health is ignorance" (IV.279-80). The secondary beauty and wonder born of his repressive questing will themselves be repressed, with rare escapes, until hallucination lets them return in Part V.

Paracelsus's dualisms of knowledge and love, body and spirit, human and divine, are defenses lately and halfheartedly erected against the power of his own will. The prime mover of Parts III and IV remains what Festus rightly calls Paracelsus's self-baffled yet

> *resolute soul, which nought*
> *Avails to awe save these delusions bred*
> *From its own strength, its selfsame strength disguised,*
> *Mocking itself.*

(III.812-15)

In these intermediate and comparatively flat parts of the poem, Paracelsus harnesses himself to the cultivation of present good and does his best to repudiate the anticipations of his early quest: "I thus renounced them and resolved to reap / Some present fruit" (III.649-50). To his great credit, he finds that his best is not enough and that the quest is not so easily to be renounced. As his old questing energies repeatedly break through his more recent and weak defenses, Paracelsus's speech in Parts III and IV takes on a new, nervous vacillation. The recurrent image of himself as acting out an undesired part (III.592,736; IV.688) witnesses to a self-division, a doubleness of mind, that is displayed in ironies directed now at the quest he has abandoned and now at his futile endeavor to abandon it. It is to the interior doubleness of Paracelsus, "half stupid and half mad" (III.746), that his construction of dualistic intellectual systems most deeply answers.

Near the beginning of Part III, he twice interrupts Festus when Festus begins to remind him of his earlier striving:

FESTUS   *O you must remember,*
                               For all your glorious . . .

PARACELSUS   *Glorious? ay, this hair,*
            These hands—nay, touch them, they are mine! Recall
            With all the said recallings, times when thus
            To lay them by your own ne'er turned you pale
            As now. Most glorious, are they not?

(III.82-87)

FESTUS   *You, who of old could never tame yourself*
            To tranquil pleasures, must at heart despise . . .

PARACELSUS *Festus, strange secrets are let out by death*
            Who blabs so oft the follies of this world:
            And I am death's familiar, as you know.

(III.107-11)

74

Paracelsus's first interruption expresses a vigilance to repress ambitious desires just below the surface of consciousness; his second interruption expresses this vigilance more indirectly and with greater force. Try as he may to restrain himself from "blabbing" and from pursuing what he defensively regards as the "folly" of his original calling, the very effort of restraint presents itself to his imagination as a "death." His inability to tolerate Festus's allusions to early energies confirms the undying persistence of those energies; even in changing the subject, Paracelsus "blabs" in spite of himself. Recognizing the inconsistency between his present life of safe but deadly renunciation and the impulse within him that is most alive, he later confides, "To be consistent I should die at once" (III.563).

A more vital consistency awaits Paracelsus in the august anticipations of Part V, with its vision of humanity under the aspect of the future. Meanwhile, a glimpse of that vision comes near the end of Part III, at a welcome imaginative oasis for the reader journeying between the more fertile lands of Parts II and V. Paracelsus turns from his internal conflicts to the external scene. He describes the dawn, with a chastened but uncompromising idiom that retrieves some of his earlier power of speech, and with a careful attention that invalidates his hasty separation of knowledge from love:

> See, morn at length. The heavy darkness seems
> Diluted, grey and clear without the stars;
> The shrubs bestir and rouse themselves as if
> Some snake, that weighed them down all night, let go
> His hold; and from the East, fuller and fuller,
> Day, like a mighty river, flowing in;
> But clouded, wintry, desolate and cold.
> Yet see how that broad prickly star-shaped plant,
> Half-down in the crevice, spreads its woolly leaves
> All thick and glistering with diamond dew.

> (III.1032-41)

Paracelsus begins in these lines to shake off the snake of his self-imposed restraints. He makes his best beginning with line 1039, when he breaks with the continuity of the river of daylight—an image doubly continuous in that it recalls his naively confident use of the Mayne in Part I. Paracelsus's "Yet" interrupts the descriptive flow of the passage and introduces a new sense of responsive, struggling growth like that exploited by the Browning of *Pauline*. "Half-down in the crevice," rhythmically as well as botanically arresting, the star-shaped plant greets the coming day with a gesture that discredits the debilitating severance of love from knowledge that has ended Part II. In his last speech Paracelsus will recur to this plant for an image of the "knowledge" that "love" strengthens: "strong from weakness, like a chance-sown plant / Which, cast on stubborn soil, puts forth changed buds / And softer stains, unknown in happier climes" (V.696-701). C. Willard Smith calls the star-shaped plant "a weed wearing the shape of aspiration."[13] One should add that Browning's image takes note of the sobering conditions that make aspiration possible: the plant wears the shape of restoration in the face of loss as it represents the absent "stars" of line 1033.

Paracelsus's shaky defenses mask the painful yet optimistic truth that is his glory and the glory of Browning's humankind: that defeat in any conceivable present is a necessary condition of future triumph.[14] The crucible of Paracelsus's final illness burns these defenses away and leaves him with the original, ennobling instinct to strive, which prompts his recognition of the star-shaped plant. This instinct is never rejected by Paracelsus or by Browning, but it is reinterpreted over the course of the poem as a warrant of difference rather than sameness, and especially of the difference in time that is deferment. Paracelsus learns to distance himself from his God and to sever the too-intimate "tie" of a prescribed future, and he learns that such decisive distancing brings strength. Even from the depths of Part IV, he can voice a different conception of his relation to "God's glory," one that is both more reticent and more creative than the tie of Part I:

> 'tis vain to talk of forwarding
> God's glory otherwise; this is alone
> The sphere of its increase, as far as men
> Increase it; why, then, look beyond this sphere?
> We are his glory.

> (IV.599-603)

This passage, which sounds so like the hubristic Paracelsus of Part I, in fact carefully defers human attainment to a future of "forwarding" and "increasing." "We are his glory." This statement of identity points both ways; humankind constitutes God's glory, and the work of increasing God's glory is the process whereby humankind knows what it is.

The idea will recur to Paracelsus with another ambiguity when in Part V he declares that "We have to live alone to set forth well / God's praise" (V.569-70). This is another passage Browning revised into ambiguity by striking the commas in his manuscript copy that originally set off "alone" and marked it as an adverb. With the ambiguous placement and revised punctuation of "alone," Browning makes the word function as an adjective as well: the passage suggests both the dependence of collective identity on solitary acts of creative

76

vitality and the necessity that Paracelsus break out of the death-in-life of Parts III and IV if he is to do any "living" worthy of the name. In crying to God out of the depths of failure for "my first energy," "that invincible faith" (II.257-58), "The supernatural consciousness of strength / Which fed my youth" (V.269-70), Paracelsus humbly asks for the chance to prove what "we are." He does so in each instance by invoking a distant God as a perpetual reminder that there is plenty of human work left to be done.

LIKE A HUMAN FACE

Paracelsus attains in Part V a sustained perspective on such human work and on his own place in the continuing change and redefinition of humanity—a perspective earned through a difficult ordeal by hallucinatory fire. The passage of delirium in which Paracelsus encounters Galen and sees his own failure in that of his predecessors immediately leads to the summoning of a figure that has recognizable antecedents in Part II:

> *In truth, my delicate witch,*
> *My serpent-queen, you did but well to hide*
> *The juggles I had else detected. Fire*
> *May well run harmless o'er a breast like yours!*
> *The cave was not so darkened by the smoke*
> *But that your white limbs dazzled me: oh, white,*
> *And panting as they twinkled, wildly dancing!*
>
> (V.192-98)

While this witch has life enough of her own, she is also the offspring of two contrary figures that have represented Paracelsus's ambivalent attitudes toward his quest: the bewitching "wild nursling," tempting him to insomnia and to a denial of his common humanity (II.221-28), and the "one truth," "beaconing" and beckoning him on to the sheer joys of questing (II.161-67). Paracelsus's language works here with the speed of the transforming fire that he is ultimately attempting to describe, and whose aid he enlists in overcoming an ambivalence of his own making. Both "truth" and "witch" occur in the first line, and one meaning of the first sentence is that the witchery and the truth are accomplices in an allowable juggle that is just the reverse of the kind deception practiced by Aprile's peers. Their song from within has hidden possible regeneration under original failure; the wild and dazzling dance of the witch, as it were in response to that song, has kept alive the promise of success by keeping the necessity of failure undetected until now, Paracelsus's last hour.

Her cave, like the earlier "branching mine" (II.164) and the yet earlier "opening out" of truth's "imprisoned splendour" (I.726-35), is a fault breaking up the earth's surface, a pocket of possibility. The fire playing across her white limbs is the "centre-fire" of renewing change to which Paracelsus later refers, the element of discontinuity that

> *heaves underneath the earth,*
> *And the earth changes like a human face;*
> *The molten ore bursts up among the rocks,*
> *Winds into the stone's heart, outbranches bright*
> *In hidden mines.*

(V.653-57)

This "centre-fire" is fundamentally one with the "sheet of winding subterraneous fire" that Festus likens to Paracelsus's heroic originality (V.395). (Until 1888 the text spoke of this fire as a "winding sheet"—a pun of potential reorigination that one wishes Browning had retained.) The bright witch is a strongly imagined figure for Paracelsus's earliest defensive energies: energies more primitive than the subsequent ambivalence and dualism they have generated; more primitive, and so more memorable, than even his dedication to the "charm of charms," the object of the quest towards which they have first impelled him.

> *I cared not for your passionate gestures then,*
> *But now I have forgotten the charm of charms,*
> *The foolish knowledge which I came to seek,*
> *While I remember that quaint dance; and thus*
> *I am come back, not for those mummeries,*
> *But to love you, and to kiss your little feet*
> *Soft as an ermine's winter coat!*

(V.199-205)

With the "scattered lights" of this passage, the poem penetrates most deeply into the subject announced in Browning's preface of 1835: the "phenomenon of the mind or the passions" of its protagonist. Even Paracelsus's coveted "knowledge" is forgotten, but decisive traces remain of an impulse anterior to knowledge: a protestant impulse that Sordello will call "some existence like a pact / And protest against Chaos, some first fact / I' the faint of time" (*Sordello*, V.555-57). To quest is to protest against the fatal continuity and indifference of a shapeless, reductive chronology and to work at shaping a better future. Some seventy lines later in this passage Paracelsus will repeat the act of protest, rejecting any notion that human life may know ultimate closure: "I, for one, protest / Against it, and I hurl it

78

back with scorn" (V.278-79). In addressing the witch, Paracelsus identifies his primitive impulse to protest as an impulse also "to love"; he discards his misconceived dualism of love and knowledge and returns to a radical source of human identity. The "quaint dance" that constitutes his earliest memory is a celebration of the continuing power to make new beginnings.

This power is celebrated at much greater length in Paracelsus's final speech on the evolution of human glory as a perpetual new beginning. Each apparent completion of the evolutionary scheme is in fact an opportunity to start again. "So far the seal / Is put on life" (V.711-12), but "progress is / The law of life, man is not Man as yet" (V.742-43).

> *But in completed man begins anew*
> *A tendency to God. Prognostics told*
> *Man's near approach; so in man's self arise*
> *August anticipations, symbols, types*
> *Of a dim splendour ever on before*
> *In that eternal circle life pursues.*
>
> (V.772-77)

The least expected splendor in these three hundred lines is Browning's tacit confession that the evolutionary scheme is itself a figure of speech, a glad fiction whose very fictiveness confirms humanity's original power: "the new glory mixes with the heaven / And earth; man, once descried, imprints for ever / His presence on all lifeless things" (V.718-20). Such distinctively human imprinting lies behind the ebullient lecture on natural history that Paracelsus is even now delivering. A representative man reading the world as a text of his own issuing, he has at last found a vantage point that subsumes his earlier roles as pure author or pure auditor. The ability that attributes "deep thoughts" to "herded pines" (V.724) has just been extravagantly demonstrated by Paracelsus himself in imagining young volcanoes, "cyclops-like, / Staring together with their eyes on flame" (V.662-63). His sermon on human making implicitly refers for its text back to his own work as a sometime poet: that "the winds / Are henceforth voices, wailing or a shout" (V.720-21) is already clear from Paracelsus's parable in Part IV.[15]

Paracelsus confesses to the pathetic fallacy, then, in such a way that the very confession strengthens his celebration of the transfiguring energies that distinguish human activities as human. "The earth changes like a human face" because to change is human; this very line of poetry changes the earth in a peculiarly human fashion. The entire poem has been working towards a definition of what is human, perhaps most remarkably in the lines that follow Paracelsus's address

79

to his witch. When Festus expresses a wish for peace and for the comforting influence of Michal, Paracelsus replies,

> *Cruel! I seek her now—I kneel—I shriek—*
> *I clasp her vesture—but she fades, still fades;*
> *And she is gone; sweet human love is gone!*

(V.213-15)

The "vesture" is the "wondrous natural robe" (II.160), the "vesture gay" (II.508), with which imagination clothes a world of absence. By the end of Part V, Paracelsus will have attained the wisdom to hold the vesture fast and to locate fulfillment in the future. But the more immediate question remains, who is the absent "she"? Shelley had fewer doubts than Browning concerning such questions, and in the passage from *Alastor* to which Browning here alludes "she" stands for erotic fulfillment: "The spirit of sweet human love has sent / A vision to the sleep of him who spurned / Her choicest gifts / . . . / Lost, lost, for ever lost!" (*Alastor*, 203-9).[16] But Browning seems more radically indecisive about the proper ends of love, and his indecision creates a problem of grammatical antecedence. Is "she" Michal by the fire-side or the fiery dancing witch? The affectionate propriety of Paracelsus's "sweet human love" for the dead Michal will be readily granted; indeed, he has been half in love with her since the beginning of the poem. But it is equally impossible to overlook the witch. Paracelsus has not been a very good listener hitherto in the scene, and the speech of over a hundred lines that this passage introduces is oblivious of Festus and Michal alike. Moreover, Paracelsus's most recent words have concerned his "love" for the witch.

The difficulty of knowing who "she" is, is the difficulty of knowing what is "human" in *Paracelsus*, and in Browning generally.[17] The summoning of the witch is the most concisely successful of Paracelsus's attempts to address certain crises of his questing, which may also be considered as crises of human definition. This is in fact how Paracelsus considers them in several passages from Part II that surround the images of the "wild nursling" and the "one truth." In passages recurring at curiously, almost arithmetically regular intervals, he fluctuates between seeing human life as quest and as rest, between seeing himself as a superman "worthy beyond peer" and as a fool "wasted past retrieve" (II.40-41).

> *To lose myself*
> *Among the common creatures of the world,*
> *To draw some gain from having been a man,*
> *Neither to hope nor fear, to live at length!*
> *Even in failure, rest!*

(II.74-78)

> *behold,*
> *He bares his front: a mortal ventures thus*
> *Serene amid the echoes, beams and glooms!*
>
> (II.101-102)

> *This heart was human once, or why recall*
> *Einsiedeln, now?*
>
> (II.126-27)

> *I had just determined to become*
> *The greatest and most glorious man on earth.*
>
> (II.148-49)

> *As a man, you had*
> *A certain share of strength; and that is gone*
> *Already in the getting these you boast.*
>
> (II.208-10)

> *I covet not*
> *An influx of new power, an angel's soul:*
> *It were no marvel then — but I have reached*
> *Thus far, a man; let me conclude, a man!*
>
> (II.253-56)

With the return of the witch in Part V, Paracelsus seems to make up his mind. Once and for all he recalls the human priority of protest and discontinuity, the original defense; and he rediscovers in the irrepressible energies of his own will the expression of a genuinely human love. That the bewitching, transfiguring image of this love should be "gone" represents Paracelsus's feverish acknowledgment that his own quest has failed at last and is ready to be passed on in one climactic lecture. The message of this lecture seems an elaborate and decisive revision of the first of the passages just quoted: Even in failure, quest!

What happily spoils this satisfying picture of priority is the ghost of Michal, breaking in like Eglamor with a joyous, indubitably domestic look of "sweet human love." By insisting upon both the maternal Michal and the magical witch as meaningful human antecedents, Browning intensifies the earlier fluctuations and calls the word "human" into question, or into play. He establishes the meaning of this pivotal word as an active play between alternatives and so postpones the fullness, and the closure, of any fixed meaning. And this is as it should be in a work asserting that "man is not Man as

81

yet." Browning finds the point worth making again, in the last moments of dialogue before Paracelsus's lecture:

PARACELSUS   *I have been something, though too soon I left*
              Following the instincts of that happy time.
FESTUS   *What happy time? For God's sake, for man's sake,*
              What time was happy? All I hope to know
              That answer will decide. What happy time?
PARACELSUS   *When but the time I vowed myself to man?*
FESTUS   *Great God, thy judgments are inscrutable!*

                                                     (V.593-99)

A reader learns something central about Browning's art of disclosure when gratitude for Festus's persistence in urging the question yields to admiration at Paracelsus's refusal to resolve it. Paracelsus speaks of a vow whose meaning shimmers between self-aggrandizement and self-sacrifice. He has been happiest when committing himself "to man," to his own questing instincts as anticipations of the man to come, whose birth into the human family of the future Paracelsus has aspired to bring about. Paracelsus refers here to his earlier vow to become "the greatest and most glorious man on earth" (II.149)—a vow grown older, wiser, and more confident in the future, where that superlatively great and glorious man remains forever to be found.[18] In following the apparently inhuman instincts of his quest and in extending the hopes of humankind, Paracelsus has affirmed his deepest humanity. He has also lived the central paradox that the greatest value of those instincts is that they are doomed to go unrealized; they remain capable of being transmitted and so ceaselessly followed by a succession of secondary questers. Even the self-serving will of a Paracelsus has served itself best by learning to wait, by deferring to a "human trouble" and a "doubt" that keep the vow fresh (V.629).

If these saving frailties inscribe themselves into Paracelsus's sermon as the judgments of an "inscrutable" God, it is in order that "God's sake," "man's sake" as it were deferred, may guarantee the endlessness of aspiration that for Browning is the one goal worth attaining. The laws such a God reveals for humanity's sake are in effect prescriptions for deferment:

                I turn new knowledge upon old events,
                And the effect is . . . but I must not tell;
                It is not lawful. Your own turn will come
                One day. Wait, Festus! You will die like me.

                                                     (V.507-10)

According to a leading doctrine of the historical Paracelsus, "It is not God's will that His secrets should be visible; it is His will that they

82

become manifest and knowable through the works of man."[19] With this passage Browning relocates the divine power of concealment, as he has relocated such traditional images of the divine as the inner light and the voice from within, at the turning point where human heritage is transformed and extended. The word "turn" occurs in both the first and third lines of the passage above; and in the interval between them Paracelsus raises the reoriginating "turn" to a higher power by subscribing to the law of a living tradition. He refuses to formulate his "new knowledge" and thus converts it from a merely personal influx to a force that may influence his successors. Paracelsus joins Aprile and his peers at last in a "lawful" duplicity. He hushes himself as they have done; their conspiracy of silence means, in the phrase from *Sordello*, that there is more to say. By withholding a knowledge that the future promises to restore, Paracelsus has bequeathed to his followers the better legacy of anticipating the unexpectably new.

CHAPTER THREE

COMMUNICATION DIFFERENT: *SORDELLO*

> *I should think it impossible that such an outpour*
> *of impetuous eloquence could lie quietly condensed*
> *by the limitations of the ordinarily accepted sermon—*
> *its regular beginning, middle, and end. Indeed, as*
> *often as not, when the scheme of the projected dis-*
> *course had been stated with due precision, its merely*
> *introductory portion would in delivery not merely grow*
> *alive but expand with ever fresh and fresh accretions*
> *of fact and fancy, old analogy and modern instance,*
> *till the orator (as those gone-by divines have it)*
> sermocinando ultra clepsydram, *"would exceed his*
> *hour-glass," to the dissatisfaction of nobody.*
>
> Browning's "Introduction" to the
> sermons of Thomas Jones (1884)[1]

The culminating vision of *Paracelsus* describes a humanity defined by transformation, by the activity of its becoming human. The poem celebrates a humanizing energy that leaps into the future to over-come the sterilities of a mistaken dualism. This energy functions much as a verb functions in a sentence when it creates meaning in ac-tive transit between a pair of fixed and, in themselves, unmeaning nouns. Without straining the analogy, one may observe that the sub-ject and object of a sentence, or of a perception, or of a quest, derive their vitality from the course of action that relates them. Paracelsus discovers in the course of his poem the spatial fallacy of imagining "truth" as a noun, as something determinate that "abides in fulness" in an "inmost centre" (*Paracelsus*, I. 728-29). For Paracelsus as for Browning, "truth" is not a nominal abstraction but rather an activity of meaning that occurs, as Paracelsus's discovery occurs, in time. It is the nature of such an active truth to elude the enclosure of direct definition. Its "fulness," or meaningfulness, may be sought as an abiding possibility of the future but may never be possessed now. What may be possessed now is a confident awareness that the break between a present deferment and a future recovery lets the act of meaning keep making itself new.[2]

In *Sordello* (1840) Browning attempted a poem that incorporates these lessons into its tissues in remarkably minute detail. Stuttering interruptions, checks, anticipations, and postponements give *Sordello* a stubbornly different meaning. They are its way of meaning. The poem exhibits the processional unity of its self-conscious discontinuities, and to learn to read it is to learn to read Browning. It is a sad fact of literary history that few readers of *Sordello* have found the discipline of its style worth pursuing. In attempting so resolutely principled a poem, Browning ran the risk, and has suffered the consequences, of alienating readers who expect the presentable unities and stable meanings of more orthodox works. Readers in search of orthodox coherence, who conceive "truth" or "meaning" as a noun rather than as a verb, may find it in *Paracelsus* if they are willing to be nominal readers and to accept a reduction of the poem. But in much of *Sordello* Browning has made such reduction impossible; fixed meaning is often simply not there to be had.[3]

For these reasons plot summary, untrustworthy with any poem, is particularly useless as an approach to *Sordello*. The headnotes Browning wrote for the edition of 1863 and withdrew from the edition of 1888 represent a futile effort to provide such an approach. Although the headnotes hold a thematic interest of their own, the commentary they provide is generally of so little help, even to a reading of the story line, that one may be justified in applying the ironic first headnote not only to the writing of the poem, but to the writing of the headnotes as well: "A Quixotic attempt" (headnote, I.1).[4] Conventional structural patterns may, of course, be found in *Sordello.* The poem falls into two equal halves. At its midpoint, the final line of Book III picks up the first line of Book I and looks ahead to the last line of Book VI. The first three books execute a massive digression and return to the point of narrative origin, the scene at Verona — a pattern dutifully acknowledged in the virtual repetition of a line (I.329, III.553). The break between Books IV and V comes at a moment of illusory return, a regressive Rome-coming; this return repeats in a political context Sordello's more private but no more possible home-coming, which occurs at the break between Books II and III. In each return the attempt "once more" to restore an early security, whether of the font at Goito or of "the archetype" at Rome, ironically reveals an unbridgeable discontinuity (III.3, IV.1017-24). Moreover, each book of the poem, and not least the sixth, ends on a note of vigorous opening, beginning, or anticipation.

Structural symmetries typically reinforce central themes in poems, and one might take several of the symmetries just noted as neat elaborations of Browning's perennial message about attending to the future and making fresh starts. It would be easier to do so, however, were such tidy virtues less pervasively mocked by the glittering movement of Browning's virtuoso style—a style whose local enactments of meaning make the larger embodiments seem perilously dull. Browning defers to the formalities of orthodox coherence in such a way as to show them up, much as he flirts with a heroic couplet whose traditional equilibrium almost every other verse of the poem upsets. As he breaks away from his narrative at the point of its completing a circle, he warns,

> *Nor slight too much my rhymes—that spring, dispread,*
> *Dispart, disperse, lingering over head*
> *Like an escape of angels! Rather say,*
> *My transcendental platan! mounting gay*
> *(An archimage so courts a novice-queen)*
> *With tremulous silvered trunk, whence branches sheen*
> *Laugh out, thick-foliaged next, a-shiver soon*
> *With coloured buds, then glowing like the moon*
> *One mild flame,—last a pause, a burst, and all*
> *Her ivory limbs are smothered by a fall,*
> *Bloom-flinders and fruit-sparkles and leaf-dust,*
> *Ending the weird work prosecuted just*
> *For her amusement; he decrepit, stark,*
> *Dozes; her uncontrolled delight may mark*
> *Apart—*

(III.593-607)

"Nor slight too much my rhymes": Browning means to speak by synecdoche of his poetry in general, but he is also speaking quite literally of his rhymes themselves. In this astounding yet scarcely exceptional passage, it is not only that Browning's syntactical structures overwhelm the apparent structure of the rhymed couplet, as he will have them do in the interests of character drawing with "My Last Duchess" (published two years after *Sordello*). His technique here is, for better or worse, more willfully outrageous than that. Most of the enjambed lines above might have been end-stopped easily enough; with a minimum of rephrasing, and surely without any violence to their creative jubilation, one might impose exclamation points, dashes, or some notations for rest after the second, fourth, seventh, and eighth lines, and especially after the fourteenth.

The possibilities for closural pause or rest are so frequent that one must assume Browning's neglect of them to be intentional, nay, aggressive. And, indeed, it is his typical endeavor in *Sordello* to "spring, dispread,/Dispart, disperse," to "mark/Apart" what might so easily come together; his conjuring with images in this passage is no less remarkable than his prestidigitation with its rhymes. Time and again Browning's "rhymes"—both his local rhymes and his larger poetic and narrative techniques—extend a promise of rest and satisfaction only to whisk it away in mockery.[5] His Sordello's story may be "dull enough," as he confesses (III.984). That very confession gives additional point, however, to an investigation of Browning's technical "portraiture" and its traditionally undervalued "adornments quaint" (III.986-87). The way to meaning in *Sordello* is through its style, not around or above or in spite of it.

"Style" is of course a matter of attitude as well as technique; any setting of verses bespeaks a set of mind. The formal distance between Browning's style and the well-wrought structure it mocks, then, may bear a significant analogy to the ironic distance of spirit dividing Browning from Sordello. One way of construing Browning's irony in this poem, as in *Paracelsus*, is to take it as an indication of what his protagonist lacks. Sordello's speech, when compared to Browning's as narrator or to the speech of Paracelsus or of Browning in *Pauline*, is unrelieved by breaks or turns. Brilliant exceptions, like the oration on poetry that Sordello delivers to Salinguerra in Book V, prove the rule that each of his addresses and meditations is, "alas,/One of God's large ones, tardy to condense/Itself into a period" (II.722-24). This is not to say that Sordello is incapable of turning on himself; he does so fiercely, for instance, when the seasonal flooding of Mincio shakes him out of his inertia early in Book III. A sudden change in his surroundings, "The earth's remonstrance" (III.86), shows him how time has been wasting the very place in which he would waste time, and he scorns the futile iterations of his old attempt to court nature:

> *she meets you, somewhat pale,*
> *But letting you lift up her coarse flax veil*
> *And whisper (the damp little hand in yours)*
> *Of love, heart's love, your heart's love that endures*
> *Till death.*

(III.113-17)

Here Sordello turns on himself clearly enough. The tone of this passage, however, is if anything *too* clearly identifiable. Sordello fails, as it were, to turn on his turn — to do what Browning, as in the encounter with Eglamor near the close of the poem, does with such persistent agility.

There is a humorless simplicity to Sordello that may be related to his fatal insistence on having all the truth now. From the passage just quoted he soon moves to a generalization of his dilemma. Although like Andrea del Sarto he is letter-perfect in the philosophy of incompleteness, he lacks Browning's saving, playful sense of nuance:

> *Ah, fragments of a whole ordained to be,*
> *Points in the life I waited! what are ye*
> *But roundels of a ladder which appeared*
> *Awhile the very platform it was reared*
> *To lift me on? — that happiness I find*
> *Proofs of my faith in, even in the blind*
> *Instinct which bade forego you all unless*
> *Ye led me past yourselves.*

> (III.141-48)

The indomitable anticipation of a reward delayed, the contrast between process and permanence, even the temporalized relationship of the deferred "whole" to its present "points," all are impeccable. But a reader of Browning's more energetically problematic enactments of the same themes elsewhere in this and other poems may suspect the very perfection of the passage as an invitation to reductive interpretation. Indeed, within a few lines the fixity of Sordello's doctrinally flawless generalization has begun to contaminate and petrify the doctrine itself. He reasons thus: "I must, ere I begin to Be,/Include a world, in flesh, I comprehend/In spirit, now; and this done, what's to blend/With?" (III.172-75). The perfection of Sordello's fluid speech here betrays an appetite for perfectly inclusive knowledge that would deprive him of the opportunity to "begin to Be." In human time this is an appetite doomed to frustration, as Browning's rather unkind last enjambment suggests. Sordello's imagination has begun to devour its proper offspring, the future. He is guilty of the temporal heresy of denying himself the right to go ahead and fail, what the prophetic "low voice" of Book V will call "The basis, the beginning step of all,/Which proves you just a man" (V.97-98). In *Paracelsus* "humanity" has emerged as a term in process, whose meaning occurs along a way that is always open to new "beginning steps." Browning's is an active philosophy of sustained inquiry into what is human, and in *Sordello* he protects that inquiry against misinterpretation by playing the changes of his style against the premature and simple readings put forward by his Sordello.

REPRESENTATIVE POWER

Browning is nowhere a more willfully defensive stylist than as he approaches the thematic climax of the poem in Book VI, where he intervenes to deliver on Sordello's behalf an apparently portable parcel of philosophy. He begins by putting central questions about human perception of some ultimate reality:

> *Never may some soul see All*
> *— The Great Before and After, and the Small*
> *Now, yet be saved by this the simplest lore,*
> *And take the single course prescribed before,*
> *As the king-bird with ages on his plumes*
> *Travels to die in his ancestral glooms?*
> *But where descry the Love that shall select*
> *That course?*

(VI.579-86)

Insofar as this passage introduces the lesson of *Sordello*, it is an educational passage. It is fitting, then, that the questions it asks are as important as the problematic answer that is to follow. Students learn that the courses they take become valuable by being different from what the syllabus has "prescribed." While only the best courses lead to a regenerating surprise like that awaiting the fire-born "king-bird," or phoenix, any course worth selecting draws its worth from the way it is run in time. What makes this passage worthy of attention is the way it runs its course: it breaks with its philosophical pretensions and abandons its capitalized abstractions for the sake of exploratory travel that finds in "Love" not reified meaning, but the promise of a meaning that is yet to be "descried." This is the promise of deferment that motivates the Browning of *Pauline* and that strengthens the failed Aprile and Paracelsus when they are finally made wise. For Browning "Love," the "ever-springing fountain" of *Christmas-Eve* ([1850] 318), is a uniquely transitive abstraction. Its meaning arises in the course of its self-renewing travel between subject and object, just as at the close of *Sordello* there runs between Browning and Eglamor a "joyous look of love." The "course" proposed in these earlier lines is "single," but only with the complex singularity of Browning's "simplest lore," his governing project of original deferment and eventual recovery.

It is only in this complex sense that the ensuing "one word to end" (VI.589) may be considered as "one." Browning follows his ultimate questions with an answer that effectively puts all ultimates in question:

> *Ah my Sordello, I this once befriend*

And speak for you. Of a Power above you still
Which, utterly incomprehensible,
Is out of rivalry, which thus you can
Love, tho' unloving all conceived by man—
What need! And of—none the minutest duct
To that out-nature, nought that would instruct
And so let rivalry begin to live—
But of a Power its representative
Who, being for authority the same,
Communication different, should claim
A course, the first chose but this last revealed—
This Human clear, as that Divine concealed—
What utter need!

(VI.590-603)

These lines are difficult, though not baffling; and Browning has made them so not from artistic incompetence or metaphysical stupor, but in order to illustrate certain ideas about religion and its literary counterpart, poetry of the sublime. Who or what are these two related "Powers"? The significance of the divergent critical explanations of the powers is that they diverge so widely. To specify the powers as Eros and Sordello's accomplice and paramour Palma, or as God the Father and Jesus the Redeemer, is to violate the painstaking indeterminacy of Browning's language.[6] The substantive identities of the powers remain in doubt because Browning's interest lies not in substances but in dynamics of relationship that will be familiar to readers of his earlier poems.

Browning clearly conceives the relationship between the two powers in affective terms. Both powers are invoked at "need" and are needed at a point of failure where love is "descried": "Or may failure here be success also when induced by love? (headnotes, VI.569,598). The "Divine" first power is "still" with a fixity like Shelley's in *Pauline* and "incomprehensible" like Festus's "inscrutable" God; unlimited in its capacity to receive love, it offers to the devoted soul a career of endless worship. The "Human" second power is a totally distinct, deputized mediator. Despite its apparent secondariness, however, this mediating power is an indispensable go-between: it must minister to the human soul first, before the soul has learned to love the unknowable first power. As far as the soul is concerned, then, the second power enjoys a certain affective priority, or, in Browning's oxymoronic phrase, "authority the same." The two powers taken together prescribe for the needy soul the single course of salvation through deferment, and they do so through a Browning-esque play of mutual dependence in which each needs the other and the first and last in importance tend to change places.

90

These affective relations are intriguing in themselves, especially when they are advanced as Browning's difficult solution to the riddle of so arduous a poem. What distinguishes this passage from similar moments in the earlier poems, however, is what constitutes the novelty of *Sordello*: an unrelenting concern with language.[7] Even at this climactic moment Browning illustrates his theme of deferment by returning to questions of style. It is not merely that Browning happens to elucidate the relationship between prior and secondary powers with an analogy to silent truth and mediating, "representative" language. The analogy is a deliberately treacherous one, and once set in play it reverses direction. The vehicle turns tenor; the metaphysical relation begins to figure the linguistic one. This strange usurpation is another instance of the resourcefulness of whatever is secondary in Browning in gaining ascendancy over what it is ostensibly secondary to. In that the passage deals with the fancy and fact of linguistic representation, it is an archetypal instance, for *Sordello* and for Browning's entire oeuvre, that repays close examination.

Browning "befriends" and "speaks for" an omniscient Sordello who has passed "quite out of Time and this world" into a speechless solitude beyond language (VI.486). In his imminent meeting with Eglamor, Browning will find a promise of renewed speech, of "more to say," precisely in veering away from such sublime speechlessness, choosing to be less than omniscient, and befriending Eglamor, with his secondary, "joyous look of love." In the passage on the two powers, however, there can be no befriending the first power, which remains indefinite and supraverbal. "Utterly incomprehensible," it surpasses all imaginative conception, "all conceived by man." That is, it exceeds the grasp of what Naddo, in a specifically literary context, has earlier called "conceits" (II.12). The first power is isolated from speech; this isolation confers upon it both the sublime strength of an infinite potential and the impotence of an unbreakable silence. It is intransitive intentionality, pure meaning; and, being pure meaning, it cannot *do* any meaning; it can only refer inexpressibly to itself.

In proceeding to the second power, the passage affirms the necessity of conceits, of a mysteriously authoritative, "representative" speech, which can break the silence of sameness with the clear, human revelations of "Communication different." Browning befriends this intermediate power in several ways. He assigns it the humanizing relative pronoun "who," whereas the first power takes "which"; and whereas he speaks only of Sordello's "need" of the first power, he punningly recalls the unutterability of that power by exclaiming of its secondary representative, "What utter need!" The paradoxical play of the passage may be most concentrated in yet another verb of speech, the ambiguous "claim." It is as hard to keep the major sense

91

of repetitive "declamation" free from the undertone of originative "proclamation" as to see what characteristics of the incomprehensible first power the language of the second may reclaim or "represent" without somehow inventing them first. At least in human terms, the terms of Browning's art, the power of figuration becomes original. But it performs its acts of origination by referring (and deferring) to an antecedent power—by disguising its creative will and claiming to follow not its own choices, but what "the first chose."

Finally, and perhaps most typically of Browning, the passage surprises or differs from itself through subtle self-contradictions like those exploited in *Pauline*. Browning interrupts the sixth line to insist upon the distinction between the two powers, with the result that by the ninth line his introductory "and" has become a "but." One expects another "and" here—but, as usual, Browning's meaning calls for a more rigorous discontinuity than one expects. The "but" means that the agency of representation is no mere "duct" drawing power from what it represents but a power to be reckoned with on its own terms. The same change is implicitly made in the later line, "A course, the first chose but this last revealed." In calling attention to the difference between an initial choice and an eventual revelation, this passage "instructs" its reader mediately, not absolutely. In running its course, it performs a verbal act of "Communication different" that qualifies and complicates itself in time. It enacts the process of representation that is its subject. The discontinuities of the passage defy an interpretation that would locate wholeness of meaning anywhere but in the enriching shifts of its temporal articulation.

It may be helpful to consider the passage on the two powers as Browning's response to Sordello's earlier metaphysical questions about the locus of power:

> *External power! If none be adequate,*
> *And he stand forth ordained (a prouder fate)*
> *Himself a law to his own sphere? "Remove*
> *All incompleteness!" for that law, that love?*
> *Nay, if all other laws be feints,—truth veiled*
> *Helpfully to weak vision that had failed*
> *To grasp aught but its special want,—for lure,*
> *Embodied? Stronger vision could endure*
> *The unbodied want: no part—the whole of truth!*

(VI.111-19)

Here an impatient Sordello makes the Paracelsan error of conceiving in spatial terms the crucial temporal relations between the whole and the incomplete part, between the truth and its feigned veil, between meaning and representation. He is insufficiently alert to the presuppositions built into his own figurative "feints," the imagery of "vision" and "embodiment" in which he frames his questions. Such imagery is inadequate because it fails to account for the course of time; it necessarily leaves out of the picture the saving possibility of a truth that is eventual or a wholeness that is anticipated. If Sordello the poet is a tragic figure, neglect of temporality is his hubris. "Remove / All incompleteness!" is his demand here; and later, "Let / What masters life disclose itself!" (VI.437-38). Browning's very enjambments, quiet reminders of the discontinuity that gives meaning to passages of poetry as to passages of time, suggest the futility of Sordello's doomed grasping at a whole and continuous truth. Sordello doubly fails to defer, and time takes its revenges on him (as on Paracelsus) by granting his requests. His desires for priority and for presence are aspects of each other; to collapse the gap between himself and "external power," ordaining "himself a law to his own sphere," and to insist on "no part—the whole of truth" are versions of the same self-enclosing, debilitating act. Sordello's final fall out of time takes him out of the temporality of language; his perfect priority earns him the fatal wages of becoming, like Browning's first power, "utterly incomprehensible."[8]

It is tempting to hear an ironic echo of this last phrase in Browning's later comment to a friend who displayed a copy of the poem on his table: "Ah! the entirely unintelligible Sordello!"[9] Sordello's hubris in rejecting temporality is, after all, an inversion of Browning's hubris in defiantly cleaving to temporality and writing a poem the evolution of whose most literal meanings so often taxes his reader's patience. Time would seem to have taken its revenges on Browning first—precisely because most readers of the poem since its publication have been, like Sordello, eager for the fixity of present meaning and for the integrity of spatial form. Yet it is possible to interpret the official critical neglect of Sordello as a backhanded confirmation of an intuition that lies at the heart of the poem: that spatial and temporal modes of meaning create and answer to entirely different expectations. Sordello is notorious for disappointing the expectations of coherence that readers bring to it. By the same token, however, the generally disappointing quality of criticism written on the poem is due to the unwillingness of readers to submit to its different expectations. To call the spatial and temporal modes of meaning "opposites" would be too nearly spatial; for Browning the difference between them is itself temporal. As with Paracelsus's dualistic misconceptions, as with the first and second powers needed by Sordello, the one is the other deferred. The only spatial presence that appeals to Browning is one that he may happily wait for at the end of a long, long time.

Later in life Browning told Edward Dowden that a major thematic motive of the poem is Sordello's fault of "Thrusting in time eternity's concern" (I.566).[10] Browning's choice of image is revealing. In this image it is "time" that is precious and stands in need of protection. It is "time" that is violated by the arresting permanence of "eternity"—that is, by a kind of grotesquely frozen time or collapsed future. The passage surrounding this image associates such "eternity" with specifically spatial notions of "containment," "display," and "completeness" (I.564). In *Pauline* and *Paracelsus* one of the threatening aspects of "eternity," one of the things "time" needs protection from, is fullness of meaning itself; and so it is here.[11] The very passage from which Browning chose his line for Dowden is itself an instance of premature narration, one of the many moments in *Sordello* when Browning gets ahead of his story and catches himself up, warding off the completion of meaning by self-consciously thrusting into the poem a reminder of its temporality. That he should have directed Dowden to this complex passage for thematic clues testifies to the persistence both of Browning's skepticism about any extractable theme and of his faith in poetry's temporal way of meaning.

Browning furnishes a much more explicit clue about what *Sordello* means, and how it means, in the poem itself. In Book II Sordello experiments with a poetry of presence and wholeness. His experiment is condemned by the temporal nature of language to a failure that faithfully anticipates his climactic failure to live in a temporal universe,

> Because perceptions whole, like that he sought
> To clothe, reject so pure a work of thought
> As language: thought may take perception's place
> But hardly co-exist in any case,
> Being its mere presentment—of the whole
> By parts, the simultaneous and the sole
> By the successive and the many. Lacks
> The crowd perception? painfully it tacks
> Thought to thought, which Sordello, needing such,
> Has rent perception into: it's to clutch
> And reconstruct—his office to diffuse,
> Destroy.

> (II.589-600)

This is a simpler, backward version of the passage on the two powers. In that passage a consideration of ultimate metaphysical values

94

delicately turns into a discourse on semantics; here a description of poetic experimentation leads to philosophical questions of perception and time. Whole, simultaneous, sole "perception" proves, like the first power, to be beyond utterance in language. Language is "a work of thought," which works, as does the second power's "Communication different," through "the successive and the many."

Like the passage on the two powers, this passage turns on the squeaky hinge of representation. The secondary "presentment," or substitution, whereby "thought may take perception's place" seems at first to be a "mere" expedient, but soon enough it swells into the chief object of attention. Sordello becomes a deconstructor in spite of himself, finding that language forces him to "rend," "diffuse," and "destroy" initial wholes. He must defer to the "reconstructions" performed by others, "the crowd," and must wait for the later wholeness of recovered meaning. In Coleridgean terms, he must dissolve, diffuse, and dissipate meaning in order to make possible its recreation later on.[12] The difference inherent in any such communication gives Browning his method and his theme, now and throughout his career. "The glory and good of Art" is that it "may tell a truth / Obliquely, do the thing shall breed the thought, / Nor wrong the thought, missing the mediate word" (*The Ring and the Book*, XII.842,859-61). In *Sordello* as in *The Ring and the Book*, the oblique mediacy of language opens Browning's breeding ground and entitles him to look beyond the present, to say "shall." "Language, the makeshift" (II.681), as a medium that does its meaning in time, asserts a difference that Browning loves for making things shift and letting things happen.

That Sordello should hate this difference is not surprising; it is his being wrong in just such matters that makes Sordello's story. It is another story, though, that most criticism of Browning should follow Sordello and should be wrong in the same way. The formalist presuppositions that characterize much of the traditional antipathy to *Sordello* —for which Sordello's images of "vision" and "embodiment" offer a convenient shorthand—sometimes infect even sympathetic and appreciative readers and lead them to try taming the poem just where it is most wild. When Michael Mason writes of "the large 'simultaneous' unit" and Robert Langbaum declares that Browning "tries to achieve the effect of simultaneity through discursive thought itself," they impose a critical muzzle on Browning that is useful if only because it represents so clearly what he is laboring in *Sordello* to throw off.[13] The point of Sordello's experimentation in Book II is that, if there is to be real poetry in his or any poet's time, there must be sequentiality, deferment, and representation. Likewise, the point of Browning's passage on the two powers in Book VI is that, if there is to be human faith or love, there must be imperfection, utter need, and the growing pains attendant upon reorigination. Browning's poem means nothing if not that simultaneity is a temporal manifestation of the threat that poems, like people, become themselves by eluding: a sameness in closure, an end to play, a denial of beginning.

SOME FIRST FACT

Sordello is tragically wrong about the importance of deferment and deference, and what makes his error tragic is his being so nearly right about closely related matters. He is admirably right when in Book V, stung by Salinguerra's scorn, he launches a defense of poetry that reaffirms the very early defenses underlying his own origin as a poet. The best introduction to those defenses is Browning's more leisurely and detailed description of Sordello's poetic origin in Book I. At first "a simple sense of life" has "engrossed" Sordello in the innocent presence of "his drowsy Paradise" at Goito (I.626-27). Soon, however, Sordello rips away the "fringe" of an apparent continuity between himself and nature and discovers "the true relationship,/Core with its crust," to be one of alienation from nature: "Amid his wildwood sights he lived alone" (I.702-4). Leaving his polymorphous, natural life behind, he learns "to circumscribe/And concentrate, rather than swell, the tribe/Of actual pleasures" and to exercise "mere sympathy," "tasting joys by proxy" (I.723-28). He learns, that is, to make choices, and to time his experiences.

Sordello makes the further discovery that such timing opens new possibilities, possibilities that Browning explicitly associates with language:

No simple and self-evident delights,
But mixed desires of unimagined range,
Contrasts or combinations, new and strange.

(I.780-82)

So must speech expand the dumb
Part-sigh, part-smile with which Sordello, late
Whom no poor woodland-sights could satiate,
Betakes himself to study hungrily
Just what the puppets his crude phantasy
Supposes notablest, —popes, kings, priests, knights, —
May please to promulgate for appetites.

(I.796-802)

Sordello's "phantasy" is not so crude that it lacks the genuine complexities of poetic imagination. "Speech" breaks Sordello's dumbness, as his "disenchanted" will breaks the continuity of natural, "simple presence" (I.710-12). Language, the makeshift, constitutes an expansive compensation for the loss of "actual pleasures." It offers a strange new reenchantment whereby Sordello may aspire to satiate the unimagined range of desire. So it is, as Browning says in introducing this moment of change, that human imagination responds to an original loss by pursuing its subsequent artistic course; that "we" —

> *diverted from our natural course*
> *Of joys — contrive some yet amid the dearth,*
> *Vary and render them, it may be, worth*
> *Most we forego.*

$$\text{(I.680-83)}$$

With the dash in the second line Browning diverts the passage from its "natural course" and so contrives to enact the rupture that inaugurates his "single course" of secondariness and variety. The valuable variety that these lines discuss is further exemplified in Browning's hesitant aside, "it may be"; he contrives to differ from himself even in asserting the worth of difference.

It is remarkable, yet remarkably characteristic of the poem, how quickly Sordello starts up a fanciful play wherein he may be secondary to creatures of his own fancy and to the decrees they "promulgate." Near the end of Book I this play becomes quite sophisticated. Sordello imagines that the forest is performing tricks with light and shade to honor him in his favorite role as Apollo:

> *Yet could not he denounce the stratagems*
> *He saw thro', till, hours thence, aloft would hang*
> *White summer-lightnings; as it sank and sprang*
> *To measure, that whole palpitating breast*
> *Of heaven, 'twas Apollo, nature prest*
> *At eve to worship.*

$$\text{(I.922-27)}$$

Sordello's "seeing through" these "stratagems" is ambiguous. He sees through each stratagem and "denounces" it as transparently a makeshift fiction, but only after it has been supplanted by a successive stratagem. The fanciful stratagems are the artifices he sees through, the doors of perception through which he does his seeing in the first place. Sordello's retrospective denunciations themselves depend upon fictions that are bolder than the fictions they supersede, but no less necessary. The supreme fiction of Sordello's life at Goito — that he is Apollo, the lord of nature — has been introduced by Browning as a covering "patchwork" composed of the "rags" of lesser fictions (I.898).

By tracing the genesis and composition of Sordello's supreme fiction, Browning decomposes its completeness and suggests that, like the "whole palpitating breast/Of heaven" that it leads Sordello to see, it is only partial, a provisional stratagem like any other.

When in Book V Salinguerra expresses his disdain of poetry, Sordello is spurred into making an apologia for himself as a poet. This apologia follows back to its origin his earlier growth into choice and language:

> I, with my words, hailed brother of the train
> Deeds once sufficed: for, let the world roll back,
> Who fails, through deeds howe'er diverse, retrack
> My purpose still, my task? A teeming crust—
> Air, flame, earth, wave at conflict! Then, needs must
> Emerge some Calm embodied, these refer
> The brawl to—yellow-bearded Jupiter?
> No! Saturn; some existence like a pact
> And protest against Chaos, some first fact
> I' the faint of time.
>
> (V.548-57)

With the idea of "reference" in the sixth line, metaphysical and linguistic issues once again converge at a critical point in the poem. Sordello works his way back to an original occasion of choice, through a process of choosing among names for the "embodied," authoritative power. After saying "No!" to Jupiter and then to Saturn, he turns from nominal embodiment to verbal enactment and finds meaning in this very "No!" He locates his purpose and task in the assertion of a will to break with things as they are and to make a new beginning, an "existence" of his own.

Making a new beginning before Salinguerra now, Sordello remakes his sense of his own beginnings as a youthful poet. He lets "the world roll back" and privileges as his "first fact" a moment from his past, the early moment of protest when he uprooted the deceptive "fringe" or "crust" of the natural world (I.701-4)—a moment to which the "teeming crust" of this passage more elementally alludes. The passage also alludes to a speech from Keats's *Hyperion* in which Saturn confesses his inability to decipher any cause for the Titans' fall "in sign, symbol, or portent/Of element, earth, water, air, and fire—/At war, at peace, or inter-quarreling" (*Hyperion*, II.139-41). Sordello's point (and Browning joins him here) is that Saturn, or the saturnine poet, can find no cause for failure because he seeks it in just the wrong place; that he seeks it in nature instead of in himself is symptomatic of his fall.

Sordello's protestant "first fact" rescues him from two forms of stasis: from the enervation of merely natural continuity; and from Jupiter and Saturn, the figureheads of supernatural creeds outworn and of the political systems those creeds underwrite. It affiliates him instead, in the fashion of *Paracelsus*, with the kingly champions "of human will" (I.544) from the past; the poet's "words" continue the tradition established through their originating "deeds" and make him their "brother" in forwarding the general good. Sordello's defense of poetry begins as a tribunal protest to Salinguerra on behalf of the beleaguered Italian people. A passage Browning added in 1863 calls this protest "his first strife/For their sake" (V.460-61). "His first strife" stands in line 460 where "some first fact" stands in line 556, and the parallel is more than typographical. Sordello's forensic strife is "first" both because political advocacy is quite new to him and because it involves a fundamental return to priorities. His principled advocacy of the popular cause finds a precedent in his earlier advocacy of a distinctively human order, which, because it is man-made, can be changed by human effort for the better.

A first fact, if it is to be practically as well as chronologically first, must be renewable on the edge of strife; though the privileged inaugural moment lies in the historical past and in Sordello's personal past, it is also potentially always now. That is why, in the name of his first negation ("No!"), Sordello returns to his early break with the natural order, rebaptizing nature this time as a featureless "Chaos." The passage ends with a recollection of the strange truth that his anxious protest against aimless natural flux is cognate with his sense of human time. For Sordello time has begun at the crisis point of a "first fact," at his memorable decision to interrupt natural continuity and make a "pact," as it were, with his future self—a pact that by this point includes his predecessors and the Italian people as well. In turning aside from the enclosing and undifferentiated crust of nature, asserting his antagonisms and kinships, and learning to defer his experiences and satisfactions, he has made a difference that gives meaning to time.

Browning's description of the original protest in Book I begins by associating the origins of anxiety and of temporality. "Time" intrudes at Goito to interrupt Sordello's life of careless simplicity: "Time put at length that period to content,/By right the world should have imposed" (I.698-99). In saying no to natural content, Sordello says yes to temporal anxieties and brings his distinctively human consciousness into being. There is quiet irony in this second line, since Browning has painstakingly isolated Sordello from "this world" in order to isolate the original mystery of the moment of poetic choice (I.672). The heart of the mystery is that Sordello's art itself is nature, that the unsolicited, self-creating moment of the individual soul's break with natural continuity should come as the most natural thing in the world. Browning's use of the word "period," and especially of the casual phrase "at length," recalls Shelley's exposition of the same mystery in the preface to *Alastor*: "But the period arrives when these objects cease to suffice. His mind is at length suddenly awakened and thirsts for intercourse with an intelligence similar to itself. He images to himself the Being whom he loves."

For Browning, too, a poet is at length suddenly born. But, in an interesting resumption of the dark tactics of *Pauline*, Browning revises Shelley by having Sordello find his first fact through imaging to himself the being whom he hates. In calling nature "Chaos," Sordello comes to the origin of poetic name-calling. As Browning himself was quite ready to allow in lighter moments, nature may be far from chaotic. In "By the Fire-side" (1855), for example, a lyric similarly concerned with imaginative travel back "to the first of all," he renders the power of love by rendering it up to natural "powers at play" (146, 231-40). But in *Sordello*, as earlier in *Pauline*, Browning is dramatizing the incarnation of the poet proper, for whom any natural or inherited order, any order that he has not himself made, is always out of order. Sordello's claim that nature is "Chaos" is a figure of speech, perhaps *the* figure of speech: an arch-representation of the original impulse to defend imagination against experience through a stratagem of substitution and postponement. The poet begins with a conviction of external meaninglessness that makes all meaning his. By positing the aimless chaos of a homogeneous present he finds his purpose, and by peopling that chaos with names and faces he makes a future for himself. In identifying the first fact of protest, Sordello identifies a disruptive principle of continuity—a principle that is the only "calm" worth embodying since it must be continually embodied afresh. This is a dynamic principle of continuity that the restless Paracelsus might also endorse as "my purpose still, my task," and that differs markedly from the fulfilled "purpose" of Eglamor's "complete" songs and their "fixed" meanings (III.620-21, II.205). Browning's endorsement of the principle is no less sincere for the subtle humor with which he expresses it in the movement of the lines that immediately follow:

> "My deep of life, I know
> Is unavailing e'en to poorly show". . .
> (For here the Chief immeasurably yawned)
> . . . "Deeds in their due gradation till Song dawned."
>
> (V.557-60)

The parenthetical break here poetically reanimates the primordial antagonism with nature. The immeasurable yawn of Salinguerra, the natural man, brings chaos up to date and so provides protest with a future, song with a dawn.

THE BEARER'S HAND

The protest against narrative continuity enclosed in this last parenthesis typifies Browning's observance of what Isobel Armstrong has called "a decorum of violation."[14] Browning's largest violation in *Sordello* is the digression of over four hundred lines that ends Book III, and he begins his digression by discussing in temporal terms the meaning of digressive gestures in poems. The proliferation of Browning's terms for digression is a small and decorous violation in itself: "some looking-off/Or start-away," "The childish skit or scoff," "one silly line," "the bard's start aside and look askance," "that one flout" (III.631-47). Such gestures give readers cause, says Browning, to anticipate a poetry that is yet to come; a "better lay" remains to be written that will incorporate the "future gains" to which such gestures point (III.646-47). Readers will catch glimpses of the future in all "true works" (III.622) and will recognize them as violations of the poet's professed promise "to meditate with us eternal rest,/And partnership in all his life has found" (III.650-51). "Eternal rest" means the peace of perfect closure, which does not pass understanding and which is to be found in songs like Eglamor's. In such songs the artifact, with its "eternal rest," hardens into funereal ornament, and the interpretive problem is the absence of problems. Browning ends his digression with a parable about interpretation, in which John of Patmos learns with unfolding brows that in time "What seems a fiend perchance may prove a saint" (III.988), "a story to the point" (headnote, III.989). "The point" is Browning's rigorous demand for a patient reading of his poem, a reading that differs from Sordello's in knowing how to attend—how to wait and how to scrutinize.[15]

In *Sordello* narrative digressions do to Browning's story line at large what his rhetorical tropes do in miniature to literal truth. Both are forms of substitution or difference that delay the finalities of narrative closure or of received meaning. A good way of defining the significance of such delaying tactics is to consider the negative or failed instance Browning offers in the description of war-torn Ferrara that opens Book IV. On the heels of the plea for readerly patience with which he has ended his long digression in Book III, he sets a scene of brutally hasty dismemberment, one that is suggestive for the student of Browning's use of synecdoche and of rhetorical figures in general. Each of the political suitors, Guelf and Ghibellin, courts Ferrara, "the lady-city," by twisting "Her tresses twice or thrice about his wrist" or planting "in her breast/His elbow spike" (IV.2-9). An old Ghibellin finds "a little skull"; a young Guelf stumbles on "a shrivelled hand nailed fast/To the charred lintel of the doorway" (IV.15-20); a soldier's spur unearths "his own mother's face" (IV.106). Here, as elsewhere in the poem, most memorably in the simile of the cliffs and the chokeweed (I.212-33), the two political parties fall into senseless opposition, fixed like the nailed hand in space, or in the repetition of a devastating cycle. In their fixity the severed members of dead bodies and the irreconcilable parties as parts of the body politic serve as ghastly parodies of synecdoche, the rhetorical substitution of part for whole that is habitual to Browning's writing and to his vision of human time. What makes these parts and parties ghastly is just what Sordello will renew his protest against: a ruthless intemperance that impoverishes the future. What makes them parodic is that they are synecdoches with nothing to represent. Sordello's earlier reference to "fragments of a whole ordained to be" (III.141) may be taken as normative in *Sordello* for Browning's repeated use of synecdoche as a figure representing a deferred whole.[16] With the corporeal fragments of Book IV Browning furnishes examples of failed synecdoche. They are parts locked into a present that precludes any hope of a later recovery, vicious embodiments of the death that sounds so much more attractive as a meditation on "eternal rest." They are admonitory images of the "eternity" that Browning's decorum of violation inventively keeps from thrusting itself into his poem's time.

If at the beginning of Book IV Browning parodies a poetry of decorous closure, he opens his narrative in Book I with a notable "look askance," a protest against closure.

> That autumn eve was stilled:
> A last remains of sunset dimly burned
> O'er the far forests, like a torch-flame turned
> By the wind back upon its bearer's hand
> In one long flare of crimson; as a brand,
> The woods beneath lay black.
>
> (I.80-85)

The eve may be stilled, but Browning's simile is not. Even the most appreciative attention to mimetic syntax and meter in this smoldering passage will not make the "bearer's hand" from the fourth line fit anything in the pictured sunset to which it is being likened. The "brand" (the "woods") fuels the "flame" (the "sunset"), but from a pictorial point of view the "bearer's hand" holding the torch is so conspicuously superfluous that a reader may assimilate it only by locating the image in time, only by violating the pictorial present and giving the torch a history. With mention of the "bearer's hand," the

102

simile opens a temporal loophole, or, to use a word Browning repeats in this connection, an "escape" (I.883; III.595, 624). The vehicle usurps upon its tenor by offering to be, in turn, part of a larger, absent whole, which is unspecified, indefinitely deferred, yet still awaited. In other words, the figure of the simile introduces the further figure of synecdoche and so breaks the expected similitude.

The newer and more complex whole of which the "bearer's hand" forms a part is one that can only be reconstructed as a process in time. Where the nailed hand of Browning's failed synecdoche in Book IV encloses a grisly significance, this hand extends the promise of a meaning yet to be reached. As the image opens out in time, the prosodically prominent "long" becomes a temporal as well as a spatial adjective and "brand" anticipates the extinction towards which the sunset tends.[17] The simile is discontinuous with itself; and, like the "up-thrust, out-staggering" narrative eruption it follows, it refuses quite to subside into shape (I.74). It may be more than coincidental that Browning's vehicle in this discontinuous simile should be fire, Paracelsus's element of creative discontinuity, and that his agent for marring the perfection of simple "metaphor" (literally a transference or "bearing") should be the etymologically apt hand of a "bearer."

This simile exemplifies the method of Browningesque "Communication different"—the method of representation whereby the secondary, "representative" power of Book VI points beyond itself to its utterly incomprehensible "out-nature" (VI.596). Browning's writing uses the temporal resources of what Sordello has unthriftily repudiated, "the successive and the many" in language. When defending his outrageous technique during the passage discussed earlier in connection with rhyme, Browning speaks of his "rhymes" as powerful openers "that spring, dispread,/Dispart, disperse, lingering over head/Like an escape of angels!" These lingering verbs are potentially transitive; and, like the expansive "speech" that marks Sordello's early protest against nature, they disperse the threat of changeless continuity. Browning keeps *Sordello* open through versions of the "bearer's hand" that recur throughout the poem, usually to illustrate moments of transition and renewal. These similes perform the temporalizing rhetorical function of rending and destroying the intact, formal correspondences that a reader is likely to expect. The figures of the Armenian bridegroom (I.344), Eve's maker (I.414), the Soldan's daughter (II.969), and the apocalyptic corpse (V.935) are all, like Browning's escaped Ethiop (IV.864-65), "past pursuit/Of all enslavers" who would shackle their meaning too securely.

One of the most sophisticated of these rhetorical defenses against closure occurs in a complex simile at the beginning of Book III, where Browning resumes a theme from *Paracelsus* and describes Sordello's defenses against himself. In this book Sordello learns the futility of trying to come home again. His return to reestablish the old continuities of Goito is frustrated by the persistence of his deeper, more authoritative will to continue to strive: "Will, he bade abdicate, which would not void/The throne" (III.573-74). The "pact" of Sordello's early, willful "protest against Chaos" has too much original strength to permit the regressive return that he thinks he desires. Browning introduces the idea of the "pact" in order to represent Sordello's internal conflict, in a comparatively unsophisticated simile that may be useful here as an introduction to the masterful simile that it follows:

> he slept, but was aware he slept,
> So, frustrated: as who brainsick made pact
> Erst with the overhanging cataract
> To deafen him, yet still distinguished plain
> His own blood's measured clicking at his brain.
>
> (III.64-68)

Having attempted to make his peace with nature and return to silence, Sordello immerses himself in a natural flux. But this peace depends upon too late a "pact," a pact that proves to be weaker than the irrepressible "first fact" of his estrangement from nature. Here Sordello, willy-nilly, epitomizes the subjective poet from the *Essay on Shelley*, who "selects that silence of the earth and sea in which he can best hear the beating of his individual heart, and leaves the noisy, complex, yet imperfect exhibitions of nature in the manifold experience of man around him, which serve only to distract and suppress the working of his brain."[18] Thus "beating" and "working," a voice from within reminds Sordello that significant time is slipping by. The "Erst" of his later pact is not early enough: the would-be slumberer is interrupted by that original timepiece, his definitively human "consciousness/Under the imbecility" (III.62-63).

Despite Sordello's efforts to repress and drown this human consciousness, it bobs up to the surface of his thoughts in the temporal elaborations of the protracted simile at the beginning of Book III:

> Quiet those throbbing temples, then, subdue
> That cheek's distortion! Nature's strict embrace,
> Putting aside the past, shall soon efface
> Its print as well — factitious humours grown
> Over the true — loves, hatreds not his own —
> And turn him pure as some forgotten vest
> Woven of painted byssus, silkiest
> Tufting the Tyrrhene whelk's pearl-sheeted lip,
> Left welter where a trireme let it slip

104

I' the sea, and vexed a satrap; so the stain
O' the world forsakes Sordello, with its pain,
Its pleasure: how the tinct loosening escapes,
Cloud after cloud!

(III.6-18)

When Browning quixotically added his headnotes in the edition of 1863, he made a further quixotic attempt to distinguish his narrative commentary from the vocal and mental postures of his characters with the extensive addition of quotation marks. Browning's editorial project must have been maddening when it arrived at passages like this one, where the voice of the poem hovers between narrative and dramatic modes, between Sordello's private tenor and Browning's public baritone. While retaining the third person, Browning adopts Sordello's perspective and patiently lets Sordello's defensive lie against time condemn itself in the process of its articulation.

It is significant that Sordello's desire for oblivion should be figured in the literary terms of "effacing" the "print" of the past, since one of the things he most wants to forget is his recent confrontation in Book II with the temporality of language. The main simile of the "forgotten vest" resumes this graphic metaphor for memory; Aprile's term for what the imagination creates, "a vesture gay" (*Paracelsus*, II.508), has become in Naddo's snappier idiom "a poetic vest," the dress of thought (III.250). Sordello, who has thrown his poetic crown into the maternal font at Goito (II.1002-3), now figures his purgative liberation from the vexations of poetry by envisioning himself as the rejected and forgotten one. Happily awash in the cradling sea of nature, he hopes to lose the "print," "stain," and "tinct" of the world's pains and pleasures and to recover a pristine truth and purity.

But for Browning, the poet of "repristination" (*The Ring and the Book*, I.23), origins are never so simply or so mildly constituted; his complex simile reveals Sordello's regressive impulse to be self-defeating. There is already a fine irony in the fact that Sordello's ostensible break with the "factitious humours" of poetic imagination should be imagined in such extravagant detail. The shifting tenses of the passage give this irony further point. The expectant future tenses of the verbs in the third and sixth lines bring forth the present tenses with which the intricate sentence arrives at its wish-fulfilling but contrafactual close—a close that witnesses to the frailty of Sordello's fiction that he has left the "factitious" behind. The pure origin to which he returns in imagination is itself a myth, and in temporal terms it is an unreliable myth because it relinquishes the power of the future and slips instead into an uninteresting present, unpleasant, painless, and repetitive—"Cloud after cloud!"

105

Time's keenest revenges in the passage come with the past tenses of "let" and "vexed." It is "the past" that Sordello would "put aside" or displace, but the initial image of spatial displacement is too weak to withstand an imagination that temporalizes in the very act of denying time. Suddenly the "forgotten vest" acquires a history that complicates Sordello's attempted retreat from time. His imagination infringes the bounds of metaphoric space and figures its proper, temporal authority in the exotic and grandly superfluous "satrap." A satrap is a provincial official, a secondary figure, an appointee; the official's presence here, like the presence of the torchbearer in Book I, points to a whole that lies out of the exclusive picture of the simile. In looking askance to this conspicuously absent or deferred whole, the simile creates a temporal loophole, making room for the poetry of some future, "better lay."

FREER PLAY: *SORDELLO* DECOMPOSED

The "better lay" that most interests Browning from the first is, of course, *Sordello*, a claustrophobic poem acutely aware at any given moment of its need to prepare for what is coming next.[19] More than once in the poem Browning pauses to discuss explicitly the importance of provision in poetry. He furnishes a notable image of his prospective narrative stance in the cinematic self-portrait that forms part of his digression in Book III. There he compares poetry to a fantastic, half-built "engine," which is not to be finished but to be "set up anew elsewhere" in some future, "clearer clime" (III.840-54). He represents himself as a tinkering technician, an inventor of new forms much of whose worth is in their novelty:

> *while you turn upon your heel,*
> *Pray that I be not busy slitting steel*
> *Or shredding brass, camped on some virgin shore*
> *Under a cluster of fresh stars, before*
> *I name a tithe o' the wheels I trust to do!*

(III.857-61)

Browning camps in a moment drained of everything but earliness and futurity. Not only are his heaven and earth to be "fresh" and "virgin," he fortifies his position with a highly temporal synecdoche in which not even the "tithe" or part of his anticipated labors is to be named quite yet.[20]

Browning's happiness as a preliminary shredder of brass and slitter of steel, his gleeful authorship of a poetry that dispreads, disparts, and disperses, involves a tacit promise to himself. His enginery of structure and meaning will not be foreclosed, and as a poet he will always have more to look forward to saying. Browning acknowledges as much in what may be the most self-conscious of his many narrative intrusions, during Sordello's prophetic oration in Book V on the progress of poesy:

> *"Man's inmost life shall yet have freer play:*
> *Once more I cast external things away,*
> *And natures composite, so decompose*
> *That"* . . . *Why, he writes* Sordello!

> (V.617-20)

This reflexive allusion first appears in the 1863 edition, along with Browning's marginal comment that such decomposition marks the poet's turn, "in due course," from being an "analyst" to becoming a "synthetist" (headnotes, V.597, 624). This anticipated synthesis, like the "single course" of Browning's phoenix in the passage introducing the two powers, represents a whole that is to be had only by traveling forward, towards the far side of an intervening schism. In the fourth line Browning preserves the schism by interrupting his Sordello before any actual synthesis, which might put an end to the "freer play" of his poem, may be so much as mentioned.

Browning composes *Sordello* by decomposing it first, and he finds its meaning by healing schisms of his own making.

> *Who will, may hear Sordello's story told:*
> *His story? Who believes me shall behold*
> *The man, pursue his fortunes to the end,*
> *Like me.*

> (I.1-4)

Tennyson announced upon reading *Sordello* that the first and the last lines, the only intelligible parts of the poem, were both lies.[21] The joke has some justice when one considers that it is already implicit in Browning's own jocular self-interrogation. Sordello's is a "story" that is less a story than a pursuit of meaning across gaps like the one opened here in its first couplet. Later in Book I, Browning associates Sordello's origin as a poet with a decisive willing of discontinuity, a moment of choice. This thematic association of beginning and interruption is repeatedly rehearsed in the stylistic maneuvers of Browning's opening narration as he attempts to break into his story once and for all. In the arbitrary originations of these beginning paragraphs, he persistently introduces the theme of choice and accompanies it with images of violent rupture:

> *as the friendless-people's friend*
> *Spied from his hill-top once, despite the din*

And dust of multitudes, Pentapolin
Named o' the Naked Arm, I single out
Sordello, compassed murkily about
With ravage of six long sad hundred years.

(I.4-9)[22]

I might be proud to see the dim
Abysmal past divide its hateful surge,
Letting of all men this one man emerge
Because it pleased me.

(I.18-21)

Lo, the past is hurled
In twain: up-thrust, out-staggering on the world,
Subsiding into shape, a darkness rears
Its outline, kindles at the core, appears
Verona.

(I.73-77)

Still, what if I approach the august sphere
Named now with only one name, disentwine
That under-current soft and argentine
From its fierce mate in the majestic mass
Leavened as the sea whose fire was mixt with glass
In John's transcendent vision,—launch once more
That lustre?

(I.360-66)

It is interesting that Browning here presents his authorial choices, as in Book V he presents Sordello's memory of an original choice, through a series of apocalyptic namings: "Pentapolin / Named o' the Naked Arm"; "this one man" Sordello; "appears / Verona"; "the august sphere / Named now with only one name," Dante. Browning discloses his choice of a hero and setting with such fanfare of revelation that one is tempted to take his emphasis on the giving of names as a hint and to say that what these passages most reveal is the importance of this poet's incipient word, of Browning's choice to write. Like the renaming of Dante's "Cunizza" as "Palma" (V.995) and, indeed, like the idiosyncratic rewriting of Italian history that sends its undercurrent throughout the poem, these passages are assertions of an authorial choice to be free from a simply continuous past.

The initiatory moment of choice is extended as well to Browning's elite audience. Much as Sordello plans to shape his work "For faces

like the faces that select / The single service I am bound effect"
(V.655-56), Browning begins by convoking an audience of "friends"
who "only believe" (I.10), who *will* to hear Sordello's story told, and
of past, "ghostly" poets who are "mustered" at Browning's summons
(I.45-49). In this protracted opening Browning also acknowledges the
decision made in *Pauline* about what to do with Shelley, through a
distancing hyperbole reminiscent of the earlier poem:

> *stay — thou, spirit, come not near*
> *Now — not this time desert thy cloudy place*
> *To scare me, thus employed, with that pure face!*
> *I need not fear this audience, I make free*
> *With them, but then this is no place for thee!*

> (I.60-64)

The couplets of *Sordello* do not often chime so decorously; here
they sweetly but firmly enclose Shelley's exaggerated purity in the
clouds. Browning's convocation of his friends and ancestors is a sort
of invocation, too, a preliminary exercise of the will to write, which
is the will to make a new beginning. In the matter of poetic vocation,
" 'tis not for fate to choose / Silence or song" (I.37-38), but for the
poet to make fateful choices that keep breaking the silence. Sordello
will rightly attribute his failure as a poet to his own impulses towards
easeful continuity, to a tethered "will" that has "forborn" and contented itself with "any wretched spark / Born of my predecessors,
though one stroke / Of mine had brought the flame forth!" (III.188-
98).

Browning gives his narrative two false starts in order to emphasize
the importance of beginnings. Before bringing Verona forth with an
originating flame that "kindles at the core," he deliberately has his
storytelling misfire: "Appears / Verona . . . Never, — I should warn
you first" (I.10-11); "Then, appear, / Verona! stay — thou spirit"
(I.59-60). As in the first two lines of the poem, the activities of beginning and of interrupting seem to be versions of each other. Even
the successful opening, when it finally arrives at I.73-77, hurls the
past in twain with the self-interfering, tongue-twisting stutter of "up-
thrust, out-staggering on the world." Browning's style in *Sordello* reveals what is thematically made explicit in *Paracelsus*: an awareness
that failure at the origin lets origination repeatedly renew itself. A
stumbling over the threshold announces that a limit is being passed,
as Browning revels in passage after passage of narrative interruption
and renewal.[23] Here he struggles through an introduction to Dante:

> *For he — for he,*
> *Gate-vein of this hearts' blood of Lombardy,*

> *(If I should falter now)—for he is thine!*
> *Sordello, thy forerunner, Florentine!*
>
> (I.345-48)

Browning has already faltered in the stuttering first line, as he falters again in the third by indulging in a parenthetical aside about faltering.

It is a plausible conjecture that what attracts Browning to Sordello as a literary subject is Sordello's earliness, both in history, as a figure from the dawn of the Renaissance, and in poetry, as a figure from Dante's *Purgatorio*, VI-VIII.[24] Dante locates Sordello in ante-purgatory: the beginning of the beginning, the threshold of spiritual renascence, the first spot along Dante's pilgrimage where the will to begin anew finds meaning in future possibilities. Dante furthermore associates purgatorial anticipation with poetic encounter by staging a rendezvous between his great forerunner Virgil and his minor forerunner Sordello. In Dante's scheme it is ultimately Virgil whom the encounter places, poignantly but decidedly, in a limbo where the future is gray and aspiration futile. The lines last quoted from *Sordello* arrange a significantly different rendezvous, as a step in Browning's extensive introductory clearing of poetic ground. Dante has had Virgil meet Sordello; for Virgil, Browning now substitutes Dante. In revising the poetic encounter, Browning puts Dante doubly in Virgil's place. By speaking of Dante as "serenest of the progeny of God," Browning consigns him to a "consummate orb" of perfect triumph, which, in its relation to futurity, is a place rather like Virgil's limbo (I.350-54). It is true that Browning presents Dante in some of the most powerfully anticipatory settings of Dante's great poem, in ante-purgatory and the earthly paradise; but these settings are rendered respectively as "a darkness quieted by hope" and "beneath God's eye / In gracious twilights where his chosen lie" (I.370-72). In the very strength and grace of his faith, Dante lacks the anxious, faltering tentativeness that frees Browning's future from the straight and narrow path. It is a nice touch, worthy of the tactics of *Pauline*, that what Browning represents himself as productively anxious about is the serene Dante.[25]

Browning's anxiety about getting started on his own way allows him to keep getting started. In the second line of the address to Dante—"Gate-vein of this hearts' blood of Lombardy"—Browning falters by forerunning himself. The line reappears more intelligibly at III.556 in the more appropriate context of Sordello's entrance into Italian politics (and with the characteristic if capricious difference of a displaced apostrophe: "heart's"). The line is virtually meaningless in Book I—and that is part of Browning's meaning in putting it there. By apprehending himself in a moment of premature revelation, by postponing a narrative event and its meaning, he prolongs and savors the pleasures of starting all over again. A similar technique appears with his heavy-handed disclosure that Sordello's besetting sin is

> *Thrusting in time eternity's concern, —*
> *So that Sordello. . . .*
> *Fool, who spied the mark*
> *Of leprosy upon him, violet-dark*
> *Already as he loiters? Born just now,*
> *With the new century, beside the glow*
> *And efflorescence out of barbarism.*
>
> (I.566-71)

Browning's broadly theatrical attitudes of alarm suggest that, as a revelation of ultimate meaning, this passage is comparatively uninteresting. The passage comes to life, however, as a forewarning of Browning's sense that such revelation threatens to shut down his storytelling enterprise. Browning's hyperbolical alarm means that "any officious babble" is inappropriate not only at this stage of the narrative, but at *any* stage of the narrative (I.584). Because such fullness of meaning would stop the poem, Browning here stops himself. He makes a fuss that opens his narrative to the birth, novelty, and "efflorescence" of the ensuing lines on the early Renaissance. "Go back to the beginning," he self-righteously tells himself (I.587); but in the glow of those lines a newer beginning has already been glimpsed.

The dance of such closures and disclosures makes Browning's vigilant storytelling a burlesque of the conventional, a worthy counterpart to his prospectively discontinuous figures of speech. The imagery of the ensuing lines parodies the decorum of traditional narration by embodying a gruesome, literal closure:

> *Crawl in then, hag, and couch asquat,*
> *Keeping that blotchy bosom thick in spot*
> *Until your time is ripe! The coffer-lid*
> *Is fastened, and the coffer safely hid*
> *Under the Loxian's choicest gifts of gold.*
>
> (I.599-603)

"The Loxian" is Apollo, Sordello's ideal, god of a complete poetry with determinate "beginnings," "gently" blended middles, and "piteous" ends (I.587-89). But narrative time in this poem will not ripen so continuously. For Browning the ornate craftsmanship of Apollonian closure harbors the "hag" of forbidden meaning; and her presence, like that of the "sleepless harpy" from whom she is descended (*Pauline*, 624), serves him as a pretext for precipitating a fresh start.

Time and again the menace of congealing completeness thus presents itself in *Sordello* only to be interrupted by the answering shock of Browning's decorum of violation. The interrupter, time, keeps appearing in propria persona to undo perceptual wholes:

> *Time put at length that period to content*
> *By right the world should have imposed.*
>
> (I.698-99)

>   *as it sank and sprang*
> *To measure, that whole palpitating breast*
> *Of heaven, 'twas Apollo, nature prest*
> *At eve to worship.*
>   *Time stole.*
>
> (I.924-27)

>   *her eyes*
> *Turn with so frank a triumph, for she meets*
> *Apollo's gaze in the pine glooms.*
>   *Time fleets:*
> *That's worst!*
>
> (I.960-63)

Browning takes special care to make such temporal interruptions part of his discussions of poetry. In Book I, for example, he tells how "earthly forms combine" in the vision of a certain class of poets until "Visibly through his garden walketh God." At once Browning discredits such vision and dissociates himself from such visionaries with an abrupt narrative intrusion and a radical shift of tone: "So fare they. Now revert" (I.501-5). In Book II Sordello's musings about poetic discourse lead him to a naive sense of how poetry may tone and organize the auditorial mind, "Until, by song, each floating part be linked / To each, and all grow palpable, distinct." Browning breaks up this ponderous spatial integration through that more temporal organ, the ear: "Meanwhile, sounds low and drear / Stole on him, and a noise of footsteps" (II.167-70). Browning's celebration of his own springing, dispreading, relentlessly temporal "rhymes" enters Book III just as the plans of Palma and Sordello are perfected in the plenitude of a glorious sunrise. Browning compares this sunrise to a very early, very mistaken Gaul, whose repetitive "triumph" brings on defeat, "who peered / A-top the Capitol, his face on flame / With triumph, triumphing till Manlius came" (III.590-92)—and cast him down, as the story has it, to the accompaniment of cackling geese.

112

Discreditings of closure like these in earlier books prepare for the elaborate deferment and escape that is Book VI, in which Sordello opts for the instant revelation of what masters life and Browning opts more modestly for the tardy recognition of Eglamor. Chronologically the book is over before it begins, since its central event, the death of Sordello, has occurred at the end of Book V. His death has come as yet another of time's revenges against the plotting of Palma and Salinguerra:

> Triumph at height, and thus Sordello crowned —
> Above the passage suddenly a sound
> Stops speech, stops walk.

(V.999-1001)

The "sound" is the noise Sordello makes as he collapses in death. By this point in the poem it is hard not to believe that the collapse has been precipitated by what is "above" in the "passage" of poetry, by the dangerously perfect triumph of the first line. A premature sense of perfection in his characters earns Browning's raillery, and in the climate of Sordello all perfection is premature. Browning ends Book V with another reminder of his abhorrence of such perfection: "While the persisting hermit-bee . . . ha! wait / No longer: these in compass, forward fate!" (V.1025-26). The line about the hermit-bee is a piece of premature narration that belongs in the next book (VI.621). Browning blurts it out here in order to postpone it and to constitute a narrative future towards which he may start working right away.

The concluding headnotes in Book V indicate that Sordello's decision to accept or decline Salinguerra's offer of political power will furnish the matter of the book to come: "Just this decided, as it now may be, and we have done" (headnotes, V.993,1022). But this promise of narrative "eternal rest" is just the sort of thing that a reader of Sordello has learned to mistrust, with a skepticism that the opening headnotes to Book VI soon intensify: "At the close of a day or a life, past procedure is fitliest reviewed, as more appreciable in its entirety" (headnotes, VI.1,25,63). Closure, fitness, and entirety have not been easy to come by hitherto in this poem, except as they have been called into question. Since the first half of this closing book is devoted to Sordello's final decision and the second half to Browning's deciding how at last to interpret the story he has just told, it may be helpful to consider the book as an obstinate, culminating questioning of closure itself.

113

When Sordello passes "out of Time" and out of the poem in the middle of Book VI, Browning rather formally prepares to point a moral by asking, "What made the secret of his past despair?" (VI.486-87). This question about his protagonist's tragic failure is also, and more deeply, a question about the meaning of Browning's long and difficult poem. These central interpretive issues prompt Browning to write into the poem a critical response to Sordello's story, a critical response that serves as an inoculation against the determination of meaning, which has been officiously suppressed since Book I. An answer to Browning's question readily follows: the "secret" of Sordello's failure is that "Soul on Matter being thrust, / Joy comes when so much Soul is wreaked in Time / On Matter" (VI.492-94).

> *Sorrow how avoid?*
> *Let the employer match the thing employed,*
> *Fit to the finite his infinity,*
> *And thus proceed for ever, in degree*
> *Changed but in kind the same, still limited*
> *To the appointed circumstance and dead*
> *To all beyond.*

(VI.497-503)

One difficulty with this "secret" is that it depends on a specious, complementary dualism worthy of Paracelsus at the stage of his most severe delusion. The passage seems to discover its speciousness as it unfolds, to attend to the Eglamoresque ring of its third line, and to become less smug about recommending the close fit and the perfect match. The attempt to explain Sordello's failure exposes itself as a version of the intemperate thinking that has already made Sordello "dead / To all beyond." Browning's isolating enjambment lets the attempt to enclose and limit meaning reveal itself as a little death, and the passage recoils from this revelation into a lengthy cosmetic paraphrase with evasive, extenuating qualifications.

A second and saving difficulty with this "secret" of Sordello's failure is that it is much too long for a secret. The confidently advanced solution that the individual must "Fit to the finite his infinity," if it were really a satisfactory solution, ought not to require such long-winded explanation. Browning allows his argument all the rope it needs, over a hundred lines of it; but given its dualistic premises of "finite" and "infinity," "Matter" and "Soul," the argument is bound repeatedly to string itself up. In fact, as Browning's incorporated critical response proceeds, it takes less and less the shape of a discursive argument. It seems more and more to take the exploratory course of a crisis poem, albeit a minor one, that recurs to versions of

114

its original question because no fixed answer, no formulable interpretation, will suffice. "What made the secret of his past despair?" "Sorrow how avoid?" "But does our knowledge reach / No farther? Is the cloud of hindrance broke / But by the failing of the fleshly yoke?" (VI.554-56).

> *Must life be ever just escaped, which should*
> *Have been enjoyed? — nay, might have been and would,*
> *Each purpose ordered right — the soul's no whit*
> *Beyond the body's purpose under it.*
> *Like yonder breadth of watery heaven, a bay,*
> *And that sky-space of water, ray for ray*
> *And star for star, one richness where they mixed*
> *As this and that wing of an angel, fixed,*
> *Tumultuary splendours folded in*
> *To die.*

(VI.561-70)

"But how so order life?" (VI.573). Not, apparently, in conformity to this mirror image of balanced body and soul—or there would be no need for the questioning to continue. Once again the impulse to "order" finds that the "fixed," enfolded closure it desires is a mask of death.

Yet through the very image that presents this death Browning makes a saving rent in the mask. The mirror image, with its internal echoes of "water," "ray," and "star," is itself the grandest repetition in *Sordello*, a wholesale quotation of six lines from the opening of the book (VI.11-16). The repetition, however, is not quite exact. The seemingly fearful symmetries of the image offer an escape from mere spatial reflexivity by differing slightly from the earlier lines that they appear to repeat. Lines 11-12 read, "A breadth of watery heaven like a bay, / A sky-like space of water." Browning might easily have transcribed these lines verbatim in the later passage. Indeed, he did so in 1840; but with an important revision made in 1863 he chose to jar the equilibrium. The earlier similes become metaphors instead: "watery heaven, a bay," and "sky-space of water." Browning's exact repetition of the rest of the lines throws the slight difference between simile and metaphor into relief and suggests that at this moment in the poem that difference may have a special meaning. The greater imaginative boldness of metaphor releases a freer play between tenor and vehicle, between the interchangeable water and sky, between the image in the mirror and the scene being mirrored. The metaphors say that the heaven *is* a bay, and that the water *is* a sky-space.

115

It should be remembered that these metaphors are part of a larger simile, which presumably illustrates the proper and orderly proportioning of body to soul. But the free play of tenor and vehicle to which Browning's revision calls attention makes an "orderly" reading of the larger simile impossible. A reader must discard the dualistic split of body and soul, which the simile is ostensibly written to support. If one makes in the metaphoric phrase "watery heaven, a bay" the substitutions for which the larger simile calls, there emerges a spiritual substance, the playfully oxymoronic and Browningesque concept of "physical soul, a body." Browning's crisis poem thus imagines in the movement of its verse a better, livelier secret than the "secret" from which it has begun; it discovers a solution that will not bear discursive articulation. With the slender revision written into lines 565-66, Browning makes his skeptical mistrust of the tendentiously meaningful into an occasion for genuine meaning. From here it is not far, either conceptually or on the page of *Sordello*, to the fruitful difficulties of the passage on the "incomprehensible" and "representative" powers and of Browning's "single course" of "Communication different."

Browning immediately emphasizes the open-endedness of the passage on the two powers by asking what the passage can mean for the story it seems to sum up, and by answering his own question with an ambiguous fable of origination.

> *What has Sordello found?*
> *Or can his spirit go the mighty round,*
> *End where poor Eglamor begun? So, says*
> *Old fable, the two eagles went two ways*
> *About the world: where, in the midst, they met,*
> *Though on a shifting waste of sand, men set*
> *Jove's temple. Quick, what has Sordello found?*
>
> (VI.603-9)

The surprising appearance of the spirit of Eglamor briefly prefigures his encounter with Browning later in the book; on both occasions that spirit of closure serves to guarantee the possibility of new beginnings. Here Eglamor's deferential secondariness is a foil to the impatient priority of Sordello. Browning's questions suggest that Sordello "ends" by finding that a position of secondariness like Eglamor's, however "poor," is where one ultimately begins from. That such apparently opposite poetic spirits as Sordello and Eglamor should meet, as did Jove's two eagles at Delphi, implies that the relation between priority and secondariness involves not a spatial opposition, but rather a mutual dependence like that between the two powers. The meeting of Jove's eagles at a spot determined by the intersection of their dif-

116

ferent paths defines "the midst" and marks the center of the world.[26] A center is an origin, and for Browning the possibility of reorigination remains a central truth. The Delphic place of the "old fable" is central to this poem, and to Browning, because it is a place of constant change, "a shifting waste" of pure, oracular potentiality. That shifting waste, Childe Roland's tract, is Browning's landscape of poetic origination, the Meribah of the smitten rock and the diviner's "dim first oozings" (III.830). It is the place where men and women become founders of monuments to their own secondariness, monuments whose glorious impermanence leaves room for fresh foundations. In Book I Browning has introduced his account of Sordello's poetic birth by referring to secondary human joys that are contrived "amid the dearth" (I.681). In the dearth of Browning's central wasteland, there is nothing to do but begin.

Perhaps the best way of interpreting this Delphic fable of origination from Book VI is to see how it reverses an earlier "legend" of closure from Book I.

> *So runs*
> *A legend; light had birth ere moons and suns,*
> *Flowing through space a river and alone,*
> *Till chaos burst and blank the spheres were strown*
> *Hither and thither, foundering and blind:*
> *When into each of them rushed light—to find*
> *Itself no place, foiled of its radiant chance.*
> *Let such forego their just inheritance!*

> (I.515-22)

Browning writes this obscure legend to effect a transition between his discussions of two classes of poets. The first class, that of Eglamor, pour their devotion wholly into the objective world, while Sordello's class, the second, find in external things continual revelations of their own glorious priority. Browning's transitional legend is obscured by an important ambiguity. According to one reading, the prevenient light "rushes into" the blind spheres and is absorbed, losing its own "place"; according to another reading, it is "foiled" or repulsed and "finds itself no place" within the spheres. This ambiguity plays between the two classes of poets and furnishes another instance of Browning's habit of overcoming his own dualism even as he professes to be setting it up.[27]

Both the poet who is wasted on the world and the poet who is isolated from the world have lost the chance of enlightening it. Whether spatially the light is enclosed within the spheres or closed out, it is in either case closed off temporally from its "radiant chance," its rightful future. The passage is a condensation of what

Browning may have decided was too dualistically schematic in the conclusion to *Paracelsus:*

> Let men
> Regard me, and the poet dead long ago
> Who loved too rashly; and shape forth a third
> And better-tempered spirit, warned by both:
> As from the over-radiant star too mad
> To drink the life-springs, beamless thence itself —
> And the dark orb which borders the abyss,
> Ingulfed in icy night, — might have its course
> A temperate and equidistant world.

(V.885-93)

Paracelsus's imagery inappropriately frames the problem of "temperance" in terms not of time, but of geometric space. When Browning revised this passage in writing Book I of *Sordello,* he came up with a legend whose ambiguous condensation forces a reader to adopt a temporal perspective from which spatial dualism ceases to matter. What matters is that both classes of poets stand in danger of losing the future, the radiance of anticipation that is "their just inheritance." The imprisonment "past escape" of the worshipful first class by the objects their reverence feeds (I.512) and the incapacity of the imperious second class to be "surprised" or "affronted" by any object in existence (I.542-47) are from a temporal perspective distinct but equivalent conditions of closure.

What keeps this dangerous closure from closing in? What allows Browning to give the "foiled" light of his legend a second "radiant chance" and in Book VI to replace that legend with a fable extending the promise of reorigination? It is the paradoxical power of deference: the power of imagination to feed on a possibility that is neither present nor nonexistent, but deferred; to dwell on a meaning that is neither confirmed nor denied, but awaited. Neither condition of closure — Sordellan priority or Eglamoresque secondariness — is ever quite perfect in *Sordello*; either condition tends, in time, to turn like John of Patmos's likeness into its apparent opposite (III.988). Sordello can and will "end where poor Eglamor begun" in the compellingly prospective position of one who acknowledges failure and "spies / Help from above in his extreme despair" (VI.616-17).[28] There is a strength in secondariness, as Browning triumphantly shows in *Pauline*, and there is in a priority like that of Paracelsus a weakness that, in bringing him to failure, brings him to a redemptive sense of that failure.

The breaking point of "wondrous change" (*Pauline*, 185), the central point of vital exchange between these two conditions, where

Jove's eagles meet and ends yield to beginnings, is where Browning sets his "temple"—or his stylistic palace of art. That is why he builds himself "golden courts" only by insisting that he is, like the Eglamor he awaits, just a "guest" passing through (VI.799). The "transient struggle" between the two menacing permanences of "perfect triumph" and "enduring damp" (VI.807-9) is a struggle always welcome to one of the most confirmed transients in English poetry. He will find in rites of passage a place for opening future plays and poems, which, while seldom again related so overtly to his own situation as a poet, may be considered as richly various elaborations of themes and techniques already prominent in his earliest works.

CHAPTER FOUR

PRECIOUS WEAKNESS: THE DRAMAS

> *I have been all my life asking what connection*
> *there is between the satisfaction at the display*
> *of power, and the sympathy with — ever-increasing*
> *sympathy with — all imaginable weakness?*
> Browning to Elizabeth Barrett (1845)[1]

As a dramatist even more perhaps than as a poet, in the years 1836-1846 Browning had special reason to concern himself with time. Temporal themes and techniques for making beginnings, maintaining suspense, and retarding conclusions not only preoccupied him as essentials of the playwright's craft, to an uncommon degree they became the very stuff of the works he crafted. *Strafford* (1837), the seven plays of the following decade, and the one-act closet drama *In a Balcony*, which Browning published in *Men and Women* (1855) as a coda to his playwriting career, all turn on "Action in Character rather than Character in Action."[2] The psychological action that quickens their characters is often difficult to distinguish from the dramatic action, the plot of which it is ostensibly but a part. The action thus sustained by the playwright and his collaborating characters is usually complex and is more than occasionally baffling. Yet from a temporal perspective it is possible to find certain complexities of action recurring in play after play. One may describe Browning's dramaturgical performances as variations on a central action — a holding action, a dramatized version of the tactical delay that figures so importantly in Browning's early narratives.

Browning's characters typically postpone a perfection, fulfillment, or presence that they regard, however obscurely, as an undesirable end. The necessary fault, emptiness, or dislocation that keeps such an end at a distance is preserved as characters maneuver themselves into secondary positions. Deferment of the action of a Browning play involves his characters' deferential behavior toward each other. Hostile critics have judged that the result of such complicity between Browning and his dramatis personae is character in *inaction* rather than anything else.[3] So little happens in Browning's plays, however, because so much is taking place to insure that little happens. The distinctive inward action of his drama is the ceaseless generation of just that state of external inaction that has received adverse criticism. Such criticism is not wrong, then; indeed, for the common reader or theatergoer it is surely appropriate, and nothing in the following pages can or should reverse the general estimate that Browning's plays are hardly stageworthy. But the student of Victorian poetry, and perhaps the student of dramaturgy, too, will find the prevailing criticism of these plays superficial in its neglect of enduring paradoxes in Browning's writing: that any genuine human initiative is deferential and that what is humbly secondary tends to subvert the ostensibly prior forces that seem to control it.

This subversive tendency lends itself well to the language of economics in which Browning's characters repeatedly represent their predicaments. A moral and emotional economy governs the world of his dramas; and, in the agitated exchanges between his characters, success consists in the mastery of a curious deficit spending. For his dramatic protagonists, as for the Browning of *Pauline*, guilt invests the future with an interest that they contrive never to pay off but to renew continually. An inventively prolonged condition of indebtedness lets the show go on, through what *Sordello* calls "The complicated scheme to make amends" (*Sordello*, III.802). In the view of most sympathetic readers, Browning's lofty heroes and heroines sacrifice themselves to an ideal of noblesse oblige.[4] This view of Browning's characters, however, is acceptable only if one stresses the primacy of their ennobling mutual obligation as heroic debtors, the dramatic priority that is conferred upon them by their guilty secondariness. Each of them might say with Browning's Ferishtah in the late "A Bean-Stripe: Also, Apple-Eating" (1884), "The sense within me that I owe a debt/ Assures me" (414-15). Browning's leading men and women extend credit to each other, often with a stunning disregard for any objective accreditation, in order to secure secondary positions from which they may purchase the future. Eager buyers of time, they define themselves within the terms of a lease on life, a mortgage that they improvise, interpret, and revise with energetic skill. The single and unalterable limit to their activity is that fulfillment or cancellation of the mortgage means, if not the ultimate human mortality, its dramatic equivalent: an uninteresting existence, a life without anticipation and, therefore, in Browning's scheme, without the promise of meaning.[5]

121

Browning's best-known play, *Pippa Passes* (1841), is also the least typical specimen of his playwriting. It will provide a useful introductory idea of what his other plays are *not*—what, in fact, they strenuously escape becoming. Composed of an introduction, a conclusion, and four "parts," which may be further analyzed into seven scenes, the play scarcely devotes to its constituent actions enough time for any major deferment to be undertaken, much less sustained. Despite the transiency of Pippa's unifying passage through the lives of the other characters, each scene draws more neatly and rapidly to its conclusion than one might expect from the author of *Sordello*. Psychological tangles of Gordian intricacy, even in the justly admired scene between Ottima and Sebald, receive sudden clarification, with the flash of a decisive judgment that resolves all differences and leaves nothing of significance to be deferred. Furthermore, Browning takes care to make the whole action of Pippa's day very much a whole. Her passing completes an itinerary that she plans in advance and smoothly executes.

Pippa Passes was an experimental work for Browning in two ways. His juxtaposition of several discrete but loosely related vignettes represented an innovation upon the traditional dramatic form to which he adhered in all of his other plays—possibly excepting *A Soul's Tragedy* (1846), which is in any case a more traditional piece than *Pippa Passes*.[6] In breaking with traditional form, Browning also broke with the prevailing tactics of his own earlier writing. Having developed strategies of escape from imminent closure in *Sordello*, his most recently published work, in *Pippa Passes* he embraced closure as a possibility not only imminent, but repeatedly realized. It is as if he wrote the play against the current of his dominant creative impulse in order to see how an art of closure might give ironic expression or negative definition to the themes informing his characteristic art of disclosure. The effect of Browning's rush to apocalyptic climax in this play, as its readers have observed, is to create a tension "between the simplicity of its moral resolutions and the grotesqueness and complexity of its world."[7] With this tension Browning makes a characteristic dramatic statement about the perils of apocalypse. As in the later lyric "The Last Ride Together" (1855), the implicit question "Who knows but the world may end to-night?" (22) exerts such pressure on the worldly events leading up to apocalypse that the apocalyptic moment itself comes to seem a sad reduction of grotesque but deeply human potentialities. The dramatic (and theological) structure of the play wrenches highly individual characters out of themselves into conformity with a moral ideal; thus character in apocalyptic action ends by performing a disappointing action out of character. To see that this disappointment is the point of Browning's experimentation with closure in *Pippa Passes* is to give the play its proper place among his dramas, and in his poetry as a whole.

The absolute closures of the play make its initially interesting characters finally inconsequential. Inconsequentiality and closure are explicitly related in the new year's hymn with which Pippa introduces and concludes the action:

> *All service ranks the same with God:*
> *If now, as formerly he trod*
> *Paradise, his presence fills*
> *Our earth, each only as God wills*
> *Can work — God's puppets, best and worst,*
> *Are we; there is no last nor first.*

(Introduction, 190-95)

These lines may be taken as Browning's acknowledgment of the kind of "earth" or dramatic world he has uniquely created for the experiment in which they occur. Pippa's "if" deserves emphasis as a sign of the hypothetical, experimental mode within which Browning has chosen to work. When Pippa's hypothesis is applied to the writing of plays — and her term "puppets" suggests such an application — certain dramaturgical principles emerge. The filling "presence" of a supervisory God manifests itself in a "now" of sameness or indifference; Pippa's resumption of her hymn in the closing lines of the play (as emended by Browning in 1849) conveys such sameness through repetition: "All service is the same with God — / With God" (IV.ii.113-14).

In temporal terms this presence makes nonsense of sequentiality, or rather makes non sequitur: if "there is no last nor first," neither is there any reason why a given scene should precede or follow another. Nor in so immediate a world is there any ranking of "best and worst." By eliminating discriminations, the paradisal presence makes it impossible that there should exist any ultimately significant differences among characters. The last judgment reduces all characters to playing a single role, the uninteresting minor role of obedient servant. Pippa's vision of continuity and plenitude leaves no room for dramatic action, for character conflict, for play. The "presence" she posits might be better considered as a double negative: an absence of absence, a lack of the lack from which plays proceed and by virtue of which their authors are able to differentiate beginnings from ends. [8]

Certainly Browning recognizes the disadvantages of thus thrusting in time eternity's concern. Pippa's hymn echoes throughout his dramatic career, but always in contexts that display its perspective as

123

one that is to be avoided or forgotten. Luria speaks of God's close "engagement" with "his world" in "the everlasting minute of creation" as of a smothering presence with which Luria has deliberately broken (*Luria* [1846], V.233-38). When Norbert attempts to repose in a vision of "all nature self-abandoned," "fixed" under a God whose universal approval justifies "no delay," Constance rejects him with an answer worthy of her author: "And so shall we be ruined, both of us" (*In a Balcony*, 248-66). Even Pippa prefaces her hymn by pausing to ask whether her day may not be prematurely exhausted, whether it may not be over before it has had a chance to start:

> *Now wait! — even I already seem to share*
> *In God's love: what does New-year's hymn declare?*
> *What other meaning do these verses bear?*
>
> (Introduction, 187-89)

Pippa has just mentioned the enjoyment of "God's love" as a goal with which her day will culminate (Introduction, 180), yet according to her hymn that goal is already attained. Such a collapse of expectation would be intolerable to the guilty protagonists of Browning's other plays; the surest indication of Pippa's innocence is that she feels no need to obey her injunction to "wait."

The prospective, apparently Browningesque "meaning" that Pippa extracts from her verses — "And more of it, and more of it! — oh yes" (Introduction, 202) — is a meaning accessible only to unorganized innocence. Especially when Pippa is compared to such protesting spirits as Paracelsus and Sordello, her bland acceptance of a random homogeneity seems inhuman. The verbal repetitiveness of Pippa's "meaning" may be a sign that here, as in Browning's drama generally, innocence is scarcely presentable. Indeed, Browning manages to present Pippa at such length in her opening soliloquy only by compromising her innocence to the extent of involving her in a primitive psychological economy. Her present holiday constitutes a gift to her future self. Promising not to "squander" the "treasure" of her apostrophized "day," she predicts, "I shall borrow / Sufficient strength of thee for new-year's sorrow" (Introduction, 13-14, 33-34). In a very explicit passage that Browning deleted in 1849 between lines 203 and 204 of the Introduction, Pippa foresees the other characters, "Whom a mere look at half will cure / The Past, and help me to endure / The Coming." Pippa looks before and after; and, while her temporal consciousness hardly furnishes evidence for demystifying her innocence, it nevertheless indicates Browning's difficulty in sustaining the utter simplicity required by her paradisal vision of divine presence.[9]

Browning permits himself much more temporal sophistication in delineating the characters whom Pippa's songs affect; it is the inner play of these characters, and their interplay, that make up the drama. Ultimately, however, each of them returns to the origin that Pippa celebrates, and each describes a circular "Action in Character" corresponding to the action of the entire play, rounded as it is by Pippa's introduction and echoing epilogue. Each character diverges for a time from the straight way but at a climactic moment ends his or her scene by responding to the strings of Pippa's puppeteer. It is no mistake that the puppets should all fall into line with the name of divinity on their lips. "God's in his heaven!" Sebald twice exclaims after Pippa's example, and Ottima follows: "Not me—to him, O God, be merciful!" (I.i.227,229,269,282). Repetitions suspiciously like Pippa's accompany Jules's final simile of "a god going through his world": "as now—as now—as now! / Some unsuspected isle in the far seas! / Some unsuspected isle in far-off seas!" (II.i.304,325-27). Luigi departs on his mission with the assurance that " 'Tis God's voice calls," after hearing about "the very god" in Pippa's song (III.i.229,198). The god's business there is to maintain a sacred enclosure against the inroads of guilty "rogues," an enclosure analogous to the dramatic enclosure awaiting each of the protagonists in *Pippa Passes*; this god manifests divine presence with a vengeance, striding "Backward and forward, keeping watch / O'er his brazen bowls, such rogues to catch!" (III.i.200-201). The Monsignor decrees the end of his own scene and binds himself in silence when he has the Intendant gagged and cries, *"Miserere mei, Domine!"* (IV.i.178).

To be sure, an anthology of their famous last words oversimplifies Browning's characters in this play, in part by overlooking attitudes toward time that they hold in common. By turning to God's presence, they are all turning away from presence of another kind. Like Pippa, in one sense or another all of them sacrifice present satisfaction for the sake of the future. Ottima and Sebald give up their fascinating "now," "now and now," and subscribe instead to the scenario of a divinely ordained morality: "There, there, both deaths presently!" (I.i.214,276). For a reflex of immediate retribution against the painter Lutwyche, Jules substitutes a more capable, deferred revenge through the mediation of art: "Meet Lutwyche, I— / And save him from my statue meeting him?" (II.i.318-19). Luigi resists his mother's tempting offer of the desirable Chiara (III.i.151) in favor of more distant political objects. The Monsignor, similarly tempted by the Intendant (especially in the version of 1841), is reminded by Pippa's song that he must devote the brief time before him to the task of rectifying a moral economy: he has friends to "recompense," wrongs to "repair," and "whole centuries of sin to redeem" (IV.i.2, 84,100).[10]

But such temporal complications remain means to inexorable ends: the characters of *Pippa Passes* achieve a closure at once spiritual and dramatic by choosing simplicity and putting themselves in unquestioning sympathy with the tonic note of Pippa's song. That such closure is a questionable achievement may be seen as Browning's meaning in undertaking so uniquely short-circuited a play. It may also be seen in his decision to model his later plays, even those destined rather for the study than the stage, not on *Pippa Passes* but on the earlier and much different *Strafford*. This chapter centers on *Strafford* in the belief that, though not necessarily Browning's most successful drama, it has the special interest that belongs to any beginning; and in the hope that the passages and issues discussed will suggest approaches to its successors that must here remain mostly implicit. The way back to that beginning will lie through a renewed consideration of the moment of *Pippa Passes* that most nearly recalls the dramatic and psychological motives of Browning's other plays: the moment of the choice of innocence.

MEANTIME: REFLECTIONS ON INNOCENCE

In the final analysis, the characters of *Pippa Passes* invite a simple reading because finally they simplify themselves. It is, however, the peculiarity of Browning's poetry to defer final analyses, even when his art of disclosure masquerades as an art of closure. The fact is worth pondering that his characters are not simplified by some external agency but really do simplify themselves. The lines just discussed from the major scenes of the play suggest that the terminal innocence of its characters is not given but in each case chosen. The final analysis would, of course, disregard this distinction, but the difference between what one is given and what one chooses makes all the difference in Browning's world. Innocence is often conceived as a state anterior to significant choice, a state in which every alternative is equally valid—or in Blake's phrasing, a mental place where all contraries are equally true. *Pippa Passes*, Browning's songbook of innocence, questions this relation of innocence to choice. For the figures of this play, the state of innocence is a state of their own choosing: not a prelude to the necessity of choice, but its result.

Such innocence involves a consciously secondary return to the myth of primal simplicity that Pippa's songs imagine and in which her errant auditors choose to believe. They all correct a late sense of guilt with a willed faith, a faith that allows each of them to recoup a purity that feels early. For Sebald and Jules, innocence is something restored, a simple alternative to the fallen dubieties of sin or irony:

"That little peasant's voice / Has righted all again" (I.i.261-62); "Oh, to hear / God's voice plain as I heard it first, before / They broke in with their laughter!" (II.i.303-5). Luigi's rhetorical question "Are crowns yet to be won in this late time?" bespeaks the reassurance Pippa's song has supplied: despite the political decadence of the times, the return to a better, primitive state is still possible for Luigi, who regains "God's gift / Of the morning-star" (III.i.227,150). The song the Monsignor hears confirms his recently shaken conviction that "My glory springs from another source"; and his choice of a heavenly over a temporal origin, like any climactic choice, entails a suppression and rejection of the alternative not taken: "Gag this villain—tie him hand and foot! He dares . . . I know not half he dares —but remove him—quick!" (IV.i.82-83,177-78). The abrupt gagging and ejection of the Intendant physically enact the internal dynamics of choice, as the once-knowing Monsignor suddenly represses the forbidden "half" of his knowledge of the ways of the world.

In addition, then, to the discrepancy between the course of each scene and its conclusion, there is a discrepancy between the simple moral goal each character attains and the psychological complexity with which at the eleventh hour that goal is established as attainable. Not just the period of wayward vacillation preceding moral anagnorisis, but the apocalyptic anagnorisis itself, is in each case the responsibility of the leading character, who thus remains the director of his or her own apocalypse. Assassins of their own characters, Browning's protagonists commit dramatic suicide; but, as Browning already knew and would show again years later in *Red Cotton Night-Cap Country* (1873), the suicide is among the most intriguing of psychological subjects. Constrained by the closural scheme of *Pippa Passes*, Browning's characters hold the undeniable fascination of wind-up dolls cunningly devised to go through the elaborate motions of shutting themselves off. And the best of them do more: in spite of the overdetermination of the play's fable, Ottima, Sebald, and the Monsignor assume a life of their own for which Browning's "puppets" offers a more pertinent image than that of wind-up dolls. Even at the last minute God's puppets exhibit an independent activity—if only the curious activity of fastening themselves to the divine strings and then hardening into wooden simplicity. The choice of simplicity is never a simple affair in Browning, and in the complexity of its characters' willed retrieval of innocence *Pippa Passes* begins to resemble Browning's other dramas as well. The resemblance remains shortlived because each vignette stops so short, but even the short lives displayed in this experimental work incarnate paradoxes about the active will to passivity and the imaginative recreation of innocence that Browning's other plays explore at greater length.

127

The choice of innocence repeatedly presented in *Pippa Passes* serves as a device for dramatic circularity and closure. *Strafford* and Browning's later plays are more open-ended or linear in shape, and Browning keeps them that way by dramatizing the contrary choice of guilt. Seeds of the difference between *Strafford* and *Pippa Passes* lie in yet another section of Pippa's introductory soliloquy, in which she addresses a sunbeam reflected in her water basin:

> *One splash of water ruins you asleep,*
> *And up, up fleet your brilliant bits*
> *Wheeling and counterwheeling,*
> *Reeling, broken beyond healing:*
> *Now grow together on the ceiling!*
> *That will task your wits.*
> *Whoever it was quenched fire first, hoped to see*
> *Morsel after morsel flee*
> *As merrily, as giddily . . .*
> *Meantime, what lights my sunbeam on,*
> *Where settles by degrees the radiant cripple?*

(Introduction, 77-87)

Browning's happy temporalization of flowing light enlists the quickness of an innocent's perceptions in the service of a miniature dramatic theory—one that views origins more quizzically than does Pippa's new year's hymn. An initiating "ruin" liberates and disperses light by breaking it up into incomplete "bits" and makes of a once sleepy whole a fragmentary, transitory display that is "brilliant," a "radiant cripple." Although Pippa charges the reeling lights to recover their ruined wholeness, she also hints, in describing the light as "broken beyond healing," that such recuperation is impossible. Given this contradiction, it is no wonder that the problem of reintegration will task wits. What *is* wonderful, and for no one more than for Browning the playwright, is that the problem promises to remain problematic. Even as it alights and settles, Pippa's sunbeam remains "the radiant cripple," broken into a lively brightness whose first significance is temporal; the gradual settling of the light "by degrees" creates a "meantime," a mean-time, an indefinite interval of play during which wits may be tasked and meaning may occur.

It should especially task wits that the unrecoverable whole, "broken beyond healing," is from the beginning a reflection. Its original "presence," to resume the comparison between these lines and Pippa's later hymn, is already a representation. The "foolhardy" light projected from Pippa's basin onto the ceiling is, in the phrase of Browning's imagined poet Rudel, "but a foolish mimic sun" ("Rudel

128

to the Lady of Tripoli" [1842], 11). The original proves to be a copy or imitation that owes its originality, through a dialectic indispensable in *Paracelsus* and *Sordello*, to someone's half-remembered decision to be secondary to it and treat it as if it were true.[11] Pippa's apparently insignificant decision to make a game out of the light playing in her chamber illustrates the temporal movement of signification that Browning so often exploits in less innocuous contexts. She constructs her game through a willingness to begin with an assumption that she knows to be fanciful. Her make-believe, making herself believe, in turn confers meaning on time, as if in response to her earlier awareness that "here I let time slip for nought" (Introduction, 72).

This pretense, this paradoxical decision to start waiting, opens a "meantime" that Browning can extend indefinitely by never letting his characters quite forget its originating paradox. By recalling the difference between inaccessible truth and representative figuration, between a simply inherited, intact faith and a faith that is chosen and therefore uncomfortably faulty, Browning keeps conclusions at bay. It is because it is a reflection that Pippa's sunbeam "would mock the best pursuer" (Introduction, 75). Such imagery of secondariness and pursuit is a hallmark of Browning's early narratives, and its recurrence here reflects the continuity of Browning's concerns as poet and as playwright. It also furnishes an implicit critique of unmocked certainties in *Pippa Passes*, in which interesting psychological cripples lose their fractured radiance by unwittingly shirking their tasks, foreclosing their own mortgages, and growing too quickly together again. Although in *Pippa Passes* as in Browning's other plays each character chooses faith, the unique structure of this play for once sanctions the innocent fiction that a believer can forget the dubious origin of faith, and that faith can thus become as pure and changeless as the object in which the believer chooses to believe. Whether Jules or Luigi will live to repent of his repentance is not a profitable question; but the fluctuating confidence of Strafford, Djabal, and Luria is essential to their plays and to the analysis of representation that those plays dramatize.

If a supposed presence, whole, or origin may be shown to have been previously constituted through the powerful fiat of a human will to defer to it, then it is rather a representation of need than a necessary presence. Now representation, as Browning conspicuously and tirelessly teaches, forever betrays its incapacity to do anything more than represent, mediate, or substitute. It reveals, if it does not proclaim, an ineradicable, incurable difference between what represents and what is represented. Through an inevitable dissimulation, a figure of speech unsettles and supplants what it is intended to render;

because as a representation it differs from the irreducibly other thing (object or idea or person) to which it points, it can only display that thing by displacing it. Precisely because it means, it can never simply be. This fundamental difference 'between image and truth, fancy and fact, opens an interminable process of reference—one that is indeed cognate with the process of deference in Browning and that from a temporal perspective may be considered as identical with it. Insofar as meaning is a temporal phenomenon, figurative language defers what it refers to. Permanently transitory, it intends an ungraspable future that it also postpones.

Under Browning's hands this seemingly gloomy account of imagination's guilty involvement with language glows with promise. Like the "bright slave" of repressed meaning (*Pauline*, 633) and like Pippa's "radiant cripple" of reflected rays, representational language lights Browning's way by concealing what it pretends to reflect: the terminus of original meaning. As Sebald says but too readily forgets, "there's a recompense in guilt; / One must be venturous and fortunate: / What is one young for, else?" (I.i.135-37). Such guilt is a commodity on which Browning's characters capitalize in the series of venturous gambles to keep themselves young on which Browning bases play after play. The splendidly adolescent lines, for example, in which Ottima recalls the "crowning" moment of sexual consummation with Sebald derive their incantatory power less from consummation than from recollected anticipation:

OTTIMA *The day of it too, Sebald!*
When heaven's pillars seemed o'erbowed with heat,
Its black-blue canopy suffered descend
Close on us both, to weigh down each to each,
And smother up all life except our life.
So we lay till the storm came.

SEBALD *How it came!*

OTTIMA *Buried in woods we lay, you recollect;*
Swift ran the searching tempest overhead;
And ever and anon some bright white shaft
Burned thro' the pine-tree roof, here burned and there,
As if God's messenger thro' the close wood screen
Plunged and replunged his weapon at a venture,
Feeling for guilty thee and me: then broke
The thunder like a whole sea overhead—

SEBALD *Yes!*

(I.i.184-98)

Sebald's asides or cheers from the sidelines here credit Ottima's ability to revive the past without laundering it. Her speech is, like herself,

130

"magnificent in sin" (I.i.218). Her imagery of "pillars," "canopy," and "roof" enshrines their sin in ritual form; and her simile of "God's messenger" attracts from Sebald's earlier economic image the related terms of "guilt" and "venture"—oddly so, but accurately, since the function of her ritual is to bind them together to share the anticipatory "recompense in guilt."

It is appropriate that Ottima, who will later join Sebald in addressing God directly, here should speak instead of "God's messenger," an intermediate figure reminiscent of the secondary, "representative" power that Browning invokes in the last book of *Sordello* (VI.598). A world in which God sends messages is not the smoothly filled world of Pippa's hymn. It is a world better described by the titles of two later lyrics that turn on the deferred correspondences of epistolary messages: a world of "Time's Revenges" (1845) and their attendant, anxious "Fears and Scruples" (1876). From a theological perspective, the "recompense in guilt" is that it may create moral work for the lifetime of a crippled but venturous soul. The analogous creation of poetical works is, from the literary perspective that always adjoins the theological in Browning's mind, the recompense in linguistic guilt—in the fault whereby fictive image differs from, and defers, imageless truth.

A RECOMPENSE IN GUILT: *STRAFFORD*

In *Strafford* Browning so concerned himself with the fault between image and truth that he wrote less a play than a foreplay, a fitting prelude to his subsequent dramatic art. The play ends as it begins, *in mediis rebus*. Strafford's final cry, "O God, I shall die first—I shall die first!" (V.ii.351), preserves an intermediacy that differs radically from the prayerful formal closures of *Pippa Passes*. Deferring even the consummation of death with which Browning arbitrarily stops several later plays, Strafford's cry invokes God not to cancel debts, but to extend them. Its desperate anticipation is a worthy counterpart to the choral suspense with which the action, or inaction, begins (I.i.2-11,20,95). The play resolves nothing because it grows out of its author's decision to address the question of irresolution itself: a question whose psychological and linguistic manifestations it is difficult, and perhaps naive, to treat independently of each other. Browning certainly treats them as related, and he so centers their relation on the slippery common ground of the unresolved image (memory or figuration) that a consideration of his queasy imagery of the image may be the best approach to the strange play that it sustains.

Strafford is a character haunted by images—images of a moral guilt that, as it finds expression, trespasses on linguistic guilt, the original indebtedness of the poetic image. A devoted royalist who has renounced his early allegiance to the republican cause, a character who has violated continuity in order to make a new beginning, Strafford is one of Browning's greatly troubled apostates. Alternation between regret and defense of his apostasy underlies not only Strafford's most theatrical moments (II.ii.131, for example, or the frenzied close of Act III), but also the sophisticated meditations that make his play worth studying. Although Strafford's royalist conversion has occurred long before the dramatic action begins, Browning reenacts this conversion broadly by having King Charles change the hero's name from "Wentworth" to "Strafford" (I.ii.241) and more subtly by having Strafford reconvert himself on numerous occasions. At each of these reconversions Strafford resumes his attitude of ministrant secondariness to a feeble king, incapable alike of political rule and of personal loyalty, in whom he nevertheless chooses to believe. It is at these moments of reconversion that Strafford most frequently recurs to imagery of the image; casting doubt on his faith even as he reaffirms it, he betrays an intermittent suspicion that his Charles may be no more than a figurehead. Like other political apostates in Browning's plays, notably Djabal in *The Return of the Druses* (1843) and the title character in *Luria*, Strafford is an illusionist practicing the power of make-believe upon himself; like them, moreover, he is partially aware of what he is doing. [12]

This awareness gives rise to a major interpretive problem of the play. Why should Strafford persevere in such a course of impossible allegiance? The problem is identified by Harold Orel in one of the few critical readings *Strafford* has received: "Strafford, acting as minister to a King who continually betrayed him, could have been under no illusions about Charles's character." Orel seeks a solution in the hero's age and illness, in the tardy "sense of irrevocable commitment" that is expressed in Strafford's confession to Charles that " 'tis too late to think about" (II.ii.36). [13] Although Orel's explication requires further unfolding, it is valuable for the temporal perspective that it adopts toward the action of Browning's play and that it finds Browning's hero adopting: " 'tis too late." As with the young Sordello, the exercise of power within and among Browning's dramatic characters typically involves their ability to time events; their psychological conflicts are most often temporal as well. Temporal conflict is probably clearest in the first exchange of Browning's last and briefest play, in which he plots the dynamics of his dramatic writing in general:

NORBERT   *Now!*

132

(In a Balcony, 1)

With this exchange, and with this play, Browning prefigures drama-
turgically a feature of his poetic career: the tendency of his strange
and spare final poems to make abstract and explicit the richly varied
motives of his earlier work. The quarrel between Norbert and Constance pointedly suggests that for Browning exploration of character
is also exploration of temporality. It is the quick play between
"Now!" and "Not now!" that engraves character in Browning's
world, that etches features and furrows brows.

Browning's subsequent dramatic practice, then, would support an
approach to *Strafford* that attempts to see its hero's mysterious habit
of self-deception and his peculiar sense of tardiness as mutually illuminating characteristics. Strafford can be "under no illusions"
about Charles—to pursue Orel's analysis—except those illusions that
he, Strafford, has made. To practice illusion is to fabricate images
and so to engage the paradoxes of representation. For Strafford these
paradoxes serve a definite purpose, which is at once psychological
and temporal: the refreshing renewal of his youthful act of apostasy.
Strafford's illusions about the figurehead Charles are defenses against
the earlier figure of Eliot, a dead republican of an older generation
whom both Strafford and his opposite Pym acknowledge as a predecessor. The ghostly image of Eliot, with its "look" (I.ii.128) or
"brow" (V.ii.245), returns throughout the play to spur Strafford's
remorse.[14] Strafford's ability to obscure this deep remorse depends
upon his ability to make his later image of a trustworthy Charles
serve as a satisfactory substitute for the ancestral revenant Eliot.
Strafford may elude his guilt, that is, at the cost of illuding himself;
and from time to time he seems to succeed. When Lady Carlisle objects that "The King's so weak!" (IV.ii.83), Strafford counters her
objection by affirming the potency not of the king, but of his internal image of the king:

> *When Pym grew pale, and trembled, and sank down,*
> *One image was before me: could I fail?*
> *Child, care not for the past, so indistinct,*
> *Obscure—there's nothing to forgive in it*
> *'Tis so forgotten! From this day begins*
> *A new life, founded on a new belief*
> *In Charles.*

(IV.ii.97-103)

Lines like these might have ended a scene in *Pippa Passes*, in which
a world of absolutes (of God, not Charles) makes absolution or

133

"forgiveness" a present possibility. But in *Strafford*, written in 1836 during the composition of *Sordello*, such fulfilled imagining consistently exhibits openings and flaws, seams that are the traces of its own fabrication.

In *Strafford* the image upon which a hero would found his "new life" treacherously reveals itself as a substitute, and the foundation sags. Because the covering image of Charles is patchy at best, Strafford's recuperation will be partial, not total; never present, but always postponed. In the lines just quoted, Strafford's obsessive dwelling on the "indistinct" past he would abandon gives ample hints that his faith healing is already faulty. An earlier passage shows Strafford reliving his recognition that the image of Charles through which he would once and for all achieve rejuvenation has been tainted by the prevenient royal favorite Vane:

> *The one last hope — I that despair, my hope —*
> *That I should reach his heart one day, and cure*
> *All bitterness one day, be proud again*
> *And young again, care for the sunshine too,*
> *And never think of Eliot any more, —*
> *God, and to toil for this, go far for this,*
> *Get nearer, and still nearer, reach this heart*
> *And find Vane there!*

(II.ii.82-89)

"One last hope," "his heart," "one day," "all bitterness," "never" — this language invokes a single, central, and ultimate totality, which Browning masterfully condenses in the apparent afterthought of "the sunshine." Strafford fondly dreams of a return to Pippa's heliocentric universe, a return that, if completed, would rob him of what he and his dramatic creator most prize: his characteristic initiative.

A reader of this passage might accuse Strafford of saying just the reverse of what he means were such an accusation not effectively forestalled by the introductory reference to a desperate hope: "I that despair, my hope." This proleptic oxymoron concentrates what the following lines extend into a narrative episode: the absolute irresolution of the image, the dependable defection of language that makes new beginnings possible. Initiation occurs in Browning at a shadowy margin between antinomies, where "despair" and "hope," like the "Love" and "Hate" of Lutwyche's poem in *Pippa Passes* (II.i.181-237), become temporally equivalent modes of anticipation. As hope begins for the dying Sordello at a point of "extreme despair" (*Sordello*, VI.617), as Paracelsus quests from a concealed awareness of early guilt, so Browning always locates a blot in the 'scutcheon, a spider in the communion-cup, a toad in the christening-font (see

"Gold Hair" [1864], 104-5). So Strafford, who knows his own temporal requirements, deeply needs to "find Vane there." He must hope against hope: he must prevent the fulfillment of any hope that threatens to be "last," in order to give himself the gift of a future in which, having "gone far," he may go yet farther. It is in Strafford's best interest to undermine his own defenses and explode his own images. Even in imagining the total triumph of his images he must, with the surprising yet entirely appropriate thought of Eliot at line 86, yield to the priority of what they defend him against.

There is a revealing moment in the second scene of the first act when the shielding image of Charles seems to swell into a royal presence that might fulfill Strafford's hope. Charles tells him, "You shall rule me"; "Henceforth touching Strafford is / To touch the apple of my sight." At this very moment, Strafford significantly loses both his sense of time and his power of speech: "I am grown young again, / And foolish. What was it we spoke of?" (I.ii.239-49). But in the lines just quoted, he grows more wisely young by thinking, despite himself, of the irrepressible and reprimanding Eliot. It is with this infinitely repeatable thought, the thought of an original, willful apostasy, that Strafford identifies himself and becomes most truly "young again." By choosing to perpetuate his guilt and to renegotiate the terms of his ancestral debt, Strafford becomes once more hopeful and, in Sebald's sense, "venturous and fortunate." According to what is for Browning the principal, temporal version of the paradox of secondariness, Strafford's " 'tis too late" must be read, " 'tis too soon." His decision to be loyal to Charles is "too late to think about" because, as his renewable point of origin, it is too recent and therefore too early. Thanks to the guilt that prompts him to remember Eliot, Strafford's apostasy has perpetually only just begun. "What can he mean?" Lady Carlisle asks herself, and she asks further, "Rejoice at the King's hollowness?" (III.ii.143-44). Her guess is quite right, and it answers the central question of the play: Strafford does rejoice at the hollowness of his image of Charles. Strafford perseveres in his course of impossible allegiance because, of all courses, that is the course that promises to keep him at a beginning, at the rejuvenating source of his own imaginative strength.

A FLAW IN THE DIAMOND

It should come as no surprise that Browning presents the question of his hero's loyal deference as if it were a question of linguistic reference. An analogy between the psychological and the linguistic image runs throughout the play. Before going on to develop some of the

135

major implications of this analogy, it will be well to pause over some of its apparently trivial elaborations, which are far from trivial in their cumulative dramatic effect. Browning strews his plays with documents—books, papers, letters, memoranda, reports, even "rescripts" (*Colombe's Birthday* [1844], II.182)—as if to keep before the eye of his auditor and the imagination of his reader the secondary processes of "understanding" or "following" a language that has been previously set down. After his speech about desperate hope in the second scene of the second act, Strafford begins at once to pursue his own plotting, and that of his playwright, through the familiar activity of reading: "*Suddenly taking up a paper, and continuing with a forced calmness*" (stage direction, II.ii.89). Strafford draws this ability "suddenly to continue" from the position of deference that he has forced himself to resume and that the secondary activity of reading here and elsewhere reinforces. Another documentary enactment of Browning's theme, unobtrusive but ingenious, occurs later in the play with the bill of Strafford's "attainder." His rival Pym achieves political victory through a "Bill of Attainder," which he creates "As though no law existed, and we met / To found one" (IV.ii.127-28). In circumventing precedent and thus hastily "attaining" his end, Pym cedes dramatic interest to his victim, the more authentically haunted Strafford.

Strafford would not be Browning's hero if origination were as simple as Pym would have it. Genuine "founding" requires a certain foundering between alternatives that may be neither resolved nor ignored. Such duplicity applies to no one more than to the poet who would be a founder. Indeed, Strafford's irresolute vacillation between a chosen faith in Charles and an acknowledgment of Eliot's worthier priority may be helpfully conceived as a dramatized figuration of an imaginative and linguistic dilemma to which Browning was as alert as any poet of his time. Let Charles be what Strafford calls him, an "image"; and let Eliot be what the image represents, substitutes for, or defends against. Then Strafford, on one hand with his consciousness of the inadequacy of the image and on the other with his refusal to tolerate the silently rebuking presence that is his sole alternative to the image, is the poet. Or, if one adopts the charitable hypothesis that gives Browning his imaginative dozens of verbal men and women, Strafford is everyman. Acutely uncomfortable with representation, he chooses representation at every opportunity, just as if it were not second best. He chafes under the checks and delays of a secondariness that, however burdensome, he willingly continues to bring upon himself. Through his agency, usurping figuration gains an ascendancy that, because he knows figuration to be only fictive, can never be complete. He is bound to keep beginning; if a literary everyman, he may do so by "suddenly taking up a paper and continuing"; if a poet at heart, he may, like Strafford, take imagery and its discontents as his continuing theme.

Strafford encounters the significance of his life's work by puzzling over the problem of signification itself:

> *Only one name*
> *They'll curse in all those streets to-night. Whose fault?*
> *Did I make kings? set up, the first, a man*
> *To represent the multitude, receive*
> *All love in right of them — supplant them so,*
> *Until you love the man and not the king —*
> *The man with the mild voice and mournful eyes*
> *Which send me forth.*

(II.ii.287-94)

The play of "representative" substitution—whereby the royalist within Strafford dethrones the republican, Charles replaces Eliot in Strafford's love, and Charles the man supplants Charles the king—receives further figuration during this speech in a process of pronominal revision. What is "only one name," the cursed name of Strafford, reveals under Strafford's own analysis a surprising diversity. First, the "I" of line 289 becomes the "you" of line 292. This revision bespeaks the internal division that characterizes Strafford's curious faith: Strafford is by turns iconoclast and worshiper, skeptic and zealot. The "fault" about which he asks in line 288 may no more certainly be attributed to either one of his antagonistic selves than may the pronouns that witness to its existence. This "fault" is rather the guilt that separates those selves from each other, "I" from "you." Strafford's meditation not only points to an interior difference, it goes further and defers psychic wholeness to the future—the future into which Strafford here sends himself "forth," and by reference to which he brings his fractured sentence to rest.

Browning uses pronominal confusions to similar effect in the central interview between Thorold and Mildred Tresham in *A Blot in the 'Scutcheon* (1843). Obsessed by the threat his sister's projected engagement poses to his abnormally strong affection for her, Thorold speaks of his fraternal love from the safely generalizing distance of the colloquial second person, calling himself "you" for some fifteen lines. But at length Thorold's passions break down his grammar with the intrusive thought of the potential husband:

> *the newcomer!*
> *The startling apparition, the strange youth —*
> *Whom one half-hour's conversing with, or, say,*
> *Mere gazing at, shall change (beyond all change*

137

This Ovid ever sang about) your soul
. . . Her soul, that is,—the sister's soul!

(II.173-78)

With this pronominal slip Browning picks up the romantic theme of the psychic identity between loving siblings, with the added suggestion, borne out later in the play, that Thorold has even shared (and suppressed within himself) his sister's clandestine affection for "the strange youth," her suitor Mertoun. Since it is Thorold's fatal possessiveness about his family name, and even family members, that motivates the catastrophe of *A Blot in the 'Scutcheon*, it is quite appropriate that his error should involve possessive pronouns.

In the case of *Strafford*, in which the hero's identity emerges through a prolonged crisis of authority, the characteristic pronominal slip involves relations of subject and object. Strafford is much possessed with what in a later play Valence will call "the fancy how he could subject / Himself upon occasion to—himself!" (*Colombe's Birthday*, III.336-37). "The eternal subject" (V.i.16), Strafford earns his place as the archetypal subject of Browning's dramatic art through his power of self-subjection. In the grammatical turbulence of the passage last quoted from the second scene of the second act, he regains the provisional integrity of the first person by shifting pronouns again and becoming a "me." With Browningesque self-accusation, he regards himself as a passive object that the confessedly derivative, usurping image of Charles suffices to "send forth." Strafford's question "Did I make kings?" is one that he cannot address directly, in part because "I" seems too clumsy a term for the fine phenomenon of belief he is trying to analyze. It is nonetheless a question that the passage as a whole answers with a powerful affirmative. With its transition from interrogation to declaration, Strafford's sentence in effect remakes a king, in the figure of a "mild" and "mournful" Charles whom Strafford may again begin to love, and so may begin

To breast the bloody sea
That sweeps before me: with one star for guide.
Night has its first, supreme, forsaken star.

(II.ii.294-96)

With these concluding lines Browning transfers Strafford's earlier pronominal confusions onto the brilliantly confused image of the star. What does it represent? It would be too great a concession to the flimsy amorous intrigue of the play to suggest that the guiding star is Lady Carlisle, whose words of friendly encouragement Strafford here recalls from her speech at a recent exit: "Well, when the eve has its last streak / The night has its first star" (II.ii.267-68). It is almost as difficult to attribute guiding stardom to Charles, who

138

seems in context to be the most likely candidate. The contrast between the weak, compellingly human figure of line 293 that sends Strafford forth and the primary astral light that here draws him on is a violent one even for Browning. The distant, prior supremacy of the star recalls Charles less than it does the influential Eliot—whom Strafford has indeed "forsaken" as a guide but who is nowhere to be found in the preceding lines.

In the absence of any clear referent, it may make most sense to take the star as Strafford's scarcely conscious figuration of himself.[15] Without insisting on the fact that this is a curtain line written by Browning for the "star" William Macready (the theatrical sense of the term was current by 1836), one may interpret the image of "one star" as Strafford's attempt to find the "one name" for himself with which the passage has begun. In its unitary splendor, the image almost reduces Browning's hero to simple innocence. In that the image supplants by a single symbol the complex "multitude" of persons and pronouns that is Strafford, it seems to exemplify precisely the illusory simplicity of representation that he has been analyzing in lines 288-92.

Yet the image is neither quite single nor quite simple. Strafford, greatly to his dramatic credit as a tragic hero, is not altogether innocent in his bid to see himself once plain and whole. He cripples his otherwise radiant image with the startling temporal epithet "forsaken." Even at this height of imaginative glory, he cannot dispense with the nagging thought that something is missing. Even in picturing himself as "supreme," he spites and forsakes himself for the sake of that better supremacy that a conviction of absence or hollowness permits him to defer. Strafford arrives in the course of this passage at the verge of an abysmal truth: that his life's work has been to guide himself into illusions through which he may continue to enjoy a future as magnificently open as the prospect of this sweeping sea. If he is a star, it is in order that he may live under his own intricately diverted influence.

Doubling himself by thus splitting his image apart, Strafford makes that image worthy of the psychological action in character that sustains him and his play. The "forsaken star" is a disfigured figure, a broken image that draws strength from confessing the condition of its inadequacy: the gap between what represents and what is represented. To characters as shrewd about time as Browning's, this semantic gap presents itself as a semantic delay, which in turn furnishes limitless opportunities for postponing closure. For instance, the conventions of dissimulation and disguise that Elizabethan and Jacobean playwrights conjured out of this gap and that their romantic successors in England often inherited with a weary sense of duty, regain a certain vitality in Browning's plays.[16] In his hands those conventions are persistently temporalized. Linguistic dissimulation and physical disguise offer ways of making reservations and asserting differences that let Browning's characters withhold conclusive truths from themselves and from each other. These conventions are especially active in the happily guilty delaying that is practiced by Mildred and Mertoun in *A Blot in the 'Scutcheon*. The cloak-wearing Mertoun indelicately, inconsistently, but accurately identifies his prolonged, illicit love affair with Mildred both as "perpetual dawn" and as "this protracted agony" (*A Blot in the 'Scutcheon*, I.iii.128, 166). In the two parts of *A Soul's Tragedy* disguise is a mainspring of the psychological machinery binding Chiappino, the would-be cloak-and-dagger man, in a stasis both erotic and political. In all of Browning's plays dissimulation serves to defer fullness of meaning with a rigor that makes the most meaningful activity of his characters an anxious waiting for what they have expended considerable resources in delaying.

In the second scene of the second act, Lady Carlisle puts this characteristic phenomenon of dissimulation into a central simile. She resolves to bare her loving soul to Strafford in the following terms:

> *Could you but know what 'tis to bear, my friend,*
> *One image stamped within you, turning blank*
> *The else imperial brilliance of your mind, —*
> *A weakness, but most precious, — like a flaw*
> *I' the diamond, which should shape forth some sweet face*
> *Yet to create, and meanwhile treasured there*
> *Lest nature lose her gracious thought forever!*
>
> (II.ii.232-38)

The close relation of temporality with linguistics, psychology, and economics in these lines creates an embarrassment of riches for a temporal reading of Browning. The delaying play of figuration, which a desperately hopeful Strafford has earlier lamented, here enjoys the celebration it merits. An alien, stamped "image" saves the "imperial" self from its own brilliance, and the saving power of this image resides in its imperfection. As he does so often when he writes about the reciprocal play of figurative difference, Browning here exploits a play of grammatical reference. The ambiguous appositive of line 235, "a weakness, but most precious," pivots between the "one image" itself and the inexplicable readiness of the "mind" to take its stamp. The ambiguity of this central phrase ripples through the passage to quicken ideas that otherwise might crystallize too soon. Browning's subject here is the intercourse of "image" and "mind" that one may call "imagination." The virtue of Browning's free-standing appositive is that it lets him describe his delicate subject without specifying it explicitly and thereby lending it a deceptive, nominal substance. Browning wishes to render "imagination" not as a posited entity, but as an act occurring in time, a deed; not as a structure, but as a function that must be conceived temporally.

The value of imagination so conceived will lie in its consequences, its indeterminate relation to the future. Browning turns to these consequences with the lovely simile of the diamond. He boldly flaws his diamond; and, in doing so, he gives it a future. He weakens and sets in flux the diamond, perennial poetic emblem of strength and permanence, in order to find in it the different power of renewing change.[17] By seeing in its hardened carbon facets an evolving "face," he makes the emblem radically human. This passage names no source for the diamond's flaw or cause for the "precious weakness" of imagination, because for Browning these defects are primordial versions of the anonymous, unmotivated, original fault on which every beginning takes its stand. The passage establishes instead an imagination that is both groundless and initially flawed; a shaping faculty that is "blank," for the present, because it reserves potential energy for a "sweet face" or figure that it has "yet to create"; a provisional "treasuring" of the nascent, incomplete images that are for Browning the priceless wealth of human "nature." The original fault of imagination is co-extensive with the semantic gap that severs image from truth and with the psychological guilt that saves Browning's lost souls from terminal salvation. As the simile of the diamond suggests, a fault at the origin makes of the present a "meanwhile" that opens a significant future.[18]

Browning takes the principle of semantic delay seriously enough to work it into the texture of his dialogues, much to the dismay of critics who object, for instance, to "the irritating mannerism whereby one speaker finishes the sentence of an earlier speaker, and in turn has his sentence finished for him by a third speaker."[19] It may be argued that such conversational devices are never merely manneristic in Browning's drama. Like his ubiquitous documents, they may be taken as elaborations, however awkward or unlikely, of the transfer of power between those who come first and those who come second. During the lines following Lady Carlisle's confession in the passage last quoted, Browning turns dialogue to typical dramatic use:

STRAFFORD *When could it be? no! Yet . . . was it the day*
We waited in the anteroom, till Holland
Should leave the presence-chamber?

LADY CARLISLE *What?*

STRAFFORD *—That I*
Described to you my love for Charles?

141

LADY CARLISLE   *(Oh, no —*

One must not lure him from a love like that!
Oh, let him love the King and die! 'Tis past.)

(II.ii.239-44)

This abortive exchange, like so many of Browning's stumbling conversations, enacts the semantic postponement that has been the
subject of the preceding speech. Prompted by that speech, Strafford
finds, then represses ("no!"), and then brings to articulation a highly
appropriate memory of the "anteroom" where he once anticipated a
delayed royal "presence." Lady Carlisle furthers the delay of meaning by asking, like a good reader of Browning, for an explication:
"What?" When she receives it, she does some quick repressing of her
own and resolves to defer indefinitely the revelation with which the
entire dialogue has begun.

The dramatic ironies of this dialogue and of others like it are plain
enough, and readers have been right to note the degree to which
irony pervades Browning's dramatic writing.[20] It should be worth
noting further, however, that for Browning irony is not merely a
matter of tone, though of course it is that. It may also, indeed may
primarily, be considered a temporal figure of speech that suspends
unresolved alternatives, that opens and extends meaning in his plays
as it does in the early parts of *Paracelsus* and throughout *Sordello*. It
is, therefore, insufficient to complain about the nullity of "action"
in exchanges like this one between Lady Carlisle and Strafford. Such
complaints were met long ago by one of the first serious students of
Browning's plays, a master of irony and stagecraft alike, George Bernard Shaw: "Browning, when the mere action of his play flags, lifts
and prolongs apparently exhausted situations by bursts of poetry."[21]
When prolongation is Browning's poetic theme, even such rapid
"bursts of poetry" as these interjections and asides may justify their
claim on an audience's attention. They are the minutiae of action in
character; and, if they fail to interest a reader, so will the plays that
they prolong — and so, probably, will the distinctively inward art of a
dramatist who was to turn from the stage to the closet drama and to
the yet more explicitly psychological form of the dramatic lyric.

Browning prolongs what Barbara Melchiori has called his "poetry
of reticence" by imagining in astonishing detail dramatic characters
who make reservations, constitute reserves, and so appropriate their
own futures.[22] In the last act of *Strafford* the protagonist looks beyond the confines of his lifetime to anticipate just such detailed
reservations. "Fame, the busy scribe, will pause" (V.ii.52) in order to
register

The curious glosses, subtle notices,
Ingenious clearings-up one fain would see

142

> *Beside that plain inscription of The Name —*
> *The Patriot Pym, or the Apostate Strafford!*

(V.ii.55-58)

There is a sense in which all of *Strafford* is an explanatory qualification of the deceptively "plain" name of "Apostate."[23] The difference between such a "Name" and the sophisticated internal transactions that it represents gives pause to Browning as well as to his hero. This pregnant pause in which, as Strafford predicts, an ingenious biographer may bring forth his story does more than acknowledge Browning's labor as an historical dramatist in this first play. As the scriptorial terminology of these lines suggests, the scribe's "pause" is also a more general acknowledgment of the suspenseful hesitation that presides over Browning's activity as an expectant writer, perpetually absent from felicity awhile.

The terminology of "ingenious" writing in which Strafford conceives his historical future is punningly implied in the "Genius" and "Term" of an earlier sculptural image invoking "Time" itself:

> *Time, who in the twilight comes to mend*
> *All the fantastic day's caprice, consign*
> *To the low ground once more the ignoble Term,*
> *And raise the Genius on his orb again.*

(V.ii.40-43)

Browning's explication of this passage for Emily H. Hickey's 1884 edition of the play is both concise and revealing: "Putting the Genius on the pedestal usurped by the Term means—or tries to mean—substituting eventually, the true notion of Strafford's endeavour and performance in the world, for what he conceives to be the ignoble and distorted conception of these by his contemporary judges."[24]

Browning's care in timing his introduction of the notion of "truth" into this sentence is exemplary. His "Time," his meantime, depends on a deferred substitution, when even "the true notion" may come into its own only "eventually" and only by becoming a substitute— and therefore ceasing to be in any simple sense "true." Browning's deferential parenthesis ("or tries to mean"), an attempt to substitute his own genius for his earlier terms, may indicate his dissatisfaction with the possibilities of closure implicit in Strafford's imagery. If the "Genius" should be restored to its true place in orbed perfection, if "the fantastic day's caprice" should eventually be mended (or if Pippa's broken lights should be healed), then the time of imaginative play would be ended as well. With the ultimate overthrow of the "Term," of the linguistic "term" that is both a limit and a beginning, there could be no more to say. Perhaps the old poet's commentary should be regarded as a revision making this speech consistent with

143

radical insights of his dramatic work: that meaning may be stored up but never restored, that the only significant present is one in which presence is awaited.

TORTUOUS DEALING:
KING VICTOR AND KING CHARLES

In effect Browning wrote such a revision large into the next work he intended for the stage, the unproduced and still practically unread *King Victor and King Charles* (1842). The plot involves a bizarre transfer of power between the royal father and son after whom the play is named. In order to avoid certain embarrassments of his self-serving diplomacy, Victor of Sardinia abdicates in favor of his son Charles. Despite painful doubts of his own competence, Charles proves to be a good and liberal king, who extricates Sardinia from its difficulties and rules with unerring skill until his father approaches the court to demand that he be restored to sovereignty. Charles's queen Polyxena and his minister D'Ormea persuade him to make preparations for opposing Victor's challenge; but, in the presence of his father, Charles's resolution deserts him and he yields the crown. The aging king is apparently overcome by such generosity, and his sudden death ends the play.

The contorted intrigues and improbable reversals of this political play seem less extravagant when one reads it as a play of representation in the tradition of *Strafford*. The long first scene teems with the language of representation. Polyxena serves Charles "in place/Of monarch, minister, and mistress" (I.i.70-71); Charles anxiously replaces his dead elder brother (I.i.36), wonders how he himself will "figure" (I.i.115), and resents the "intervention" of D'Ormea and his "contrivances" (I.i.253,118). Such language may justify a translation of the major action of the ensuing scenes into terms of the image. As in *Strafford*, a later figure substitutes for an earlier: Victor speaks of Charles as "referring" back to him (I.ii.246), and at the end of the play the queen says of Charles to his father that "he acted you" (II.ii.340). Moreover, the source from which Browning almost surely derived his ideas about Charles, the *Biographie universelle ancienne et moderne*, introduces Charles through a metaphor of figuration ("dissimuler") as a willingly secondary figure of just the kind likely to intrigue Browning: "lest he arouse his father's suspicious ambition, he forced himself to dissemble his natural talents."[25]

The dethroned figure, the former King Victor, regards Charles's substitute sovereignty as a usurpation of the image upon the truth and attempts a return that will restore to him his original power,

144

"the crown whose shadow I gave" (II.ii.286). Victor makes, or attempts to make, an explicit identification of "truth" with his person:

> Truth, boy, is here, within my breast; and in
> Your recognition of it, truth is, too;
> And in the effect of all this tortuous dealing
> With falsehood, used to carry out the truth,
> — In its success, this falsehood turns, again,
> Truth for the world. But you are right; these themes
> Are over-subtle.

(II.i.288-94)

This return of "truth" from "falsehood" corresponds to the return of unsullied earliness or presence of meaning that closes scenes in *Pippa Passes*, that is envisioned in Strafford's lines on the "Genius" and "Term," and that makes Browning uncomfortable when commenting on those lines in 1884. It is a return that always makes Browning uncomfortable because it means the end of that "tortuous dealing/With falsehood" that is a play or a poem. As the title of his next play suggests, *The Return of the Druses* confronts this discomfort directly. The Druses' return to their homeland is still only beginning as the play ends; in the meantime, with more theological boldness than many readers have given him credit for, Browning has made it quite clear that the religious "truth" motivating their return is a costly falsehood.

It is in clarifying the problematics of the return of truth from falsehood that *King Victor and King Charles* takes its most interesting twist, a twist away from its predecessor *Strafford.*. Browning calls the later play a "statement" in his preface. The reversals of its plot are not "over-subtle" for the semantic theme they state: that the sovereign truth may return into a principality or a poem only after submitting to conditions that deprive it of its veritable sovereignty. Victor's definition of "truth" involves a double standard, which he expresses in the first two lines quoted above. Whether or not truth may in fact be present in itself, known here and now, as Victor claims, it is also to be "recognized," known then and there, in the form of the postponing, displacing image. This double standard straddles the semantic gap that is always present in Browning's drama; but one of its implications is worked into the plot of this play with particular insistence. The truth (Victor) is reduced to soliciting the image (Charles). The prior figure must become a "suppliant" before the secondary figure to which it asserts its priority (II.i.364). In order to earn "recognition" as the "whole, sound, and impregnable" entity that it claims to be, the truth resorts to figuring as a "pretense" and a "delusion" the restoration that it seeks (II.i.341-55). Victor finally prevails after pleading that he is friendless and "weak" (II.ii.287-91). Only after assuming the humiliating guise of the image, the precious weakness of *Strafford*'s fluid diamond, does truth reclaim its place in Browning's "statement."

This play revises *Strafford* by disposing of the notion of Strafford's that is least worthy of a Browningesque hero: that the "Genius" of truth may return without first sacrificing its simplicity to terms and so compromising its truthfulness. In *King Victor and King Charles* the truth must contrive to represent itself falsely if it is to obtain a hearing at all. The later play offers a further and more radical revision by calling into question a lineally related notion, one that dwells in the shadows of the earlier play: the notion that truth has ever had a simplicity to sacrifice. Whatever truth is inherent in the figure of Charles I that Strafford has created is obviously compromised. The figure of Eliot, however, seems inexplicably to enjoy a privileged status and to retain the pristine, truthful simplicity that *Strafford* as a whole repeatedly questions. If *King Victor and King Charles* is a reworking of *Strafford*, the pressure of Browning's revisionary labor bears most heavily on this curious inconsistency. The crucial difference between the two plays is that Charles's Victor assumes in a single figure the functions that Charles I and Eliot have severally performed for Strafford. Victor then stands in his play where Eliot stands in his, at the privileged place of origin. Yet Victor, one of the least trustworthy villains in all of Browning, is split in two from the first; he exposes his characteristic duplicity in the "slip, a fault, a trick" of his first speech in the play (I.ii.12). By condensing Charles I and Eliot into the double-dealing Victor, Browning dispenses with the misleading hint of simplicity that lingers in his first play and clears the way for future dramatic works that will be unequivocally rooted in complexity and founded upon an original fault.

In the revised reading of *Strafford* that the later play suggests, even Strafford's memory of Eliot may be an imagined figment; the very origin against whose authority Strafford constructs his defenses may have originated in Strafford himself. It is difficult to exaggerate the shocking freedom or the ponderous responsibility that Browning's revision bestows upon imagination. The paternal power of Eliot and Victor is invested in them by the filial deference of Strafford and Charles, who in this sense father their own fathers. In the case of Charles this feat of filial creation is especially noteworthy since he knows so exactly what he is doing. As he tells his queen near the end of the play,

> The best is, that I knew it in my heart
> From the beginning, and expected this,

146

And hated you, Polyxena, because
You saw thro' him, though I too saw thro' him.

(II.ii.233-36)

In flat contradiction to the observable and not very respectable facts of Victor's character, Charles makes a paternal image to which he may defer; and at the end of the play, confronted with even more damning facts, he remakes the image and defers again. It may be that the improbability of Browning's plot in this play is quite deliberate. Where the origin has no simplicity and truth is feigned to begin with, imagination will be anterior to probability and indeed anterior to fact.[26]

Any figure or memory that is prized as Charles prizes the "dark form" of his father (I.ii.356)—any image with the status of what Sordello calls a "first fact" (*Sordello*, V.556)—will owe its priority to the act of imagination that has established it as "first." An awesome solipsism lurks in the idea of so authoritative an imagination, but it is a solipsism that Browning increasingly adopted as the ground of his evolving dramatic poetry. From Pippa's bowl playfully filled with the sun, the path lies clear to Charles's recreation of his own father, to Luria's dizzying isolation with a private "illusion" of an impersonal civilization (*Luria*, IV.266), and to Djabal's musing, for the sake of an uncomprehending and otherwise inert people, "That a strong man should think himself a God!" (*The Return of the Druses*, II.1). And from these it is but a short step to Browning's lyric speakers: defiantly solitary individuals, each of whom utters a world that is peopled with creatures of his or her own quarrelsome spirit.[27]

CHAPTER FIVE

SUCH VARIOUS INTENTIONS: THE DRAMATIC LYRICS

Ah but traditions, inventions,
(Say we and make up a visage)
So many men with such various intentions!
        Browning, "Master Hugues of Saxe-Gotha"
        ([1855] 121-23)

No poet was ever more fascinated by intentions than Browning or more willing to insist upon their significance.[1] In *Sordello*, in his prose essays on Chatterton and Shelley, and elsewhere, Browning asserts that what a poet writes is less than what he means, that realization betrays impulse, that form even at its best expresses purpose inadequately.[2] Criticism written in recent decades, in its just recoil from superficial assessments of poetic intentionality like those issued by the Browning Societies, has been ill at ease with those who would champion intentions. Criticism has not been slow to draw from Browning's assertions the conclusion that he so prized the poem-as-intention that he disdained the poem-as-artifact; nor has it been slow to disdain him in turn as a slipshod writer. One aim of the following two chapters is to be slower on the critical draw while investigating the insistent care with which Browning worked motives of intentionality into poems that he published between 1842 and 1864 and never surpassed: the dramatic monologues or, to adopt the less restrictive term that Browning retained throughout his career, the dramatic lyrics.

Attempts to describe lyric poetry sooner or later pay express or tacit homage to a certain irreducible intentionality that is inherent in the genre. Venerable commonplaces about the urge that spurs a poet into song hover about any discussion of lyric, and it may be useful to hover briefly with them before proceeding to consider individual poems. Every poem implies a will to be heard; this will may sound most simply and clearly in a lyric. But not every lyric speaker begins by announcing such a will, and few lyric poets have created such boisterous announcers as Browning's. It is remarkable how frequently a lyric by Browning will begin with an assertion of will, an initial resistance or difference:

> *Plague take all your pedants, say I!*
> ("Sibrandus Schafnaburgensis" [1845])

> *It is a lie!*
> ("The Confessional" [1845])

> *My first thought was, he lied in every word.*
> (" 'Childe Roland to the Dark Tower Came' " [1855])

> *Stand still, true poet that you are!*
> ("Popularity" [1855])

> *Would it were I had been false, not you!*
> ("The Worst of It" [1864])

> *No protesting, dearest!*
> ("St. Martin's Summer" [1876])

> *I will be happy if but for once.*
> ("Dubiety" [1889])

These opening lines from poems otherwise diverse share the property of being aggressively first: they are lines that defy, interrupt, plead, yearn, or somehow intend a beginning. They register discontinuities that are no less striking for the fact that a reader is totally uninformed what they are discontinuous *with*. Browning's vociferous openings, breaking the preceding silence, lay bare the intentionality of lyric voice, its will to silence any and all prior claims. All of Browning's lyric monologists begin with more or less overt versions of the willful insistence that opens "Dis Aliter Visum" (1864): "Stop, let me have the truth of that!" The monologist's world begins with that imperially possessive "me," explicitly or implicitly hushing anterior voices; there is no other "truth" to be had than that which each speaker wills into the poem.

The very genre of a lyric gives its speaker an initial monopoly on truth, a commanding control over interpretation, that exceeds any comparable power in the characters of the narratives and dramas written in Browning's earlier and later years. In these longer works, ironic narrative commentary, or the discrepancy among the perspectives of various characters, serves to diminish the voice of any one character by placing it in a choral or social context. That may be

149

why Browning's longer works tend to begin with gestures not of definitive repudiation, but of sociable inclusion. Compare the lyric openings collected above with these first lines from poems in Browning's more expansive modes:

> Pauline, mine own, bend o'er me.
>
> (*Pauline* [1833])

> Come close to me, dear friends; still closer, thus!
>
> (*Paracelsus* [1835])

> You're my friend.
>
> (*The Flight of the Duchess* [1845])

> Do you see this Ring?
>
> (*The Ring and the Book* [1868])

> O trip and skip, Elvire! Link arm in arm with me!
>
> (*Fifine at the Fair* [1872])

> And so, here happily we meet, fair friend!
>
> (*Red Cotton Night-Cap Country* [1873])

These lines warm to their readers, while the lyric lines burn or freeze on the page in splendid isolation. The lyric speakers are defined by their solitude; these speakers, on the other hand, introduce themselves as members of a community, if only a community of two: lover and beloved, storyteller and listener. The tonal difference between the two kinds of beginning underscores the difference between two kinds of intimacy: the public or shared intimacy that narrative and drama have traditionally assumed to constitute their audiences, and the private or meditative intimacy of the sole self, the charmed ground of lyric.

Browning's turn to lyric poetry in the volume of *Dramatic Lyrics* he published in 1842 is sometimes welcomed as a fresh start, particularly by readers with little use for his prior achievements. But of course "dramatic lyric" is an oxymoron, and it suggests, without altogether blurring the distinction between lyric and other modes, that Browning's lyric concerns should be viewed in the light of the long poems and dramas he wrote before and during his early lyric period. Without exception, the longer works are intricate subversions of the power of imaginative autonomy, personal priority, unadulterated intention—which is also, in generic terms, the power of lyric speech to monopolize truth and govern its interpretation. Browning's earlier works and his dramatic lyrics may be read alike, then, as responses to the psychological and poetic challenges posed by such power: the challenges of learning to see its monopoly as *only* initial, of loosening its control, and of deferring its truth. To remember how Browning meets these challenges in the early works is both to see the remarkable continuity of his poetic career and to appreciate what is distinctive in the lyrics he called "dramatic."

Paracelsus and King Victor, for example, would monopolize a "truth" both original and ultimate, seated in the will, "an inmost centre," "within my breast" (*Paracelsus*, I.728-31; *King Victor and King Charles*, II.i.288). The significant action of the works in which Paracelsus and Victor appear is the dissolution of their monopolies. Browning's machinery of events, including the actions and commentary of other characters, discredits his protagonists' ultimata and replaces an original truth with different possibilities of reorigination. Paracelsus redeems the failure of his quest for absolute knowledge by discovering his place relative to past and future questers in a tradition whose definitive gesture is the affirmation of a fresh beginning. Victor, with a gloomier frenzy, discovers the folly of attempting to resume an original place without expecting to find it altered and uncontrollably new.

Discoveries like these never lose their importance for Browning, and the turn from earlier genres to the more condensed and isolated genre of lyric represents his decision to isolate the internal processes whereby such discoveries may happen. Stripped, from its inception, of external event and commentary, the dramatic lyric leaves Browning with the will alone; and it is Browning's genius never to find the will monotonous company. Under the deliberately straitened circumstances of lyric, Browning faces in refined and concentrated form the problems of deferment he had met in his earlier works: the thematic problem of how the will yields up its apparently unitary truth in exchange for a better yield to come, and the formal problem of how a poet avoids the enclosure of meaning and so keeps writing. It is the privilege of poetry to treat thematic and formal problems as aspects of each other, and it is Browning's special distinction in lyric poetry to have pursued the problematics of will so deeply through the sustained utterances of so many imaginary persons. The will of a Browning monologist is rarely unitary or single. In exploring the vagrancy and even plurality of intention within a single speaker, in celebrating the mysterious readiness of the will to revise itself, Browning discovers the thematic and formal motive that impels the great poetry of his middle years.[3]

The enormous range of Browning's dramatic lyrics on themes of nature, history, art, religion, and love—to name only the broadest possible categories—presents speakers in a variety of interpretive roles. Browning's characters are often literally, and always at least figuratively, readers. They puzzle over the phenomena of the physical world, the vestiges of the past, the forms of the several arts, grand hints of the divine, and the humbler signs men and women make to each other; and in the wealth of their inspired or troubled constructions of the life around them lies Browning's plenty. Moreover, as his lyric speakers interpret the world without, they are also in the best romantic tradition interpreting themselves, whether they like it or not. An analysis of the dynamics of self-interpretation offers a way of approaching Browning's multitudinous and sometimes bewildering plenty, and seeing it whole. A dramatic lyric by Browning is a tissue of what the fugue-weaving organist in "Master Hugues of Saxe-Gotha" calls "various intentions." It shuttles back and forth between intention and speech; between a speaker's primary lyric impulse towards self-expression and a speaker's secondary, more dramatic and Browningesque impulse towards self-analysis; between vision and revision. It is the various record of a fictive will's grapplings with a language that it can never quite embrace. The variety of the record grows out of the imperfection of the embrace, out of gaps and slippages that let the will rejoin the fray with strength renewed.[4]

For testimony to this renewing struggle let King Victor be summoned once more as one of Browning's witnesses to linguistic representation and its frustrations:

> *Fool! What way*
> *Could I intend or not intend? As man,*
> *With a man's will, when I say "I intend,"*
> *I can intend up to a certain point,*
> *No farther.*
>
> (*King Victor and King Charles*, II.i.274-78)

The idea of a revisionary will receives gratifying substantiation when one observes that in the original text of 1842 the third line read, "a man's life." Browning's choice in 1863 to concentrate on a man's *will* acknowledges just the thematic concentration that had shaped his poetry in the intervening years. The difference that spurs a Browning monologist into speech is the difference, felt acutely by Victor in these lines, between a moment when he *intends* and a moment when he *says*, "I intend." The two moments need not arrive in this order; their difference may be felt on either side of speech, before or after. Indeed, the shuttling alternation fundamental to Browning's dramatic writing depends most upon the later difference between an unsatisfactory past articulation and a fresh attempt yet to be made—upon the residual difference after speech that so piques Victor in these lines and that in fact motivates him to speak them.[5]

The "certain point, / No farther" that Victor glimpses in this passage is the definite, limited meaning into which Browningesque intention fears to collapse. As in *Pauline* (the first of his dramatic monologues, Browning later insisted), this last, certain point can become a first, waking point when monologists refresh their intentions or—to use a phrase whose strangeness is refreshed by a reading of Browning—change their minds.[6] The possibility of closure in "I intend" prompts the speakers of the dramatic lyrics to change their minds, to alter their wills, to make a difference that permits their speech to continue. No matter how assuredly they may trumpet their opening announcements, Browning's speakers soon begin to regret or qualify them. The need for a repentant, secondary beginning is Browning's *dramatic* lyric inspiration. It leads him to imagine speakers for whom the commanding lyric power of interpretation is most revealing when exerted over their own previous utterances.

According to the most influential study of the dramatic monologue that has yet appeared, Robert Langbaum's *The Poetry of Experience*, Browning's speakers never change their minds.[7] In the largest terms, Langbaum is right; Browning's broadly consistent characters do not reverse their positions on major issues or sacrifice their first principles. But they do often refine their positions or develop a clearer sense of their principles; Mr. Sludge speaks for many of Browning's monologists when he says, "Really, I want to light up my own mind" ("Mr. Sludge, 'The Medium' " [1864], 811). The lights whereby Browning's characters illuminate their own minds are most often struck by the friction of their inarticulate intentions against the hard surfaces of the words in which they would frame those intentions. The essential stasis of a Browning monologist, like the bristling inaction of a Browning drama, depends upon a host of lesser revisions within and between the poetic lines. Browning's speakers change their minds into the currency of speech, the way one changes a bill of a uselessly high denomination into more readily negotiable amounts—and the losses and gains such transactions entail are a part of the poet's lyric theme.

The lyric speaker begins by turning his or her will into words, but begins to be a Browningesque speaker when this conversion leads to a turning of the will *against* words. This inversion, or perversion, of the will against its own expression requires a reader to entertain a complex notion of the relationship between intention and language—or, more accurately, to hold in suspension two competing versions of that relationship. A reader learns not only to conceive interpretation in the simple lyric sense, as a prevailing assertion of the will, but also to conceive any given assertion of the will, any intention given over to articulation in language, as an interpretation and therefore a potential falsification inviting further refinement. The playful competition that Browning urges between these two conceptions of intentionality frees meaning to wander somewhere beyond the ken of

153

lyric speaker, somewhere in the future of lyric utterance. Mean-
to the dramatic lyric what action is to the drama proper; and
much as the curious action in character of Browning's dramas defers
dramatic action and makes room for play, so Browning defers meaning in the lyrics by enlisting the patterning forces of the self-interfering will.

"SOLILOQUY OF THE SPANISH CLOISTER"

If human intention were ever quite pure and could be stabilized
against the vagaries of interpretation, then men and women would be
as angels, or as demons perhaps, but would not be as Browning presents them. If hate killed men, there would be no reason for the
monk in Browning's "Soliloquy of the Spanish Cloister" (1842) ever
to begin soliloquizing. But even the simple hatred felt by this most
obviously intent of Browning's lyric speakers must submit to language, and the first and last lines of his soliloquy record the submis-
sion. The monk literally growls his way into utterance and out again,
ending his poem in the expression of unspeakable hatred with which
he has started. "Gr-r-r—there go, my heart's abhorrence!" (1); "*Ave,
Virgo!* Gr-r-r—you swine!" (72). The transposition of consonants
from "Gr-r-r" to "there go" enacts the transition between mute intention and actual articulation upon which Browning lays such stress
in his lyrics, and the "*Virgo*" and "Gr-r-r" of the last line repeat this
transition in the opposite direction. The monk lapses out of language
to the accompaniment of the tolling bell that here, as at the end of
"Childe Roland" ([1855] 193-98) and of *Prince Hohenstiel-Schwangau* ([1871] 2072-73), rings the knell of defeat. Yet these detailed
phonetic reversals suggest the renewing possibility of reversal that is
the poem's larger theme. The monk's straightforward hatred becomes
the pretext for a series of murderously inventive interpretations that
let him enjoy the power of his own revisionary will.

Although ultimately every one of Browning's monologists practices the will to interpretive power as indefatigably as the growling
monk, few of them practice so ingenuously or cleave so loyally to
the interpreter's power of finding a difference between what one receives and what one may make of it. Utensils, glances, gestures,
speeches, scriptures, novels, and pledges are all parts of a great text,
which the monk reads with authorial delight. With each stanza he
gleefully situates himself in a gap between phenomena and their
significance that lets him exercise power by performing an act of
naming, or renaming. In replacing Brother Lawrence's "*Latin name
for 'parsley'*" by "the Greek name for Swine's Snout" (15-16) or

154

making "L. for our initial" stand instead for something more original, a snapping lily (23-24), the monk warms to the tasks of wholesale interpretation awaiting him in later stanzas:

> Saint, *forsooth! While brown Dolores*
> *Squats outside the Convent bank*
> *With Sanchicha, telling stories,*
> *Steeping tresses in the tank,*
> *Blue-black, lustrous, thick like horsehairs,*
> *—Can't I see his dead eye glow,*
> *Bright as 'twere a Barbary corsair's?*
> *(That is, if he'd let it show!)*
>
> (25-32)

The monk's will to desanctify Lawrence's saintly name is strong enough here to open a mode of interpretation that is distinctly creative. His parenthetical nod to actuality in the last line makes it clear that the monk can see what is not there to be seen. That line is less an admission of defeat than a measure of his imaginative success in revivifying Lawrence's "dead eye," despite the absence of any empirical warrant for doing so. Commentators who search in vain for all twenty-nine of the monk's scriptural damnations (51) or for the source of "*Hy, Zy, Hine*" (70) might return with profit to consider how in this stanza the monk makes something of nothing.[8] The superabundance of his creative vitality receives incidental expression in his attribution of narrative powers to the women "telling stories."

The truly powerful storyteller of this poem is, of course, the monk. A maker nourished by the finding of meanings, as are the performer of "Master Hugues," Fra Lippo Lippi (1855), and Mr. Sludge in their various ways, the monk sustains his tale through a cheerful willingness to believe in an inexhaustible supply of possible meanings, "One sure, if another fails" (52). Like other storytellers in Browning, he knows how to distinguish and defer: he drains his cup in three sips, illustrating the Trinity with a lively eye on ulterior motives, while his simple Brother Lawrence (unthinkable as the subject of a Browning monologue) "drains his at one gulp" (39-40). Like other storytellers in Browning, the monk achieves his best narrative moments by opening eventful temporal intervals, by interrupting apparently assured continuities to insert interpretations fabricated by his surprisingly different will:

> *There's a great text in Galatians,*
> *Once you trip on it, entails*
> *Twenty-nine distinct damnations,*
> *One sure, if another fails:*
> *If I trip him just a-dying,*

> *Sure of heaven as sure can be,*
> *Spin him round and send him flying*
> *Off to hell, a Manichee?*

(49-56)

The virtuous Brother Lawrence may be sure as sure can be, but his soliloquizing observer is determined to give such assurance a spin and to show how one "sure" moment may be forced worlds apart from another. The separation in the text between the monk's "sure" and Lawrence's constitutes the fancied delay at the deathbed in which Lawrence may have time to trip. The monk discovers a temporal opening through the same discriminating ability that discovers faults between letter and spirit amid the crags of Galatians.

This stanza celebrates the power of the monk's exultant will to dwell in an instant of reversal. The final stanza of the poem presents a climactic anticipation of such power:

> *Or there's Satan! — one might venture*
> *Pledge one's soul to him, yet leave*
> *Such a flaw in the indenture*
> *As he'd miss till, past retrieve,*
> *Blasted lay that rose-acacia*
> *We're so proud of!*

(65-70)

Not satisfied with hoping to pervert Brother Lawrence's reading of Galatians, here the ambitious monk proposes to overgo the father of lies, to out-Satan Satan in a struggle for hermeneutic supremacy. What marks the proposal as Browning's and enables it to end a poem as obsessed with interpretation as this one is its characteristic coupling of interpretive with temporal issues. An opening between text and interpretation generates an opening between present and future, a mean-time that is at once petty, spiteful, canny, and significant. The monk imagines a wager for time, with the future at stake, which he will win through a masterful delay in construing the terms of the wager. The "flaw in the indenture" will let him refuse to close the deal by pointing to a difference between hidden intention and apparent execution that Satan, presumably still too angelic a reader to arm himself against the wiles of Browningesque humanity, will have overlooked. The syntactic unfolding of the stanza induces, in the duration of a reader's experience, just such a mysterious semantic flaw as that which will trip up Satan. The stanza defers meaning until the "till" clause completes its explanation — as it were, after the flaw has had the time to do its subversive work. The flaw in the terms of the indenture corresponds precisely to the flaw or warp in time that is to be the monk's prize. It also corresponds to the extension of poetic

156

time between a pair of inarticulate growls that is Browning's prize, the monk's soliloquy. The vesper bell may toll time's triumph, but in the meantime the monk has exploited time's revenges. By complicating and humanizing time through wily strategies of delay, he has obtained an imaginative purchase on the future.

"ARTEMIS PROLOGIZES"

To extend poetic time is to extend the sense of possibility that has persistently attracted readers into Browning's relativistic or pluralistic universe.[9] The possibility of reinterpretation celebrated by his Spanish monk, the renewable possibility of exchanging one's past mind for a different future mind, runs throughout Browning's lyrics. This possibility frequently receives stylistic expression in syntactic flaws like the one ventured in the monk's last stanza. It has been remarked that the leaping rapidity of stylistic changes and reversals that gives Browning both his power and his obscurity is among the poet's greatest compliments to the mental agility of the human race.[10] One might substantiate this remark by turning, for an example of a mind exceptionally slow, to the nonhuman speaker of "Artemis Prologizes" (1842), the one monologue Browning ever ascribed to a deity. Even the divine Artemis, however, finds her way into the company of lyric men and women in order to testify to the sense of possibility. She takes the stage as an anticipator, speaking a prologue for a play Browning never went on to write; and her prologue tells the story of how she has changed her mind. Her story flows with such an unusually measured rhythm that it offers a unique opportunity to study in slow motion the temporal dynamics of a Browningesque change of mind.

At the request of Theseus, who has been falsely provoked against his son Hippolutos, Poseidon has sent a sea monster to madden the youth's horses and so to bring about his gruesome death. Hippolutos is Artemis's votary, and she has acted twice on his behalf; first she has appeared before Theseus to reproach him, and then she has summoned Asclepios to restore the dead youth to life. Her prologue consists of two long verse paragraphs narrating her two actions, and each paragraph exhibits its distinctive narrative mode. A passage late in the first paragraph contains examples of both modes in miniature:

> But when his sire, too swoln with pride, rejoiced
> (Indomitable as a man foredoomed)
> That vast Poseidon had fulfilled his prayer,
> I, in a flood of glory visible,

157

> *Stood o'er my dying votary and, deed*
> *By deed, revealed, as all took place, the truth.*

(64-69)

"The truth," in Browning, often implies the figurative death of enclosed meaning; here that death is made quite literal. That Hippolutos is dying a horrible and senseless death is a truth that Theseus and Artemis both wish to resist, and their wish is expressed in the poignantly halting movement of the last two lines of the passage. These lines exemplify the narrative mode that has typified Artemis's first paragraph; in the relentlessly continuous sequence of lines 47-61, she has detailed the grisly ruin of Hippolutos "deed / By deed," "as all took place," from the perspective of a helpless onlooker (62). Her sequential repetition of the truth in the later passage reveals the weakness of that narrative mode, its inability to answer to desire and stave off closure. At the end of Euripides' *Hippolytus*, Browning's source for the myth, Artemis leaves Hippolytus and his grieving father with the most beggarly of all consolations, an appeal to inevitable fate. [11] In Browning's poem Artemis's first mode, the deed-by-deed, sequential revelation of events, constitutes a narrative analogy to the idea of fate. What it gains in tragic inevitability, it gains at the cost of something with which Browning is never willing to part: the romantic sense of possibility.

Browning accordingly turns away from his source and away from the deterministic cast of the classical spirit to which he could no more reconcile himself in this poem than in "Old Pictures in Florence" (1855) or in the late "Parleying with Gerard de Lairesse" (1887). [12] He makes Artemis turn with him to a second, stronger narrative mode. This mode appears briefly in the second line quoted above—"(Indomitable as a man foredoomed)"—a line that owes its strength to the different attitude that it takes, not only toward the man it describes, but also toward narration itself. Browning never wrote iambic pentameter that sounds less like *Sordello* than does "Artemis Prologizes," but with the insertion of Artemis's parenthesis the digressive tactics of that narrative begin to inform this dramatic lyric. Artemis's parenthesis violates the deed-by-deed mode of storytelling in the same way that her comment about Theseus invalidates his reliance on predestined results. In form and theme her remark encloses the idea of fate and reveals it as but one way, among other possibilities, of finding meaning for human time and its losses. When Artemis pauses in her account of Theseus's grim joy to call him indomitable as a man foredoomed, she substitutes for sheer sequence a marked discontinuity. She suspends straightforward comprehension of the story line and evinces instead a narrator's indomitable will to

158

forestall foregone conclusions and to shape a different doom for Theseus and his son in the paragraph to come.

Artemis looks to the future; and, with a divine anxiety lest she lose the homage of her worshipers, she majestically changes her mind:

> I interposed: and, this eventful night, —
> (While round the funeral pyre the populace
> Stood with fierce light on their black robes which bound
> Each sobbing head, while yet their hair they clipped
> O'er the dead body of their withered prince,
> And, in his palace, Theseus prostrated
> On the cold hearth, his brow cold as the slab
> 'Twas bruised on, groaned away the heavy grief—
> As the pyre fell, and down the cross logs crashed,
> Sending a crowd of sparkles through the night,
> And the gay fire, elate with mastery,
> Towered like a serpent o'er the clotted jars
> Of wine, dissolving oils and frankincense,
> And splendid gums like gold), — my potency
> Conveyed the perished man to my retreat
> In the thrice-venerable forest here.

> (84-99)

Between her hint of a new will to interpose a second time in human affairs and her narrative of the execution of that will, Artemis interposes an eventful thirteen-line parenthesis. This narrative interposition displays potency beyond the reach of an art bound to sequential continuity. It is the different potency of a discontinuous mode, the strong second narrative mode of the poem, to shape human time and give it meaning. The night described in the parenthesis is "eventful" in a peculiarly Browningesque sense; the evolution of Artemis's sentence endows the parenthetical details not with significance in themselves, but with a larger significance that is about to be manifested. The lines are filled with the eventual, and rich with outcome. They occupy the gap between expectation and event in which Artemis rests at the end of her prologue: "While I/Await, in fitting silence, the event" (120-21). Browning first wrote, "In fitting silence the event await": his 1849 revision literally defers "the event" and lets Artemis wait a little longer. In either version the energies of divine expectation are finally strong enough to defer even grammatical closure; Artemis speaks a fragmentary sentence, a temporal clause anticipating an outcome Browning never bothered to write out.

He did not need to write it out. The miraculous new beginning that was to have been his subject is already potentially present—

159

present, that is, in the way that meant most to Browning as a poet. Matthew Arnold praised "Artemis Prologizes" as an "antique fragment."[13] Like the grammatical fragment that concludes it and like *Pauline: A Fragment of a Confession*, it is a potent piece of deliberate anticipation. In the long passage last quoted, Artemis exalts the power of fragmentation. In describing the funeral pyre, she incidentally describes an emblem of her potency even as she exerts it, much as the Spanish monk sees a dead eye glow while women happen to be telling stories. The fire, Paracelsus's element of renewing change, is itself renewed in the course of Artemis's parenthesis. At first it is a "fierce light," which only illuminates the inevitability of human bondage to death; it then cedes a temporary authority to the disabling repetitions of grief by giving place to an extinguished hearth: "Theseus prostrated/On the cold hearth, his brow cold as the slab/ 'Twas bruised on." But, with the dash in line 91 and the crash of the "cross logs," the ritual structure of grief becomes fuel for an energy overmastering grief. "The gay fire, elate with mastery," resumes its place in Artemis's parenthesis as a representation of her ability to reopen the question of closure, to break old seals and dissolve old certainties. Her interposition on behalf of Hippolutos intends to fill the night with other events than have hitherto been imagined by the attendants of funerals.[14]

Artemis's parenthetical pause, a capacious extension of poetic time, accommodates the mighty revolving of alternatives whereby a divine mind turns itself over and comes to its decision. Browning originally signaled her decision by introducing the second paragraph with a "but." By substituting "so" in 1849, he retarded the decisive moment and so diffused it over the course of a stately passage that the moment becomes impossible to specify. The indeterminacy of Artemis's moment of reversal creates a valuable delay in a reader's gradual passage to her perspective from that of Theseus and the mourners. Those darkly bound figures stand as reminders of an unprivileged, alternative interpretation of Hippolutos's fate—that the youth is irretrievably dead and gone—an interpretation that for a time the similarly unprivileged reader entertains as valid. Only after Artemis's grand sentence has reached its period may one realize how from her narrative perspective this interpretation is a hollow mockery. At an unspecified moment during the performance of the rites, the potency of Artemis has spirited Hippolutos away. The glorious pyre must then be vacant, the funeral ceremony emptied of its object. Theseus and the populace are left mourning not a corpse, but its absence, a flaw that has already extended a promise of regeneration.

The power of Artemis's second narrative mode is the power to defer events, syntactic events among them. Her parenthetical deferral of meaning counters the failure of Theseus to defer and suggests that he may be as premature in grieving for Hippolutos as he has been in condemning him to death. Her narrative, elate with mastery, enforces a divinely comic point of view from which the "cold," "heavy" mourning of Theseus becomes a slightly ridiculous form of punitive and unavailing therapy. To grieve may be human, but to defer is to exercise the more definitively human, creative power that matters most to Browning as poet and as analyst of the losses and gains of men and women. Theseus's self-absorbed grief is a denial of possibility, an abandonment of intention, which Browning has to discredit in order to write. In *Balaustion's Adventure* (1871), a reworking of Euripides' Alcestis myth, Browning suggests that all grief ends with the mourner's painful rebirth into possibility, with the decision to lose the past for the future's sake.

Browning encloses tragic fate and grief as he does in this early lyric because it is only after grief has come to an end that the romance of the future may begin anew. But the indeterminacy of the future means anxiety as well as possibility. If the best is ever yet to be, then it is never now. It is a token of Browning's greatness that the creative possibilities that excite his dramatic speakers are ultimately indistinguishable from their besetting anxieties. As he puts it with the disarming bluntness that marks his later poetry, "Who knows most, doubts most; entertaining hope,/Means recognizing fear" (*The Two Poets of Croisic* [1878], 1257-58). Browning's speakers stand at the brink of the unknowable future by pitting hope against fear, and their ambivalence about the future creates the internal action in character that Browning traces in their speeches—with a deep respect for their courageous assertions and with a compassionate curiosity about the motives that inhibit such assertions and cause them to fail. To grow old along with Browning will be to live with Artemis and with Rabbi Ben Ezra (1864) in the ageless anxiety of awaiting, in fitting silence, the event.

"HOME-THOUGHTS, FROM ABROAD"

"Artemis Prologizes" is a study in deliberate anticipation—an oxymoron that may be used to describe the situations in which all of Browning's lyric speakers find themselves. Although other speakers are never so deliberate in pace and never roll out their various intentions so smoothly, they share Artemis's choice to defer conclusions by complicating the present in which they speak. This choice appears quite clearly in one of Browning's most limpid lyrics, "Home-Thoughts, From Abroad."

Oh to be in England
Now that April's there,
And whoever wakes in England
Sees, some morning, unaware,
That the lowest boughs and the brushwood sheaf
Round the elm-tree bole are in tiny leaf,
While the chaffinch sings on the orchard bough
In England—now!

(1-8)

The oddest thing about this beautiful first stanza is that Browning felt the need to revise it, as he plainly did, in the stanza that follows. These lines enjoy the important earliness of morning and awakening; moreover, they gracefully bear the burden of surprise ("unaware") that Browning was always happy to shoulder. But an obstacle on which lyric voice may trip into the wider surprises of the next stanza appears in the last line: "In England—now!" "Distance all value enhances," as King Francis yawns in "The Glove" ([1845] 2); or as the dreaming lyric "I" has it in "Women and Roses" (1855), "What is far conquers what is near" (41). This stanza seems to indicate, however, that spatial distance in itself may not be of sufficient value to set in motion an imagination as temporal as Browning's. "England" only rhymes with "England," "lowest boughs" slopes only to "orchard bough," and the "some morning" hopefully ventured in line 4 turns out to be only the same "now" with which the stanza has begun. There is a simple simultaneity of flora, and fauna, and lyric voice, which traps this speaker in a last line that can do nothing more than repeat the words he has just said.

The first stanza implicitly poses a question of repetition, and the second stanza answers it by redeeming repetition in a mode reminiscent of the second narrative mode from "Artemis Prologizes." The second stanza is a vindication of latter beginnings, and it gets started by breaking with the present that has stopped its predecessor:

And after April, when May follows,
And the whitethroat builds, and all the swallows!
Hark, where my blossomed pear-tree in the hedge
Leans to the field and scatters on the clover
Blossoms and dewdrops—at the bent spray's edge—
That's the wise thrush; he sings each song twice over
Lest you should think he never could recapture
The first fine careless rapture!
And though the fields look rough with hoary dew
All will be gay when noontide wakes anew

162

> *The buttercups, the little children's dower*
> *—Far brighter than this gaudy melon-flower!*

(9-20)

Browning's second stanza follows his first as May follows April, working with much the same materials, spring foliage and bird song, but in a more self-conscious and sophisticated fashion. Like the whitethroat, the speaker now *builds* his lyric, rather than simply singing with the chaffinch. The keystone to his revised structure is the six-line sentence that hearkens after the thrush. "Hark," in line 11, stands where "Sees" has stood in line 3; and the change from visual to auditory perception betokens the difference between spatial and temporal imagining that makes this stanza new. "Hark" is followed by three lines describing the natural scene, as the first stanza might have described it, in pictorial terms; the internal repetitions of that stanza are recalled by the repetition of "blossomed" in "blossoms."

But the second stanza adopts the manner of the first only temporarily in order to place it in context. Lines 11-13 lead to an "edge" on the other side of which the predominant temporal language of the stanza reasserts its control. The effect of this control is to preempt the spatial language of the first stanza and make it serve different, temporal ends—to make the demonstrative "where" of line 11 function as a delaying "while." For the speaker is listening all the while for the wise repetition of the thrush's song; Browning's syntax forces a reader to take the inset descriptive passage, however lovely and fresh it may be, as filler, as a means of keeping time until the thrush will sing again. Furthermore, the stanza charges these descriptive lines with purpose and direction; no longer a mere object in space like the elm-tree of the first stanza, the pear-tree "leans" and moves towards a goal or "edge." "Blossoms" and "dewdrops," with a punning transformation that Hopkins may have observed, align themselves with "leans" and "scatters" and borrow the force of active verbs. A better and wiser builder here than in his first stanza, the speaker has recaptured the beauty of that stanza, its first fine careless rapture, and has made it part of an ampler, more careful temporal scheme that may preserve it from its own tendency to collapse into "now."

Repetition may be conceived as a formal expression of the revisionary or secondary will that lies at the heart both of Browning's aesthetics and of his psychology—and also, it might be argued, at the heart of what is most enduring in Victorian poetry generally. It is the virtue of this brief lyric so to conceive repetition, and to argue that any wise repetition bespeaks an intention to revise what is ostensibly being repeated. The difference between "Hark" and "That's the wise thrush" represents a difference between two versions of the bird's song; the latter version possesses the additional, distinguishing power of having recaptured the former. In the first stanza someone "wakes in England"; but in the second stanza the verb becomes transitive: "noontide wakes anew/The buttercups." The anew-ness, a novelty in repetition, is the difference to which Browning's strategy of delay draws attention. Or, more precisely, since the new awakening of the buttercups is a future event anticipated from the already future perspective of May with which the stanza opens, anew-ness may be considered an article of the temporal faith that keeps Browning a writer. It is his faith that the future will wake new blossoms "Far brighter than this gaudy melon-flower"—brighter, that is, than the gaudy present, which has been suspended in order to let this finer stanza occur.

At least until the detached last line, there is no "now" in the second stanza whatsoever. The final presence of "*this* gaudy melon-flower" lets one perceive the absence behind "*That's* the wise thrush"—a phrase that comes after the fact, as does "Hark," to indicate a song that has already been sung. The thrush may sing his song twice over; but the poem, intent upon other game, never sings it even once. The speaker's break with the present consigns the thrush's song to moments of fitting silence between the different moments of lyric utterance, much as the descriptive filler in lines 11-14 points to the existence of a void that is very much there to be filled. This silence and this void are traces of a present deliberately lost, and the loss of the present gives legitimate cause for an anxiety of which the second stanza faithfully takes note. Its thrush (unlike Shelley's skylark, for example) is a worried bird, fearful *lest* its song be undervalued; and the promise that "all will be gay" comes only after the blank misgiving of "though the fields look rough with hoary dew."

A reader of this stanza learns to interpret its anxieties as essentially creative, as original conditions that spur both bird and poet to renew their song. But other men and women in Browning, who find presence more difficult to relinquish, balk at the tasks of renewal. For every speaker like the Spanish monk who exploits the difference between intention and language, or between present and future, as his inalienable revisionary right, there is a speaker who suffers that difference as an inexorable doom. Though the monk hops like a demonic Ariel from "or" to "or," from one stanza of his soliloquy to the next, and though the speaker of "Home-Thoughts" exchanges now for then and homes in on the future, the vacillations of other speakers are signs of a self-division that chastens and subdues. Less wise than the speaker of "Home-Thoughts," less inventive than the

Spanish monk, or just more resignedly human than Artemis, they submit their own revisionary impulses to revision and commit themselves to elaborate versions of stasis that it is Browning's business to explore.

"PICTOR IGNOTUS: FLORENCE, 15--"

"Pictor Ignotus" (1845) tells the story of another change of mind, with the interesting variation that this mind keeps reenacting its change as it tells its story. "I chose my portion" (57), says the unknown painter from whose failure to make a name the poem takes its title; and, like Browning's Strafford, he chooses to repeat his self-crippling choice again and again. Unlike Strafford, however, the painter is not in a drama but in a dramatic lyric. Under the different conditions of lyric, there is no one for the Pictor Ignotus to defer to but himself.

> *I could have painted pictures like that youth's*
> *Ye praise so. How my soul springs up! No bar*
> *Stayed me—ah, thought which saddens while it soothes!*
> *—Never did fate forbid me, star by star,*
> *To outburst on your night with all my gift*
> *Of fires from God.*
>
> (1-6) [15]

The Pictor's initial confusion of verb tenses is remarkable; but, to a man who seeks consolation for past failure and future oblivion, it may be an advantage not to know what time it is. A sense of past possibility, the Pictor persuades himself to believe throughout the poem, is more comforting than no sense of possibility at all. The Pictor's sorry apologia depends on his perceiving a difference between his potential and actual achievements in art; these opening lines attempt to establish that protective and soothing, if saddening, difference. Yet his shifting tenses and the unsoothing movement of the verses he speaks disclose that there is a more urgent cause than past failure for the Pictor's self-reproach. "How my soul springs up!" If his soul springs up, right now, it does so because his past possibilities are also present possibilities, which a reader may watch him crush all over again in uttering the poem.

That the time is the Florentine High Renaissance, a time in which he could still, if he chose, paint bolder and better pictures, is a fact against which the Pictor defends himself with all the might of his quietly perverse will. "No bar" has stayed him in the past from higher achievement, and no bar stays him now—except a self-censuring will that is listening as he speaks and that inhibits him again, in its small way, when the bar lowered in line 3 stays his soul from springing very far across the poetic line. The ambiguity of the adverbial phrase "star by star" in the fourth line further illuminates the inwardness of this artist's failure. The stars were presumably to be his fiery gift to the grateful world he goes on to imagine in lines 25-40, but there is also an astrological connection that would link his "star by star" back to the idea of "fate" and its deed-by-deed inevitability. The ambiguity of Browning's grammar suggests an entanglement of forbidding fate with outbursting imagination, of prohibition with expression, that underlies both the Pictor's creative catastrophe and the futility of his attempt to understand himself in this monologue.

Further entanglements appear a few lines later, when the Pictor undertakes to describe what he might have rendered in his unpainted works:

> Each face obedient to its passion's law,
>> Each passion clear proclaimed without a tongue;
> Whether Hope rose at once in all the blood,
>> A-tiptoe for the blessing of embrace,
> Or Rapture drooped the eyes, as when her brood
>> Pull down the nesting dove's heart to its place;
> Or Confidence lit swift the forehead up,
>> And locked the mouth fast, like a castle braved, —
> O human faces, hath it spilt, my cup?
>> What did ye give me that I have not saved?
>
> (15-24)

Beneath the superficial composure of these lines plays a drama in which the Pictor repeatedly punishes himself for transgressing his own taboos. Not only do his imagined human faces obey ruling passions, the passions themselves manifest a strange obedience to rule. Browning's imagery of enclosure always repays attention, and the images in this passage give evidence of the censorious, self-blocking activity of its speaker's complex will. "Hope" must be aggressive to survive in Browning's world; but here it rises all at once, as the Pictor's soul has sprung up in line 2, only to be tamed between lines into a wish for a hug. "Rapture," which should be somewhat fine and careless, is no sooner mentioned than pulled down, midline, and taught its place by the violently idiosyncratic simile of the nesting dove. The image of "Confidence," the passion that the timid Pictor most needs to feel, undergoes the cruelest revision of all. In line 21, with a momentary burst of confidence he rekindles the outbursting divine light from lines 5-6; by the end of the next line, however, he

166

has fallen silent. He proceeds to change the subject—but not the governing imagery of enclosure—and avoids the imperfections of artistic creation by taking solace in the perfection of his memory, which he likens to a retentive "cup." Meanwhile in line 22, as if fearing the hypothetical power that he has released, he has shut up his own light with an image at once of enclosure, of silence, and of the internal warfare in which he has just defeated himself one more time: "And locked the mouth fast, like a castle braved."

This very final image recalls the earlier line "Each passion clear proclaimed without a tongue" and suggests that there is more to its conventional paradox of a speaking picture than meets the eye. The Pictor wishes to keep passions tongueless, and to lock up the mouth of the confidence he desperately needs, because he fears the originating power that is represented by voice. In approaching the central voice of the poem, the intruding "voice" that governs the difficult confessional passage beginning at line 41, it will be useful to bear in mind the simple authority of lyric voice from which all Browning's monologues begin. In the preceding passage the Pictor has recounted a youthful dream of preeminence in which "old streets" were to have been "named afresh" after his fancied artistic successes (32); the dream has grown "frightful, 'twas so wildly dear" (40). In the original edition of 1845, Browning put line 40 into the present tense as a reminder that the Pictor is still engaged in repressing present possibilities. But the revised reading of 1849 makes it clearer that even as a youth the Pictor already found something frightening in the thought of success, even before he replaced it with the figure of an inhibiting voice:

> But a voice changed it. Glimpses of such sights
> Have scared me, like the revels through a door
> Of some strange house of idols at its rites!
> This world seemed not the world it was before:
> Mixed with my loving trusting ones, there trooped
> . . . Who summoned those cold faces that begun
> To press on me and judge me? Though I stooped
> Shrinking, as from the soldiery a nun,
> They drew me forth, and spite of me . . . enough!

$$(41-49)$$

The apparently unmotivated voice that has summoned these judicial faces remains as mysterious to the Pictor as it is at first to the reader. If the Pictor could identify the source of this voice, then his alibi for failure would disappear because the voice would no longer be alien. He would be left with no apology, and Browning with no poem—or

167

at any rate with a very different one called "Andrea del Sarto." For the voice is no one's but the Pictor's, a powerfully condensed representation of his cruelly cognate impulses to express himself and silence himself.

In an instance of the sure tact that makes Browning's verse worth reading slowly, the voice summons faces that enter the poem as figures both of beginning and of repression: "cold faces that begun / To press on me and judge me." The voice issues a call at once of origination and of prohibition, a call anticipating the divine voice that ends Browning's "Prologue" to *Asolando* ([1889] 41-45). The old poet there will hearken to the originating challenge of the voice and will interpret the call prospectively, as an injunction fit for a prologue. Here, however, his unknown painter hears only the voice's forbidding commandment and shrinks in obedience. The Pictor's creative impulse to effect change, to rename old streets, to make this world "not the world it was before," turns inward and, with an increasingly strong revulsion, revises itself out of existence. Beginning intentions are figured through the opening door of line 42 in a disturbing image of rebelliously broken closure that nevertheless offers "strange" possibilities. The open door might be read by a Fra Lippo Lippi as the break in continuity whereby artistic tradition extends itself. But in the Pictor's perverse consciousness, before long such creative violation becomes a threat directed at the would-be creator, "Shrinking, as from the soldiery a nun." The mind turns its forces against itself, with an image of physical violation that figures the Pictor's iconophobic recoil. He flees from "some strange house of idols at its rites," from a vision of the house of fame as peopled with images of his own making, and seeks asylum in "the sanctuary's gloom" (63), under the shadow of a prescribed iconography.

By the last line of the passage, the Pictor's original dream of emerging into creativity has been completely overturned. Instead of "going forth" in his art, as he has dreamed in line 26, he now tells with nightmarish intensity how he has imagined violent outsiders drawing him forth against his will. The assertion that "they drew me forth" lets the Pictor absolve himself from responsibility for the dream of self-expression to which he has given voice in earlier lines. If some alien force has made him emerge into his own in spite of himself, then he cannot be held to have transgressed. In these lines the authority of voice, the identity of the lyric "me," is transferred from the Pictor's will-to-originality into the keeping of a stronger will-to-silence: a will that triumphantly ends the passage with its authoritative "enough!" Browning's 1849 revision emphasizes this unproductive identity crisis; the original version reads, "Mixed with my loving ones there trooped—for what?" The Pictor well knows *what* has happened to his dream of power and *what* the poor results of his creative conflict have been. He bears witness to more provocatively personal questions in Browning's revision through his inability to complete the sentence broken off at the end of line 45. The question of *who* has prevented him from realizing his youthful potential in the past and the more menacing question of *who* is preventing him from making a new beginning now are questions that the murky central passage records the Pictor's successful struggle to resist answering.

The obvious answer to both questions, the Pictor Ignotus, should be joined to the less obvious qualification that "the Pictor Ignotus" is interestingly plural.

> *They drew me forth, and spite of me . . . enough!*
> *These buy and sell our pictures, take and give,*
> *Count them for garniture and household-stuff,*
> *And where they live needs must our pictures live*
> *And see their faces, listen to their prate,*
> *Partakers of their daily pettiness,*
> *Discussed of, — "This I love, or this I hate,*
> *This likes me more, and this affects me less!"*

(49-56)

Readers have observed that with the abrupt switch from intimate confession to expansive rationalization in these lines the Pictor makes an unconvincing attempt at covering his tracks.[16] His pronominal switch from "me" to "our" should be observed too; the Pictor attains his lofty dismissal of unsympathetic criticism by mounting the stilts of the editorial "we." The "we" of these lines speaks for the Pictor more truly than he can let himself know. It speaks in the confident tones of an editor because it is the voice of the internal censor that has been performing its redactions throughout the poem. Having vanquished his creative impulse once again, the Pictor's will to fail enjoys its victory by rising to the surface and speaking seven lines of mediocre satire unlike any others in the poem. It adopts the first-person plural because it is now empowered to speak on its own behalf and on behalf of its recent victim.

When the more familiar "I" returns at line 57, it is to acknowledge defeat at its own hands: "Wherefore I chose my portion." Formerly the soul has sprung up, but now

> *My heart sinks, as monotonous I paint*
> *These endless cloisters and eternal aisles*
> *With the same series, Virgin, Babe and Saint,*
> *With the same cold calm beautiful regard.*

(58-61)

Monotony, eternity, and sameness are well-established analogues for closure in Browning's earlier poetry. What is new in a lyric like this one is a heightened intensity of internalization, which lets Browning look beyond the formal finish of the Pictor's art to the dynamics of the expressive failure that such art masks. Browning's exploration of the intentionality behind art reveals that even the devotional works of a Pictor Ignotus may constitute a kind of self-portraiture. The Pictor puts into his religious subjects the same "cold calm beautiful regard" that he has already encountered in "those cold faces" from line 46. He paints, and will continue to paint, images of his own inhibiting need for closure. He will take satisfaction where he may in a soundless retreat from time's "vain tongues" where "only prayer breaks the silence," " 'Mid echoes the light footstep never woke" (64-68). This last line inverts Browning's more usual procedure of divining new possibilities through temporalizing light and space. By spatializing sound and time, by fixing unawakened echoes like blackened pictures in the gloom, the Pictor commits himself to the certainty of a futureless present—which, for Browning's purposes, is death. "So, die my pictures! surely, gently die!" (69).

It is appropriate that the final lines of this poem should include images of a trumpeting cry and an unlocked mouth: "Blown harshly, keeps the trump its golden cry? / Tastes sweet the water with such specks of earth?" (71-72). The Pictor intends these as images of the worthlessness of human fame, but by this point in the monologue it is difficult to confine his words within the orbit of a single intention. Both of the metaphors chosen by the Pictor to represent critical response evoke celebrated biblical images for the creative process, and for Browning in 1845 recent poetic reworkings of these images were important antecedents. Shelley had called for the apocalyptic trumpet of a prophecy in his "Ode to the West Wind"; and, in a central passage on poetic origination in *Sordello* (III.806-32), Browning himself had used the story of the prophet Moses' smiting the rock and bringing forth water from the earth (Numbers 20). By ending his poem with these images of prophetic creativity, the Pictor may be asking a question less rhetorical than it first appears. He may be asking the "youth, men praise so" (70) what it feels like to proceed with artistic creation despite imperfections in the artist's environment and, indeed, despite imperfections in the artist.

The question remains unanswered; but, recalling that Browning has suggested answers to the Pictor's other questions in the poem, one hazards the guess that proceeding with artistic creation feels rather like speaking a dramatic monologue. The Pictor's most interesting moments are those in which he wrestles with his own imperfections and tastes his own specks of earth, and his poem is better than any of the cold calm beautiful works he has painted. [17] No one, and least of all Browning, has ever pretended that prophecy is "golden" or "sweet." The deliberate anticipation that often makes Browning's lyric writing a kind of prophecy depends (as in "Artemis Prologizes" and "Home-Thoughts, From Abroad") upon sacrifices, temporal exchanges that may seem harsh or bitter. Speakers trade the past or present for the future with a strict prophetic economy that "holds the future fast, / Accepts the coming ages' duty, / Their present for this past" ("Popularity" [1855], 13-15). When the Pictor Ignotus insists, "At least no merchant traffics in my heart" (62), he would like to believe that he has abstained from all such economies. But, if he were right, his poem could never have been spoken; it would never have had the time. In fact there is a merchant incessantly trafficking in the Pictor's heart who practices prophetic economy in reverse and trades the different future for repetitions of the bungled opportunities of his past. The Pictor is one of Browning's bargainers in spite of himself, and his sad bargain makes the poem. By lending his mind out in a haunting monologue, as he will not do in his painting, the Pictor illustrates the temporal economy that Fra Lippo Lippi will identify as the very gift of art.

"JOHANNES AGRICOLA IN MEDITATION"

The continuance of lyric speech for Browning always proceeds from discontinuities of intention like those dividing the Pictor Ignotus against himself. By economizing time in their various ways, his men and women create the future of their poems, the poetic time in which they may speak. This process is complex but clearly apparent in "Pictor Ignotus," in which the fact that the speaker is internally split is never in doubt. The sublime confidence of Johannes Agricola, however, seems to leave no room for a change of mind:

> There's heaven above, and night by night
> I look right through its gorgeous roof;
> No suns and moons though e'er so bright
> Avail to stop me; splendour-proof
> I keep the broods of stars aloof.

(1-5)

Johannes's seems the extreme case of a monologist who has circumvented human economies altogether and, therefore, a suitable test case for the present argument about Browning's lyric intentions. In 1842 Browning acknowledged the extremity of "Johannes Agricola in Meditation" (originally published as "Johannes Agricola" in 1836)

171

by retitling the poem a "Madhouse Cell." But in the collected edition of 1868 Johannes found his rightful place, in the volume of later "Men and Women" from whom he finally differs only in the fierce simplicity of his dilemma.

It is the dilemma of the Antinomian apologist, or even of the soliloquizing Antinomian meditator, to have to put into language a doctrine that sets itself against language, against the name, against the written law and the problematics of interpretation.[18] Johannes wishes to take his stand on a guilt-free, faultless, unmediated relationship to God,

> *God, whom I praise; how could I praise,*
> *If such as I might understand,*
> *Make out and reckon on his ways,*
> *And bargain for his love, and stand,*
> *Paying a price, at his right hand?*

(56-60)

With these concluding lines Johannes rejects interpretation and indebtedness in the same breath because, in speaking the poem, he has come to see how knowing and owing imply each other. To make God out and reckon on his ways is to pay a price that Johannes is determined to withhold: the price of admitting an interpretive reckoning, a mediation that, in its linguistic as well as its religious manifestations, would undermine his Antinomian position.

Recognition of his own will to interpretive power entails a loss of innocence that Johannes can ill afford. In the course of his meditation he loses his innocence, nevertheless, and loses it more than once; the drama of the poem is the play between this loss and his stubborn refusal to accept it. The defensive paraphrases of the last three lines, like everything else Johannes says, indicate both his heroic determination to oppose mediation and his ludicrous inability to exclude it. The semantic differences among "understand," "make out," and "reckon" or among "reckon," "bargain," and "pay" are less important than the mere proliferation of synonyms; even in denying interpretation with these paraphrases Johannes reinterprets himself. He would cling to a conviction that God's love is nonnegotiable, that the spirit is all and the letter nothing. In seeking to spell out this conviction, however, Johannes finds that the letter is not nothing but something to be reckoned with. He becomes a negotiator despite his best intentions, and what he negotiates is the linguistic fault between meaning and expression.

Johannes begins his meditation imperially enough by disregarding the visible universe of "suns and moons." All works, including the works of God, are irrelevant to his faith in predestination. For the visible universe Johannes substitutes a universe of mere intentionality:

> For I intend to get to God,
> For 'tis to God I speed so fast,
> For in God's breast, my own abode,
> Those shoals of dazzling glory, passed,
> I lay my spirit down at last.
> I lie where I have always lain,
> God smiles as he has always smiled.
>
> (6-12)

Time has as little meaning in Johannes's system as does tense in these opening clauses.[19] Browning's odd juxtaposition in lines 10-11 of the present tenses of "lay" and "lie" draws attention to the fashion in which Johannes makes past, present, and future not only continuous but simultaneous. Where intention is all, a difference between intention and execution becomes unthinkable; and, where there is no such difference, there can be no distinguishing an initial "abode" from a "last" destination.

But if beginnings and ends should thus coincide to cancel time, there could be no *pre*destination either, no original past moment of divine decision. Johannes apparently realizes as much, because in the next lines he hastily retrieves the original moment, prior to creation, when "God thought on me his child; / Ordained a life for me" (15-16). Here Johannes revises himself, and in revising himself he joins the company of Browning's lyric speakers. Like them, Johannes opens a difference between intention and act, and he begins, like them, to experience the poetically productive frustrations of living with that difference—of living as an interpreter. Before long Browning has Johannes share such frustrations with the reader: "God said / This head this hand should rest upon / Thus, ere he fashioned star or sun" (18-20). It matters little whether in Johannes's meditating position his head is resting on his hand or vice versa, but it matters a great deal that the one speech in the poem telling what God has actually *said* should be so ambiguous. It may also matter that the ambiguity concerns the relation between Johannes's intending "head" and his executing "hand."

If divine predestination stands to creation in an idealized paradigm of the relation of human intention to speech, then Johannes's cosmogonical speculations may imply a theory of language. The historical Johannes Agricola denounced the written law: "All who follow Moses must go to the devil. To the gallows with Moses."[20] This is the position from which Browning's Johannes begins, but

173

the lines following his report of what God has "said" manifest a significant instability in Johannes's attitude toward language:

> And having thus created me,
> Thus rooted me, he bade me grow,
> Guiltless for ever, like a tree
> That buds and blooms, nor seeks to know
> The law by which it prospers so:
> But sure that thought and word and deed
> All go to swell his love for me,
> Me, made because that love had need
> Of something irreversibly
> Pledged solely its content to be.
>
> (21-30)

The Antinomian ignores "the law" in order to escape indebtedness: if he can but abrogate the law and its interpretation, he may be "guiltless for ever." Johannes relies upon a theory of language that confuses and collapses the intervals between meaning and expression, sign and significance, "thought and word and deed." He posits instead a faultless linguistic fluency that is analogous to the innocent and continuous intentionality of his predestinarian cosmos. The divine intention to love Johannes Agricola fills this cosmos to the brim, while Johannes exfoliates upward "irreversibly"—or, in the more explicitly linguistic term that Browning retained here until 1868, "irrevocably."

Johannes's relentless upward mobility—speeding through the roof of heaven, ascending like a tree—recalls the poet's "upward course" through the gyres of *Sordello*, a poem on which Browning was working when he first published this lyric. His encounter there with Eglamor in Book VI, when taken alongside Johannes's encounter with the temporality of language, constitutes an early definition of the Browningesque sublime. In Browning the classical sense of sublimity as elevation yields to a sense of sublimity as prolongation; the vertical dimension begins to matter in his poems when it figures a temporal one. His sublime is an effect of endlessness that a poet achieves by putting the temporally infinite within time, by so wording his text that the flow of language becomes an image of the perpetual beginning or ceaseless becoming that animates Browning's world. Such sublimity may be considered as either a textual or a psychic effect, since any living text exists, as the human soul exists, in time and not as an atemporal abstraction. Browning intimates the infinite through the oddly time-warped space of his meeting with Eglamor or more traditionally through imagery of voice and hearing, as at the conclusion to "Childe Roland" or the "Prologue" to *Asolando*.

174

In this temporal sense of sublimity Browning hearkens back through Shelley, Wordsworth, and Milton to the biblical prophets and ultimately to Moses, the lawgiver whom the historical Johannes Agricola had so emphatically rejected. To see how this sublime tradition bears on "Johannes Agricola," it is instructive to set against Johannes's denunciation of the Mosaic law the response of Longinus to the book of Genesis:

> The lawgiver of the Jews, no ordinary man—for he understood and expressed God's power in accordance with its worth—writes at the beginning of his *Laws*: "God said"—now what?—"'Let there be light,' and there was light; 'Let there be earth,' and there was earth."[21]

Longinus's fine critical question, "now what?", dwelling on the temporal gap opened by the creative word, is one that Browning's poetry continually requires. The sublimity Longinus finds in the text of Moses depends on a repetition that occurs in time even as the event described by Moses shapes time. Browning would endeavor to recapture this repetition at the end of his most explicitly Hebraic poem, "Saul" (1855), in which all of nature feels "the new law" and murmurs with David its rhythmic amen: "'E'en so, it is so!'" (331-35).

As the book of Genesis presents it, the force of eternity is in love with the productions of time; and, in committing itself to the temporal mode of production that is language, it makes its utter power manifest in ways that empower Moses' text. The difference between "God said, 'Let there be light'" and "there was light" corresponds to the difference between God's performative word and God's effective intention, or the difference, in literary terms, between form and content. This is just the difference that Johannes Agricola fondly hopes to deny by collapsing language into intention. In theory, as a result of the indifference of "thought and word and deed," the Antinomian soul enjoys a condition of pure "content." The soul con*tents* the divine love that has created it, and it shares in the divine intentionality by remaining an unmediated *con*tent, free of the restrictions of form. Johannes's extraordinary doctrine of unformed intentionality, then, exalts a sublimity that is not endless but beginningless.

In giving form to this doctrine, however, Johannes meditates his way back into a recognition of formal restrictions. If the soul is "pledged" to content God's love, then the whole doctrinal fabric rests on a pledge; and, where there is a pledge, there may be a flaw in the indenture, something to be made out and reckoned on. With the next lines Johannes eagerly attempts to bury the possibility of a flaw under the reassuring continuity of his earlier organic metaphor:

> *Yes, yes, a tree which must ascend,*
> *No poison-gourd foredoomed to stoop!*

175

I have God's warrant, could I blend
All hideous sins, as in a cup,
To drink the mingled venoms up;
Secure my nature will convert
The draught to blossoming gladness fast.

(31-37)

Metaphor is so subtly powerful a governor of interpretation that when it leads to unacceptable consequences, as it does for Johannes here, it can be dislodged only by another, more powerful metaphor. In the first line Johannes desires to think of himself as a tree because he hopes that trees cannot be guilty. To be not Adam, but the tree of knowledge itself, is to evade Adam's interpretive confrontation with God's prohibition and with the choice of good or evil.[22] This desire for unconditional innocence is blasted as Johannes ponders the implications of his metaphor through the apparently unsolicited but revealing thought of the "poison-gourd" in the second line. He needs above all to distinguish himself from the damned; yet his organic metaphor will not permit him to do so. Trees and gourds alike, as they bud and bloom, participate in the deed-by-deed continuity of a fate "foredoomed." In order to make a saving distinction between himself and the damned, Johannes must become a reader of fate and not a mere participant in its evolution. With the third line he is driven back to the earlier image of the pledge, "God's warrant"—an image that is strong enough to uproot the organic image because it is nearer than the organic image to Johannes's source of power as an interpreter. When he says, "I have God's warrant," he reverts to a recognition of his "nature" as a willful reader and finds himself again amid the discontinuities of interpretation.

Perhaps this recognition motivates the superfluous appearance of the "cup" at the fourth line in a simile expressing within small compass Johannes's awareness of his dilemma. It should not be in the "nature" of a tree to drink from a cup; indeed, if the cup recalls anything in nature, it recalls the gourd, which for Johannes represents the damned. Whatever its natural origin, a cup is the decidedly unnatural work of an artificer, a vessel (or vehicle) deliberately formed to hold a content (or tenor). It is precisely the sort of object that should have no place in the realm of pure and formless "content," which Johannes has imagined only four lines earlier. Besides, there is nothing in the passage to which the cup may be assimilated; Johannes clearly differentiates it both from the sins that it contains and from the drinker who uses it. It stands outside the terms of the organic metaphor and reveals an oddly intermediate activity of "blending" or "mingling"—an intermediate activity like that of the mind as it finds metaphors in the first place.

The cup resists assimilation to any concrete referent in the passage because it refers instead to the deliberate imaginative process that makes the passage possible. It represents the inherently word-bound metaphoricity of Johannes's doomed campaign against the treacherous faults of language. In thus confessing to the inevitable slip between cup and lip that is Browning's lyric point of departure, Johannes's imagination is more honest than his disputatious intellect. The imaginative insertion of the cup simile within the extended simile of the tree means that the organic metaphor, whereby Johannes has tried to absolve himself of will and guilt, is but a vehicle, a linguistic convenience to be adopted or replaced at will. By replacing his organic imagery here with the imagery of artifice, as later with the imagery of economics that ends the poem, Johannes testifies, against himself, to the very trading in meanings that he remains anxious to disown.

"MY LAST DUCHESS"

In *Sordello* Browning uses the careers of the poets Eglamor and Sordello to show how the contrary attitudes of devotion to form and flight from form may lead alike into oppressive poetic enclosures. Such a resemblance between contraries links Johannes Agricola's furious attack on form to the polished speech of Browning's most famous monologist, the formal Duke of "My Last Duchess" (1842). The two speakers, the Antinomian and the aristocrat with "a nine-hundred-years-old name" (33), approach the gap between form and content, name and meaning, from opposite directions. By the end of their monologues, nevertheless, each of them is a firmly entrenched inhabitant of that gap, and each of them draws vitality from an apprehension of his frustrating intermediacy. Throughout the Duke's monologue the contrast between his rhymed couplets and a syntax that enjambs more lines than it stops bears witness to a conflict between conventional form and informing spirit. The duke's internal division appears more clearly still at moments when the polished surface of his speech begins to crack:

> She had
> A heart—how shall I say?—too soon made glad.

> (21-22)

> She thanked men,—good! but thanked
> Somehow—I know not how—

> (31-32)

Even had you skill
In speech — (which I have not) — to make your will
Quite clear . . . .

(35-37)

Browning never created a more patently skillful speaker, and it is a measure of the Duke's conversational skill that his critics have generally dismissed the hesitant gesture repeated in these lines as an item from his rhetorical stock of commonplaces. But when a skilled rhetorician reaches three times in the space of fifteen lines for the same commonplace, especially for this one, the commonplace is no longer common but the expression of a private struggle.[23]

A man endowed with a nine-hundred-years-old name must know at any price what names mean. Like his less forbidding counterpart in *The Flight of the Duchess*, the Duke is the heir of a heavily traditional sense of himself, which prescribes fixed relations between form and meaning. He is bound by this sense of himself to find in any obstacle to interpretation a personal threat, and it is because the presence of the Duchess has constituted such a threat that he has put her out of his life. His hesitations in the three passages quoted above make the threat quite clear: they move from the Duke's difficulty in interpreting his Duchess's heart to a more intimate difficulty in interpreting his own heart or "will." If the Duke's will is law, then any hesitation in laying down the law must indicate that his will is somehow at fault. His inability to make his will quite clear to her and say, "Just this/Or that in you disgusts me; here you miss,/Or there exceed the mark" (37-39), has revealed an indeterminacy of intention within himself that he cannot tolerate. Unpardonably, the Duchess has made him see that he, too, in committing his intentions to language, may miss or exceed the mark. At last the Duke has turned from the discomforts of flawed interpretation and simply obliterated the growing difference between intention and speech: "This grew; I gave commands;/Then all smiles stopped together" (45-46).

The portrait of the Duchess remains, however, to taunt the Duke with his incapacity to find its meaning. He seats the envoy before the portrait as an interpreter, and he treats the reader in similar fashion by compulsively bringing interpretive issues into discursive prominence. During the first few lines alone the painted Duchess looks "as if she were alive"; the Duke calls attention to the way he "calls" the painting a wonder; he mentions the painter's name "by design"; and he says that other strangers have "read" "that pictured countenance" (1-7). These preliminaries lead to the center of the maze, the meaning of the portrait, with the question "How such a glance came there" (12) — a question that is itself open to some interpretation. The Duke

178

introduces the question as if it concerns Frà Pandolf's artistic technique: how did the painter achieve the effect of such depth and passion? But, to the Duke's eternal credit as a Browningesque interpreter, he takes the question back beyond artistic technique into artistic genesis: what was the source of the depth and passion the painter saw in his subject? It is a question the Duke can no more answer now than he could answer it when the Duchess was alive. He calls "that piece a wonder, now" (3), as he called it a wonder then. His inconclusive wondering is the mainspring of his monologue; and, with his choice to turn aside from an unanswered question and stop wondering, the monologue comes to a halt.

In the meantime he knows that the Duchess's face figures some meaning forth, but he knows too that he cannot say what that meaning is. The Duke expresses his difficulty in reading her countenance by the variety of names that he, the autonomous namer, must use to describe what defies description: it is an "earnest glance" (8), a "faint/Half-flush that dies along her throat" (18-19), a "look" (24), a "blush" (31), a "smile" (45), and, most revealingly, twice it is a "spot of joy" (14-15,21). The Duke's question, how such a glance came there, is a question about origins. Genitive constructions may indicate origins, and with the phrase "spot of joy" the Duke comes as close to the mystery of the Duchess as language will take him. As he notes with growing exasperation, her joy has been wildly disproportionate to any cause for joy in her external circumstances; it has been its own independent cause. "All and each/Would draw from her alike the approving speech,/Or blush, at least" (29-31). With that blush beyond speech the Duchess has evinced her inaccessible intention to rejoice. The "spot" is the interval that has prevented the Duke from taking her meaning and from determining in a name the significance of her intent, earnest glance.

In "that spot of joy" on the Duchess's face Browning finds one of his happiest names for the difference between figuration and meaning out of which poems are written. As always in Browning, this difference has the power of opening temporal intervals; the spot of joy makes possible spots of poetic time like this one:

> My favour at her breast,
> The dropping of the daylight in the West,
> The bough of cherries some officious fool
> Broke in the orchard for her, the white mule
> She rode with round the terrace.
>
> (25-29)

Despite the Duke's efforts to contain the Duchess, her joyful energy breaks into his discourse and charges these eventful lines with a mystery to which everything in the surrounding poem defers.[24] Their mystery is hers: the mystery of a meaning withheld, for which even the Duke here pauses a while in expectant wonder. In a sense the better part of the entire monologue has occurred in such a pause. The Duke concludes his speech by "repeating" an assurance "that no just pretence / Of mine for dowry will be disallowed" (48-51). Between repeated assurances that the future will conform to his expectations, the Duke has paused to dwell in the possibility that expectations may not be fulfilled. Between two moments of "just pretence," he has given play to a better pretense; like the wise thrush, the Duke has become most interesting in the anxious interval between self-assertive moments that extends his poem.

The Duke's characteristic unwillingness to sustain anxiety brings the poem to closure with a series of more confident, less immediately revealing interpretations. He experiences no difficulty in reading the "ample warrant" of the Count's "known munificence" (49-50), and he very quickly reduces the "self" of the Count's daughter to the status of an "object" (52-53). The Duke's final turn to the statue of Neptune has rightly been identified as his ultimate self-interpretation, an oblique recognition of his own power over Claus of Innsbruck, the envoy, and Duchesses past and future.[25]

> Notice Neptune, though,
> Taming a sea-horse, thought a rarity,
> Which Claus of Innsbruck cast in bronze for me!
>
> (54-56)

But this self-interpretation is obviously a misinterpretation and, like those immediately preceding it, a drab one at that. A reader who accepts such an assertion of ducal power as an adequate motive for Browning's forceful monologue makes exactly the reductive mistake made by the Duke. By implying that he is a masterful potentate like Neptune ("My statue of the god was cast in bronze to stand for me"), the Duke attempts to trim his complex, curious self to a simpler mold than he deserves. With the phrase "thought a rarity," he attempts to substitute the placid detachment of the connoisseur for the mingled frustration and wonder that have motivated the rest of his speech. This last-minute attempt of the Duke's to cast himself as Neptune owes its interest to its inaccuracy; he is nowhere more human and nowhere more worthy of suspicion than as he reaches thus for godlike, repressive power over protean circumstances that he would like to forget.

The poem's authentic power, one central to Browning's dramatic writing, is the power of untamed meaning. The wild spot of joy has set this power free for good, to draw readers back to the poem as the

Duke is drawn back to the portrait, in order once again to undertake the task of figuring his last Duchess out. The Duke in his monologue and other source-hunting speakers in theirs track this power to its dwelling in a gap between signs and meanings—a gap indicated by the Duke in referring to the Duchess's inexplicably joyful "speech, / Or blush, at least." It is with that eloquent blush, when the sign she makes is irreducibly "least," that the mysterious power of the Duchess is greatest; for then it hints most strongly at the potential energy of a meaning that persistently eludes formulation. Her "earnest glance" gives an earnest of her escape from any interpretive confines.

In later life Browning declined to confine himself to a single interpretation of the Duchess's fate at the hands of the Duke: "I meant that the commands were that she should be put to death. . . . Or he might have had her shut up in a convent."[26] The poet's nonchalance about his Duke's mere act exemplifies a lifelong preference for questions of motivating intention, "the seed of act" (*The Ring and the Book*, X.272). Nevertheless, the apparent equivalence in Browning's imagination between mortal closure and physical enclosure suggests that "My Last Duchess" may have some bearing on a subject about which he was anything but nonchalant: poetic closure. If one accepts Louis S. Friedland's conjecture that the model for Browning's Duke was Alfonso II of Ferrara, there may be historical warrant for relating the enclosure of the Duchess to the enclosure of poetic meaning. As Browning knew from his research for *Sordello* and the *Essay on Chatterton*, Alfonso II was the duke who incarcerated the poet Torquato Tasso. Browning may have made this patron of the arts and imprisoner of poets the subject of a dramatic lyric in order to dramatize his concern with the patronizing tendencies of readers to imprison the meanings of poems.[27]

Browning had recently given this perennial concern much play in *Sordello*, and he would return to it with a vengeance in the monologues of the coming decades. The foreclosure and enfranchisement of meaning in poems from his greatest book, *Men and Women*, will form the subject of the next chapter. But first, by way of introduction to those poems and issues, it may be helpful to draw out an analogy between the interpretive activities of the Duke and of the reader of a poem, especially of a Browning poem. It is safe to assume that the Duke would not make an enthusiastic reader of Browning. Still, part of the appeal of Browning's Duke is that there is someone like him somewhere in every reader; and, although Browning knows better than to attempt an outright exorcism, his poetry has a salutary if not always flattering way of making readers confront this ducal reader or Duke within.

"My Last Duchess" may be considered a study in the reductive study of poetry, with the face of a Duchess as a highly figured text and the Duke as a "reader" of "that pictured countenance," a student impatient of uncertainties who would fix the meaning of a text beyond doubt, regardless of the cost to its vitality. By giving commands to obliterate the spot of joy, the Duke's reductive reading would reduce what all reductive reading reduces: the difference, where poetry grows, between intention and execution; or, in temporal terms, the difference between "meaning" conceived as a beginning and as an end. By seizing on the latter conception (meaning as end-stopped conclusion, the point of a poem), a reader may neglect the former conception (meaning as originating intention, the motive of a poem). For Browning, with his undying conviction that "the prize is in the process" ("A Pillar at Sebzevar" [1884], 22), meaning is not something poetry possesses once and for all; it is what poetry does and keeps doing. In haste to determine *the* meaning of a poem, a reader like the Duke risks losing touch with the *activity* of meaning, with the renewing pulse, the "faint / Half-flush," of a poem's evolving possibilities. To return to Browning's comment on the Duke: the ducal reader puts the poem to death—or he shuts it up in a conventional formula.

If this analogy is a just one and if in Browning's view to neglect a poem's impelling motives is to foreclose its meaning, then Browning should be obliged by his own principles to invite further questions about motives. What motivates the Duke, or the ducal reader, to neglect motives? What is the intent behind such a disregard for intentions, such a mistaken possessiveness about meanings? These questions are proper to the subtleties of *Men and Women*, but a provisional answer may be ventured here. According to the interpretation of "My Last Duchess" offered above, the Duke's reductive impulse arises in response to pervasive fears of meaninglessness. He literally encloses his Duchess in a tomb or convent and imaginatively encloses himself in an icon of possession, a bronze statue of Neptune, in order to avoid confronting what he perceives as an absence of meaning in his surroundings, in his marriage, and in himself. By analogy, then, the ducal reader, that impulse within every reader that would settle for a formulaic reduction of poetic meaning, acts out of self-defense in order to allay a private suspicion that without such a reduction meaning may be quite absent. The Duke's perception is unimpeachable, given the premise of his interpretive method: the premise that the facets of experience, or the figurations of a portrait, either possess a readily graspable meaning or else lack any meaning whatsoever. To a mind equipped with such a premise, the Browningesque world of temporalized, eventual meaning must seem inscrutable and absurd.

182

As Browning proves on the pulses of *Paracelsus*, of his plays, and pre-eminently of *Sordello* and *Men and Women*, the absurdity lies not with the Duke's world, but with the Duke's all-or-nothing premise — and with the analogous premise of the ducal reader that meaning occurs all at once or not at all.

CHAPTER SIX

TAKING MEANINGS:
MEN AND WOMEN

*If I have any instinct or insight — if I can retain and
rightly reason upon the rare flashes of momentary conviction
that come and go in the habitual dusk and doubt of one's
life — (and this in spite of a temper perhaps offensively
and exaggeratedly inclined to dispute authoritative tradition, and all concessions to the mere desires of the mind) —
if the result of all this can no more be disputed as
something — or even, as much — than pretended to be* everything,
*then I dare believe that you and that I shall recover what
we have lost: I am not given to hope, nor self-flattery: and
my belief is a very composite and unconventional one, and
I myself am most surprised at detecting its strength in the
unforeseen accidents of life which throw one upon one's
resources and show them for what they exactly are.*
Browning to Julia Wedgwood (1864)[1]

The end of the preceding chapter suggested an analogy between
Browning's Duke and the ducal reader of poetry, who defensively
chooses "never to stoop" to the pursuit of eventual meaning but insists instead on extracting and possessing meaning now. For such behavior, at least in Browning's world, the ducal reader pays the heavy
price of possession. In taking meaning as an entity to be possessed,
such a reader is possessed by that meaning and bound — bound to
miss, among other rewards, the invigorating play between what a
poem says and how the poem says it. Or to adapt an epigram of
Blake's that is highly pertinent to Browning: in binding to himself a
joy, or that spot of joy that is poetic meaning, the ducal reader
destroys it and destroys with it his view of eternity's sunrise, the perpetual promise that comes of kissing the joy as it flies.

184

In Browning's world of postponed meaning, wise speakers and readers learn ever to stoop by embracing expectancy and deferring to an unapprehended significance that the future holds in store. This world is the world of *Men and Women* as of *Sordello*; but, despite Browning's hopes of making *Men and Women* "a first step towards popularity," he had to wait years before readers were disposed to adopt its wisdom.[2] The charges of obscurity that greeted the later work in 1855, as they had greeted the earlier in 1840, should be attributed not only to Browning's abrupt and evasive style—though it is unquestionably a more difficult book even in this sense than either of the shorter lyric collections of the 1840s—but also to the sheer spiritual difficulty of abiding in the provisional present that Browning's style figures forth. Critics in 1855 were objecting to the metaphysical as well as to the technical efforts that Browning's works required of them; they found his poetic world meaningless in a deeper sense than that of diction or syntax. Their objections will probably always be valid among certain readers; for the theme of *Men and Women* is the making of meaning, the give-and-take of signification—especially in its religious, erotic, and artistic aspects—between the individual mind and the other minds that constitute its world. By suggesting the fictional status of meaning in general, Browning's theme thrives on the dangerous edge between absurdity and certainty and is likely to strike some contemporaries, in any era, as threatening.[3]

Only with the appearance in 1864 of *Dramatis Personae*, a volume of men and women no more immediately accessible or untroubled than their predecessors, did Browning begin to enjoy a moderate success with the British public. The success of the volume was perhaps due in part to a spreading sense of religious crisis among Victorian readers. This sense of crisis may have gradually prepared them for the poetry of perpetual crisis that Browning had been writing all along and that he directed specifically to contemporary religious issues in 1864 with such poems as "A Death in the Desert," "Caliban upon Setebos," and the "Epilogue." The last of these provides a fascinating sample of what Browning offered the British public in response to its crisis of faith. The "Epilogue" to *Dramatis Personae* occupies a climactic position at the end of Browning's two most impressive collections of lyrics, and Browning makes a rare appearance in his own person to speak its final stanzas. It may serve here as an appropriate introduction to the ways in which several of the dramatic speakers from Browning's great middle years engage, according to their variously refracted lights, in the giving and taking of meaning.

Following the liturgical pomp of King David in the first section of the poem and Renan's lament for a lost faith in the second, Browning answers both speakers with an intimation of ceaseless becoming, a redemptive vision of imperfection. Through a total immersion in the destructive rush of time, the splashing brilliance and violent play of "Arctic seas" (73), he emerges with this vision:

> *That one Face, far from vanish, rather grows,*
> *Or decomposes but to recompose,*
> *Become my universe that feels and knows.*
>
> (99-101)

With seven verbs swirling through its three lines, the stanza nearly renders pure process. The poem's earlier "presence of the Lord" (19) has been replaced here by a series of present tenses, exceptionally fugitive even for Browning, which keep spilling ahead into the future. The purposive infinitive constructions of "recompose" and "become" are temporally ambiguous; they poise the final line at the very place of becoming, on the threshold between present and future states. These verbal energies of decay and regeneration all but consume the matter they work on, the two substantive nouns of the passage. "Face" and "universe," neither of them very concrete to begin with, finally defy visualization—not because they vanish into the abstract, but because they continually grow together towards new particularity in the unforeseeable future. As befits such a blinding vision of incessant revision, Browning recomposes the stanza in transit, revising the already volatile imagery of the first line with an "or" introducing the alternative predicate of the second.

The passage confronts a crisis of religious meaning by triumphantly embracing crisis as its element. Its shifting figurations elaborate its meaning: that the universality of Browning's "universe," the unity of "that one Face," is an eventual unity, to be felt and known only by and by. Constituted through the flux that the stanza both describes and enacts, "that one Face" (like the face of Eglamor at the close of *Sordello*) is the simplest of possible figures for the play of absence and presence, the processional destruction and recreation that lets meaning live. Or, as Browning explained more succinctly to Alexandra Orr, "That Face, is the face of Christ. That is how I feel him."[4] This religious interpretation is incontestably appropriate but liable to misunderstanding if one forgets how the poet's nonsectarian Christian feeling involved a radical historicizing of Christianity. In "A Death in the Desert" and yet more cogently in the Pope's monologue from *The Ring and the Book*, Browning insists that the face of Christ owes its continuing significance precisely to its figurativeness, its capacity for adaptation. Less an historical figure than a figure of history, Browning's Christ is the promise of meaning, as "that one Face" is the mercifully changing face of time.[5]

In the "Epilogue" Browning diagnoses Renan's fears about "dread succession" (62), the meaningless secularity of profane time, as the symptoms of an insufficiently elastic imagination. Renan and religious skeptics like him exercise too little skepticism toward their own conclusions. They have stopped the play of meaning too soon by exchanging the future for the present, the figurative for the literal, the representation for the void.

> Why, where's the need of Temple, when the walls
> O' the world are that? What use of swells and falls
> From Levites' choir, Priests' cries, and trumpet-calls?

> (96-98)

In giving the answering "fall" to the orthodox "swell" of David, Renan's work suffers the fate awaiting any facile deconstruction; enslaved within the terms of the meaning that it would dismantle, it can do no more than lament that the mantle is fallen. If to a better tempered imagination the mutable "walls / O' the world" may take the place of a deconstructed "Temple," then profane time may be no more than a delusion of nihilistic melancholy. Meaninglessness may be but a temporary shadow through which a skepticism as romantically confident as Browning's sees the traces of a meaning deferred.

Browning suspects the nihilistic skepticism of a Renan, like the "Mesmerism" (1855) and "Transcendentalism" (1855) he also wrote lyrics about, because he suspects the totalitarian character of any predetermining system. By dogmatically proclaiming the death of meaning, nihilism falls into the error of reifying a meaning of its own that precludes further possibilities. Optimism may fall into the same error, as Browning's later poetry is only too capable of demonstrating. Despite bursts of remarkable energy that recur far more frequently than is acknowledged in the prevailing critical estimate of the poet's old age, his later optimism often degenerates into dogma and so goes the way of all systems. Browning's best writing, however, abundantly justifies Yeats's observations "that he was only an optimist because he was an artist who chose hopefulness as his method of expression" and that "thought and speculation were to Browning means of dramatic expression much more than aims in themselves."[6] It is a healthy distrust of thought and speculation as aims in themselves that makes personal pronouncements like the "Epilogue" so rare in the best of Browning, and so rarefied, so skillfully inconclusive, when they do occur.

Time and again when he raises his own voice with the ostensible purpose of delivering his message, Browning seems to be talking about his medium instead. He concludes "The Statue and the Bust" (1855) by lecturing his reader on the worth — even the inevitability — of figuration: as a standard for the motivation and judgment of

187

conduct "The true has no value beyond the sham: / As well the counter as coin, I submit" (235-36). Browning's images for value should be taken quite seriously here: a "coin," his metaphor for the standard of truth against which the sham "counter" is measured, is itself already a signifier, another "counter." Both counters count in Browning's poem by virtue of the value invested in them by human needs and passions, whether generally sanctioned or illicit. Likewise, Browning resolutely declines to apologize for the mystifications of "Bishop Blougram's Apology" and returns to the semantics of Blougram's "not having in readiness / Their nomenclature and philosophy: / He said true things, but called them by wrong names" (994-96). And when Browning comes to rest in *Men and Women*, his "One Word More" is a poem about the power of unarticulated meaning, "the novel / Silent silver lights and darks undreamed of, / Where I hush and bless myself with silence" (195-97). The final lines from *Dramatis Personae*, like those at the thematic climax of *Sordello* (VI.590-603) and at the end of *The Ring and the Book* (XII.835-67), discuss artistic means—composition, figuration, representation, obliquity—as if to suggest that the proper end of Browning's poetry is to foster an awareness of the means whereby meaning may happen.[7]

The value of the dramatic method for sustaining such an awareness is one subject of a concluding poem in *Men and Women*: " 'Transcendentalism: A Poem in Twelve Books.' " Here Browning questions the capacity of a nakedly philosophical poem to "repair our loss" of youthful perception (34). He praises instead the magically restorative power of the blossoming poetic image, "the sudden rose herself" (40), to arrest and refresh the mind and to win readers away from their desiccating, reductive quests after "subtler meanings of what roses say" (36). Yet Browning notes in conclusion that such reductions have an attractive power of their own when they are viewed as psychological phenomena, from a dramatic perspective:

> So come, the harp back to your heart again!
> You are a poem, though your poem's naught.
> The best of all you showed before, believe,
> Was your own boy-face o'er the finer chords
> Bent, following the cherub at the top
> That points to God with his paired half-moon wings.

(46-51)

To refuse to find the song and singer one, to look "o'er the finer chords," beyond the pretensions of argument to its underlying intentions, is to be rewarded by the sight of a human face, here the "boy-face" of rejuvenating aspiration. As Yeats well knew, Browning is the great poetic *dramatist* of thought and speculation, to whose peculiarly ingenious and generous imagination even the most philosophic of men and women may become as roses. The interest of their meaning-making speeches lies not in the conclusions such men and women reach, but in the difference between their conclusions and their ampler human selves. Though their conclusions may be naught, Browning's probing of intentions lets him say to each, "You are a poem."

"A TOCCATA OF GALUPPI'S"

One of the clearest illustrations of the dramatic difference that gives Browning's imagination its start comes in the opening stanza of "A Toccata of Galuppi's" (1855). Disappointed by a meaning that is somehow not what he has meant to find at all, the speaker is torn between conflicting senses of meaning as conclusion and meaning as intention.

> *Oh Galuppi, Baldassaro, this is very sad to find!*
> *I can hardly misconceive you; it would prove me deaf and blind;*
> *But although I take your meaning, 'tis with such a heavy mind!*
>
> (1-3)

The "meaning" to which the speaker refers is that of Galuppi's toc-cata, a "touch-piece" or elegant display of keyboard virtuosity by "a master" (27). That such a musical composition should have a given "meaning," which a listener or performer may "take," seems as questionable as that a poetical composition should be so "taken."[8] Browning's speaker disarms critical suspicions on this account, however, by entertaining them from the first himself. "But although" is already too intricate a locution for one who will be satisfied with a meaning as unequivocal as "dust and ashes" (35); "I can hardly misconceive you" is a way of saying that there must be some mistake. In this stanza as in the poem as a whole, the speaker repersuades himself that there has been no mistake; yet a part of him, the fugitive "boy-face" over the finer chords of this tightly strung text, remains unpersuaded to the last:

> *"Dust and ashes!" So you creak it, and I want the heart to scold.*
> *Dear dead women, with such hair, too — what's become of all the gold*
> *Used to hang and brush their bosoms? I feel chilly and grown old.*
>
> (43-45)

This speaker earns his place in *Men and Women* precisely because he does not, in any simple sense, "want the heart to scold." Confessing in the first line a lack of heart, a deficiency of desire, the speaker revives his desire and names its object in the lines that follow. His return in this final stanza to the erotic energies at the heart of the poem is a protest against his own mistaken reduction of those energies and of the music that has called them forth—albeit the protest of one who begins and ends in subjection to himself.

If the speaker could rest content with "dust and ashes," his burdensome consciousness of error would be lightened. What gives him "such a heavy mind" and the chilling sense of premature old age is the internal conflict that gives Browning his poem. It will prove helpful in investigating this dramatic conflict to recall how often in Browning's dramas psychological conflicts present themselves as conflicts about time. Music is preeminently the medium of time, and the interpretation of life that the speaker hears in Galuppi's music may be conceived as an interpretation of human time.

What? Those lesser thirds so plaintive, sixths diminished, sigh on sigh,
Told them something? Those suspensions, those solutions — "Must we die?"
Those commiserating sevenths — "Life might last! we can but try!"

"Were you happy?" — "Yes." — "And are you still as happy?" — "Yes. And you?"
— "Then, more kisses!" — "Did I stop them, when a million seemed so few?"
Hark, the dominant's persistence till it must be answered to!

So, an octave struck the answer.

(19-25)

Like any music Galuppi's has its closes, but to the ear of Browning's speaker it seems to have little else. He hears in Galuppi's toccata an obsession with closure, with the necessity that it come to an end. The music as performed and heard by the speaker interprets time by imposing upon it a rigorous eschatological obligation that creeps "thro' every nerve" (33). As the speaker's repeated reference to "the answer" suggests, the touch-piece he fingers is nothing if not responsible; its primary responsibility appears to be the application of finishing touches, the discharge of its formal obligations, mirrored by Browning in fifteen stanzas of fifteen-syllable lines. Galuppi's creaking speech in stanzas XII-XV actually imitates musical form; it states, varies, and exactly restates its "dust and ashes" theme. Even in the stanzas just quoted, the music arrives at a conclusion — "So, an octave struck the answer" — as logical as the speaker's conclusions when he reasons about physics, geology, or his "pastime," mathematics (38), and when he triumphs "o'er a secret won from nature's close reserve" (32).

The closeness of this correspondence between the speaker's interpretive activities in music and in other fields should serve as a reminder of what Browning's tinkling prosody makes it easy to forget: that Galuppi's music enters the poem only as subject to the speaker's lyric sovereignty over interpretation. There are, after all, other and suppler ways than this speaker's of interpreting an artistic obsession with closure. The most pertinent counterexample here would be the poetry of Robert Browning, where the possibility of closure also creeps through every nerve but where the finality in closure is nervously qualified, the death in closure indefinitely delayed. For Browning "the dominant's persistence" remains a challenging question that predominates over the striking of answers; the delaying, "commiserating sevenths" of his odd music preserve opportune intervals in which "Life might last! we can but try!" In comparison with Browning, the speaker becomes a man who refuses to try; in comparison with the flexibility of Browningesque time, the speaker's metronomic sense of passing moments, "in due time, one by one" (28), becomes hopelessly, or laughably, rigid.

A poem that invited such an ironic critique of its speaker would be a simpler and a lesser poem than the one that Browning has written in "A Toccata of Galuppi's." An adequate interpretation will recognize that the readerly balancing of sympathy and judgment, which figures so prominently in recent critical appraisal of the dramatic monologue as a literary genre, is here anticipated and deeply internalized within the speaker.[9] To read the poem is to follow a prior balancing act, in the course of which Browning's complex speaker unsteadily commiserates or condemns the various intentions that make him up. This speaker is quite capable of conducting a partial critique of his own conclusive rigidities; what enables him to do so is the irrepressible erotic susceptibility that surfaces in the central stanzas quoted above. It is only through his imagination in those stanzas that the ghosts of the Venetian lovers present themselves and make their haunting speeches; and it remains a moot point whether, even in the speaker's own mind, the mutual responsiveness of their playful questions and answers may not scold him more than the sober responsibility of his intrusive "Hark" scolds them.[10]

Although in the penultimate movement of the poem the speaker safely distances himself from his imagined lovers, regarding them collectively as a dying generation "born to bloom and drop" in "mirth and folly" (40-41), the delicate specificities of his earlier stanzas have already given such deterministic generalization the lie. He has heard in Galuppi's music not the monotone of a single meaning, not the alliterative and rhythmic repetitions of "Dust and ashes, dead and done with, Venice spent what Venice earned" (35), but the different meanings of antiphonal voices. These voices can alter time as their colloquial freshness alters the prosodic timing of Browning's verse. " 'Were you happy?'—'Yes.'—'And are you still as happy?'—'Yes. And you?' " This line uniquely violates a caesural pattern maintained everywhere else in the poem; a question rides across the expected pause at midline in order to celebrate the unique continuity of lovers' play. The line introduces different pauses, filled with erotic anticipation, which enforce an awareness of the lovers' freedom in time, their power to elude the tacit step of "Death" (30). They "break talk off" so that the better taciturnity of such pauses may afford full range to the play of their more intimate voices, while they turn in the meantime to the external props that represent the play, "She, to bite her mask's black velvet—he, to finger on his sword" (17).

By extending imaginative sympathy to his Venetian lovers, the speaker extends his poem. His willingness to give play to their voices lets him attend to those "suspensions" in Galuppi's toccata that stave off its "solutions." He entertains in imagination the possibility of an amorous delay, of "more kisses," and so temporarily postpones the reductive, rational conclusion that "the kissing had to stop" (42). Despite the seeming finality of this reduction, in the last stanza the speaker's earlier sympathy with suspended time returns in the only enjambed line in the poem, the powerfully physical suspension of "all the gold / Used to hang and brush their bosoms." The image emerges through the dust and ashes of passion spent, to represent the apparently lost vitality of musical and erotic time and to resuspend the speaker in the rich irresolution from which he has begun.

It is significant that the dead women should be "dear" and that their sweeping hair should finally be prized as "gold." Throughout the poem the speaker's ambivalences have received economic figuration reminiscent of the leading imagery of Browning's plays. The maestro Galuppi is introduced as a musical merchant of Venice, "where the merchants were the kings"; and his toccata is a vessel laden with questionable cargo: "Here you come with your old music, and here's all the good it brings" (4-5). Here the speaker deliberately depreciates Galuppi's merchandise; he will do so again in his reductive closing of the account: "Venice spent what Venice earned." Meanwhile, however, his running account of the music discloses a "superb abundance" (15): the commercial ebb and flow of an erotic liquidation, where "the sea's the street" and "the Doges used to wed the sea with rings" (6-7). The Venetian lovers base their sexual to-and-fro not on a summing up of what is spent and earned, but on a generous and creative credit in the future: "When they made up fresh adventures for the morrow" (12). It is this basis of credit, the untold promissory wealth of more than a million kisses, that lets them "afford" to pause for Galuppi's recital.

Where the speaker may "triumph o'er a secret wrung from nature's close reserve," his lovers' triumphs are yet to be drawn from each other, from the open reserves of a human nature that scorns natural time and place. Later the speaker hears Galuppi "creaking where a house was burned" (34), creaking a tale of how death has taken the lovers "where they never see the sun" (30). The best commentary on this eschatological reading of the toccata will be found in the earlier passage that it halfheartedly revises:

> *Did young people take their pleasure when the sea was warm in May?*
> *Balls and masks begun at midnight, burning ever to mid-day,*
> *When they made up fresh adventures for the morrow, do you say?*

(10-12)

These lovers have *begun* where they never see the sun; burning with a fresh brilliance of their own, they defy the temporal structures of the solar clock and find night day. In this supernatural commerce, midnight becomes their morrow and the natural plenitude of noon becomes only a provisional moment, an occasion for further planning. As the young people "take their pleasure" in creating a distinctively human time, so the speaker manages, at least momentarily, to take Galuppi's meaning without leaping to conclusions and to accept the imaginative currency of the toccata.[11]

For "I take your meaning" at line 3, Browning originally wrote in 1855, "I give you credit." Although an economic image is certainly suitable here, one may guess that Browning struck this particular image from the poem because it gives the speaker too much credit a little too soon; it represents too full a realization of his dilemma. The speaker does give Galuppi credit, with the deep imaginative investment of stanzas II-VIII; but the burden of his first and last stanzas is that he is a timorous investor, ashamed to realize that he has withdrawn his credit and let the fluctuating economy of the toccata collapse. The final sadness the speaker finds in Galuppi's music is that it opens him to a self-reproach that he is too prudent to investigate and too honest to ignore.

> *But when I sit down to reason, think to take my stand nor swerve,*
> *While I triumph o'er a secret wrung from nature's close reserve,*
> *In you come with your cold music till I creep thro' every nerve.*

(31-33)

In the immediately preceding lines the speaker has dismissed the lovers to sunless death. If the chill in Galuppi's music simply resulted from the meaning that all men and women are mortal, the speaker's sentence should begin with "so" or "and"—not with the puzzling "but."

The "but" must signify a discontinuity between his interpretation and what he hears lingering beyond interpretation in the music, a dissatisfaction with what his reason tells him must be true. By saying "but," he testifies to something unsettling in the toccata that makes him swerve from rational inevitability: something like a superfluous grace note, recalling the "graceful" generosity of the lovers in deferring to Galuppi's performance as a welcome digression in the course of love (16). The speaker is chilled here and again at the last line of the poem by an unspoken conviction of his own poverty. He dimly sees that by a failure in credit that is also a failure in imaginative desire, he has abandoned the august anticipations that keep "young people" young for the tight-fisted meanings of one "grown old."

"ANDREA DEL SARTO
(CALLED 'THE FAULTLESS PAINTER')"

"I am grown peaceful as old age to-night. / I regret little, I would change still less." By the time one comes upon these apparently restorative lines (244-45) from the last movement of "Andrea del Sarto" (1855), one should find them as chilling as anything in Galuppi's music. Spoken by an old master of painting rather than a musical maestro, these lines evince a cold and quiet control beyond the reach of Galuppi's unsettled auditor. Instead of saying, "I feel chilly and grown old," Andrea del Sarto masters his emotion from the more safely contemplative distance afforded by a similitude: "I am grown peaceful as old age." The object of Andrea's detached, aesthetic contemplation here is his own life, a well-wrought study in "common greyness" (35), a masterpiece of willed defeat. In reviewing his failed art and ruined marriage and finding them good, Andrea exercises the perverse power of impotence, which gives his picturesque still life its closed and repetitive meaning.

An analysis of Andrea's jealously guarded impotence may begin with his assertion that, in the practice of his art, the intention and the execution are one:

> I can do with my pencil what I know,
> What I see, what at bottom of my heart
> I wish for, if I ever wish so deep —
> Do easily, too — when I say, perfectly,
> I do not boast, perhaps.

> (60-64)

An assertion of this kind is at best difficult to substantiate; Andrea refers Lucrezia to the approving criticisms of "the Legate" and of connoisseurs in France (65-66), and scholars refer to Vasari's warm praise for Andrea's technical excellence.[12] If one refers instead to the evidence of Andrea's rhetoric, at this as at every other point in

194

the poem, it becomes impossible to believe his assertion in any direct sense.

Andrea's "low-pulsed forthright craftsman's hand" (82) may indeed be able to work without preliminary "sketches" or "studies" (68), but the hesitations and repetitions that characterize Andrea's speech indicate that impulses may reach his hand only after being carefully stepped down through a preliminary process of internal conversion. A forthright assertion of technical perfection should not end, as Andrea's does, with a qualifying "perhaps." Nor should such an assertion call attention to its diction by questioning the terms in which it is framed. When Andrea says, "when I say, perfectly, / I do not boast," his language opens the very fault between meaning and formulation that he ostensibly denies in his faultless painting. What seems to begin as an unconditional pronouncement that Andrea can translate any wish into paint, even if he wishes ever so deep, issues in a conditional clause introducing a doubt as to the depth of any of his wishes: "if I ever wish so deep" suggests that he is a habitually shallow wisher who has left the lower reaches of his will unsounded. Andrea's works are faultless because he has let his technique dictate to his creative intention. He can do with his pencil what he knows because he has chosen to know only so much as he can do: "I, painting from myself and to myself, / Know what I do" (90-91).

This explanation of Andrea's shortcomings in art would link him with the earlier Pictor Ignotus. Yet to compare their monologues is to mark a difference in sophistication that distinguishes the best of *Men and Women* and *Dramatis Personae* from the lyrics of 1842 and 1845. In the later volumes Browning gives his characters a far greater degree of the reflective self-consciousness that Cleon identifies as "the sense of sense" ("Cleon" [1855], 224). The Pictor Ignotus and the Duke at Ferrara are largely unwitting victims of their own defenses, and a reader emerges from their monologues understanding a great deal about them of which they remain unaware. In the later volumes of dramatic lyrics Browning elicits finer measurements as he narrows the gap between conscious and unconscious motives. By bringing his speakers closer to self-understanding, he brings them closer to his reader—and perhaps to himself as well. Browning's later speakers exhibit an advanced awareness of the stratagems through which they make sense of their various worlds—an awareness that requires that their monologues be read as *knowing* self-interpretations, consciously fabricated and tendentiously put forth. "Andrea del Sarto" and "Cleon" are "Pictor Ignotus" and "My Last Duchess" raised to the higher power of "the sense of sense," and they reward a higher-powered scrutiny of their speaker's motives.

When Andrea says, "I know what I do," he not only means that like the Pictor Ignotus he has failed by conforming his aspirations to his supposed abilities, he also means that he has done so knowingly and for a purpose. He knows the value of his artistic works and knows as well the value of that more ambitious work that is very much in progress throughout the poem, the shaping and disposition of his life:

> Eh? the whole seems to fall into a shape
> As if I saw alike my work and self
> And all that I was born to be and do,
> A twilight-piece.

(46-49)

These lines establish the dialectic that it is Andrea's supreme achievement to create and sustain, between "my work and self" and "all that I was born to be and do," between what he is and what—but for the obstacles he has painstakingly placed in his own way—he might have been. The practice of a faultless, minor art is only a part of "the whole," the scheme of life that Andrea articulates with every stroke of his poem: his intricate yet faultless accommodation of a need to fail.

In the background of Andrea's accommodating autobiographical scheme lies his version of the Browningesque philosophy of the imperfect: "Ah, but a man's reach should exceed his grasp, / Or what's a heaven for?" (97-98). That these lines, along with Pippa's "God's in his heaven" (Pippa Passes, I.i.227), should have been untimely ripped from context and delivered up as Browning's moral of life is not quite the irony of literary history that it would appear; or, if there be irony, it is Browning's and is already written into his poetry. It is remarkable that Browning should have entrusted his cherished beliefs to so devious a speaker as Andrea. Betty Miller steps with convincing ease from poetry to biography and finds the poem a confession of Browning's besetting psychosexual weaknesses.[13] Yet the very proximity of Andrea to Browning, and the remarkable extent of Browning's dramatic trust in writing this monologue, may also be taken as indexes of poetic strength. "Andrea del Sarto" represents one of Browning's most intimate engagements with a threat he greatly feared: the tendency of poetic meaning generally, and of his own deep-running convictions in particular, to precipitate a doctrine—or, in Andrea's phrase, "to fall into a shape."

Nothing could be more appropriate than that Andrea's words should have acquired dogmatic weight over the decades, since it is Andrea who, with more persistent ingenuity than any other monologist, dogmatizes and therefore betrays Browning's leading ideas.

196

Andrea is a perfect Browningite, and his praise of incompleteness in lines 78-114 presents a summation of the poet's lesson that is at least as reliable as those attempted by later and less capable speakers at gatherings of the Browning Society. A doctrine of incompleteness ought perhaps to be privileged above other doctrines to resist such complete summation, but Browning foresaw in writing this poem what the development of his reputation has subsequently confirmed: that even a doctrine of incompleteness must earn its privilege to resist formulation by remaining less a doctrine than an active teaching.

Once teaching has hardened into doctrine, it becomes a commodity that a technician as clever as Andrea can use for his own ends. Andrea has taught himself enough of the doctrine of imperfection to insure that he need never undergo the growing pains of further learning. He sees formal failings in the works of Rafael and of lesser painters in Florence (112, 71) and sees too that these failings testify to a grandeur withheld. Andrea determines to aggrandize himself by multiplying the advantage of his doctrinal lever and outfailing them all. Since "less is more" (78), he chooses to be least through the radical expedient of withholding his most.

> In this world, who can do a thing, will not;
> And who would do it, cannot, I perceive:
> Yet the will's somewhat—somewhat, too, the power—
> And thus we half-men struggle. At the end,
> God, I conclude, compensates, punishes.

(137-41)

Where others discover a frustrating gap between reach and grasp, between their excessive aspirations and the limits of their technical capabilities, Andrea frustrates himself in advance by arranging an equal and opposite gap between grasp and reach. Literally self-effacing at line 197 ("Ay, but the soul! he's Rafael! rub it out!"), Andrea purposely intends less than he can perform so that he may number himself among the "half-men," the glorious failures of art, without enduring their struggles. His doctrine of imperfection shows him the low road into a compensatory heaven, one that he ultimately prefers to the heaven of artists who "Reach many a time a heaven that's shut to me" (84) and of Rafael, "Reaching, that heaven might so replenish him, / Above and through his art" (109-10). In the celestial vision of the New Jerusalem that ends the poem, Andrea reaffirms this preference, "choosing" to be "overcome" by more aspiring artists, the better to repay himself with an afterlife providing renewed opportunity and support for a lifelong habit of regret (265-66). Such is the power of Andrea's calculated impotence that it will transform

197

"four great walls in the New Jerusalem" (261) into a cozier place where he will feel more at home: "The grange whose four walls make his world" (170).

Andrea imagines the heavenly opportunities of the future in order to anticipate the luxurious sensation of having let them slip, like Lucrezia's hand, through his fingers. This proleptic sentimentality, or anticipatory nostalgia, is the major temporal mode governing the "twilight-piece" that is his monologue. As always in Browning, temporality and psychology exhibit a close relation here; Andrea's way of organizing time is also a way of protecting himself against failure on any but his own terms.

> There's the bell clinking from the chapel-top;
> That length of convent-wall across the way
> Holds the trees safer, huddled more inside;
> The last monk leaves the garden; days decrease,
> And autumn grows, autumn in everything.
>
> (41-45)

Like other monologists, Andrea clearly associates the passage of time, marked by a ringing bell, with diminution and loss. The distinctive revelation of Andrea's monologue is that he associates time and loss with security as well. As Andrea sees the trees safely huddled within a protective wall, so he finds security within his deeply internalized temporal defenses. By anticipating his losses, he assures them; by choosing impotence, he makes the power of self-fulfilling prophecy his own.

A preemptive loser, Andrea builds his home on the expectation of loss so that with every fresh failure he may encounter not a disappointment, but the comforting, familiar return of just what he knew would happen. "Nostalgia" is etymologically a homesickness; the return of the last monk homeward from the garden suggests the nostalgic repetition of failure that is so dear to Andrea that he will sacrifice for its sake both his marriage and his work. Recurrent economic imagery indicates his knowledge of the sacrifices that keep his house in order; later in the poem he concentrates this knowledge into the cryptic sentence, "I'll pay my fancy" (226). Andrea lavishes his "fancy," both his imagination and his love, on the fancy design of a time scheme guaranteeing him a future of painless because unsurprising failure.

When Andrea turns again to the external scene, it is with all the complacency of the minor prophet's I-told-you-so:

> See, it is settled dusk now; there's a star;
> Morello's gone, the watch-lights show the wall,

198

The cue-owls speak the name we call them by.
Come from the window, love, — come in, at last,
Inside the melancholy little house
We built to be so gay with.

(208-13)

These lines, like the earlier descriptive passage, measure time's irrevocable losses by noting the "settled dusk" and the disappearance of the mountain Morello, but the earlier wall reappears here as a countermeasure of Andrea's continued success in defending himself against the pain of loss. "The watch-lights show the wall" because, as images both of civil security and of time as organized into the watches of the night, they illuminate Andrea's providential planning. The cue-owls speak on cue; while the elusive song of the wise thrush in Browning's resolutely undomesticated "Home-Thoughts, From Abroad" arouses expectation, these accommodating birds satisfy it instead, marking time by repeating what they have always said.

Andrea picks up the cue-owls' repetition in the lines that follow, bidding Lucrezia to come, again to come, and yet again to come inside: "Come from the window, love, — come in, at last, / Inside the melancholy little house / We built to be so gay with" (211-13). The repetition of this deliberately uninviting proposition, like all of Andrea's defensive repetitions, lets him prepare for the rejection that he knows is sure to follow: in telling Lucrezia to "come," he anticipates her eventual departure, as he will later encourage it with the ready question "Must you go?" (219) and finally decree it with a command: "Go, my Love" (267). Andrea's phrase "the melancholy little house / We built to be so gay with" manifests the full subtlety of his prophetic nostalgia. By inverting the chronology of his decayed marriage and putting "melancholy" first, he poisons domestic gaiety before giving it a chance. He builds into his syntax the same homesick intention to dwell in failure with which he has built his house in the first place and with which he has conducted his marriage ever since.

In the chiming of the chapel bell and hooting of the cue-owls, Andrea hears a reassuring echo of his habitual organization of life as repetition.[14] The repetitions of "autumn" and "come," in the passages cited above, bespeak his need to see all growth and becoming as toil cooperant to an end: the perfection of an anticipated loss that validates his nostalgic homing instinct. It is this instinct, Andrea's will to fail, that gives meaning to his reconstructed memory of artistic glory in France, where he has deemed the "humane great monarch's golden look" (153) and the "frank French eyes" of the courtiers (160) well lost for Lucrezia's "face" and for the promise of failure that Andrea has made her represent:

And, best of all, this, this, this face beyond,
This in the background, waiting on my work,
To crown the issue with a last reward!
A good time, was it not, my kingly days?
And had you not grown restless . . . but I know—
'T is done and past; 't was right, my instinct said;
Too live the life grew, golden and not grey,
And I'm the weak-eyed bat no sun should tempt
Out of the grange whose four walls make his world.
How could it end in any other way?
You called me, and I came home to your heart.

(162-72)

This passage reveals the perverse intent with which Andrea draws Lucrezia into the background of his scheme of life.[15] The homecoming of the final line is precisely the "last reward" that he most desires. His instinct to home in on failure finds a goal in Lucrezia's "face"—but not until his sentence has given play to that instinct in its own right. Like the strange and nameless id that it is, Andrea's homing instinct rises to the surface in the opening lines of this passage, and—for once in the poem—all but undoes his control of language and narrative time: "this, this, this face beyond, / This in the background." The compulsive return of "this," and not any sign from poor Lucrezia, represents the call that determines Andrea's vocation as prophet of his own doom. His insistent will to fail, proleptically "waiting on my work," confers upon his eventual failure the instinctive rightness of an expectation that has been perfectly fulfilled.

"How could it end in any other way?" Andrea's question is an instance of the rhetoric of self-fulfilling divination that recurs throughout the monologue. "So free we seem, so fettered fast we are!" (51); "All is as God over-rules" (133); "God is just" (213); "Let each one bear his lot" (252); "No doubt, there's something strikes a balance" (257). Delighted that character is fate, Andrea sings in his fetters a hymn celebrating the divinely poetic justice, the pleasing aesthetic balance, of the life he has freely contrived for himself. The entire monologue falls into shape as a faultlessly rounded episode in this life. Andrea bargains for his hour with Lucrezia in the full expectation that he will lose her to her lover; the opening promise that "all shall happen as you wish" (3) also foretells that all shall happen as Andrea wishes. By preempting the pain of his loss from the beginning, he becomes the knowing author of its fated inevitability and comes into the commanding strength of his final, imperative "Go, my Love."

200

"FRA LIPPO LIPPI"

In "Andrea del Sarto" and "A Toccata of Galuppi's," Browning plays a speaker's sterile assurance of meaning against his buried but unquiet consciousness of better possibilities, possibilities that each speaker denies to himself, "grown old," and attributes instead to figures of youth, to Rafael or to the Venetian lovers. In "Fra Lippo Lippi" (1855), Browning gives the stage to such a figure of youth, a painter as aware of his own position at the beginning of a new move-ment in art as he is aware "that the morning-star's about to shine" (272). The interest of Fra Lippo's monologue, and particularly of the theory of artistic representation that he expounds, lies in the strata-gems through which this youthful awareness is preserved. Like An-drea del Sarto and the speaker in "A Toccata of Galuppi's," Lippo quarrels with tendencies in himself. Although his quarrel moves in the contrary direction to theirs, he too uses lay figures—notably, as spokesman for prior masters in painting, the aptly named "Prior" of the Carmelite cloister—as determinants of his later and younger posi-tion, as guarantors of his precious sense of standing at a beginning.

Fra Lippo's escape from the clutches of the police into "the grey beginning" of dawn (392) is only the last of the series of escapes from enclosures external and internal that makes up his story. G. Wil-son Knight writes that in this poem Browning is "fighting for physi-cal reality and vitality as against a premature spiritualizing of the human."[16] This remark illuminates the poem's implicit analogy be-tween the relation of body to soul and the relation of an artifact to its meaning: Lippo's defense of pictorial realism is a fight for the in-dependence of art from a premature determination of its meaning. It will not be disputed that Fra Lippo's aesthetic opinions are ultimate-ly Browning's, but Browning keeps his poem human and defends it against hasty disclosure of those opinions by letting Lippo gradually work them out for himself.[17] Over the course of the monologue, Lippo emerges from the enclosures of received opinions into his own as an artist who has broken "out of bonds" (223, 341).

The enclosure that worries Lippo most is the familiar enclosure of artistic meaning, and one of the questions that Lippo worries most is the question of what constitutes "intensity" of meaning in pictorial representation. According to the Prior, who calls for a highly formal-ized and abstract art subordinating medium to message, the intensity of art resides in its ideological efficiency: "Your business is to paint the souls of men" (183); "Give us no more of body than shows soul!" (188). Lippo's first answer to this call is a rattling of the salaried moralist's chains:

201

> *Thus, yellow does for white*
> *When what you put for yellow's simply black,*
> *And any sort of meaning looks intense*
> *When all beside itself means and looks nought.*

(201-4)

This suggestion that there may be more than one sort of meaning for painting to render is at first encouraging in its heterodoxy, but Lippo falls into the blasphemer's error of adopting the very presuppositions of the system he wants to overturn.[18] He follows the Prior in regarding medium and message as antagonistic; what is worse, he accepts the Prior's notion of hypostatized meaning. The visual imagery of these lines—"beside" and the repeated "looks"—treats meaning as a thing, an object presented to the eye. It would seem reasonable to find a painter talking in this way; Fra Lippo, however, is not any painter but a Browning painter inaugurating the art of the future. The new movement in art that Lippo's monologue heralds will require a more radically temporal approach to the artistic process.

These lines occur early in Lippo's discussion of representation as an instance of the traditional thinking about meaning from which he is trying to break away. A few lines later he substitutes emotional for religious meanings and asks a question about a portrait of the Prior's "niece": "is it so pretty / You can't discover if it means hope, fear, / Sorrow or joy?" (209-11). The question leaves Lippo still in the Prior's traditional mode; the picture remains the sign of a given meaning. With his next overt reference to meaning, however, Lippo breaks new ground by returning to the tradition and revising it, taking a fresh look at its beginnings:

> *For me, I think I speak as I was taught;*
> *I always see the garden and God there*
> *A-making man's wife: and, my lesson learned,*
> *The value and significance of flesh,*
> *I can't unlearn ten minutes afterwards.*

(265-69)

Like other innovators, Lippo conceives his project as one of renovation. At the revolutionary moment when his "whole soul revolves" (250), he rediscovers a creative source prior to the Prior, an act of original "making" that he may restore by repeating it in his own way: "Can't I take breath and try to add life's flash?" (213). The paradoxical temporality of the passage suggests a redemptive dialectic of repetition: the habitual present tense of "I always see" governs Lippo's absolute phrase "my lesson learned" to reinforce the repeatability of his lesson, its absolute value as a creative model to which

202

he may continually return. In fact Lippo has subtly begun to imitate this model earlier in the monologue when he patterns an account of his boyish artistic genesis on the rhetoric of Genesis itself: "First, every sort of monk, the black and white, / I drew them, fat and lean" (145-46); "So God created man in his own image, in the image of God created he him; male and female created he them" (Genesis 1:27).[19] Exactly what Lippo's lesson has to teach him, what the value and significance of flesh may be, are questions that the passage leaves unresolved. The flesh, the physical world in which the flesh participates, and (by the analogy running through these lines) the made work of art, all become the bearers of an unspecified yet unforgettable meaning.

Lippo eventually comes to see that the intensity of meaning that he seeks in a new art will proceed from the artist's refusal to specify a given meaning:

> This world's no blot for us,
> Nor blank; it means intensely, and means good:
> To find its meaning is my meat and drink.
>
> (313-15)

Here meaning becomes a temporal process, a verb seeking its object outside the confines of the present. In the proof sheets of *Men and Women* the first line read, "This world's no trap for us." Browning's cancellation of "trap" in favor of the more painterly "blot" suggests that, from Lippo's perspective on the world as a continuing work of signification, the two terms may be synonymous, that such a liberating perspective commits the artist who shares it to a new realism that abhors a blot, to a new clarity of articulation in the signs of his art. The world "means good," betokening a benevolent intentionality that the wisely mimetic painter will imitate.[20]

Fra Lippo represents such a world most faithfully by conceiving his painting as an exploration; and the activity of finding, rather than any meaning found, provides the "meat and drink" nourishing the body of his work. A commercial explorer like all of Browning's venturous figures of youth, Lippo gives the world credit. His pursuit of verisimilitude is a gesture of metaphysical as well as pictorial fidelity: he trusts the world to mean. "Lending" his mind out (306) both to the visible world and to spectators whom he helps to see that world anew, he replaces the Prior's strictly hierarchical, one-way "praise" of God (191) with a more fluid, economic, and self-respecting "thanks" for the freshly apprehended beauty of God's works: "you'll find the soul you have missed, / Within yourself, when you return him thanks" (219-20).[21] Much as Lippo's iconoclastic insistence upon temporality frees painting from the Prior's hypostasis of meaning, so here his notion of perception as a grateful commerce offers an escape from the Prior's iconic reification of the soul (184-87). The human soul, like the meaning of Lippo's humanistic art, finds itself in process; both are agencies at work in time.

This world "means intensely, and means good." Here Lippo discovers that the intensity of an art that imitates the world consists in its extensity, its capacious temporal reach: it means intensely by intimating a future good. In a passage immediately following this discovery, Lippo takes note of the distance he has traveled since his spatial complaint at line 203 that "any sort of meaning looks intense."

> "Ay, but you don't so instigate to prayer!"
> Strikes in the Prior: "when your meaning's plain
> "It does not say to folk — remember matins,
> "Or, mind you fast next Friday!" Why, for this
> What need of art at all? A skull and bones,
> Two bits of stick nailed crosswise, or, what's best,
> A bell to chime the hour with, does as well.
>
> (316-22)

As in the earlier passage, Lippo wishes to assert the importance of technique, but now he has a stronger basis for his assertion. If this world's meaning is always in the making, then the artistic technique that elaborates its meaning must assume a new dignity and responsibility. Fra Lippo no longer places his medium in competition with an externally imposed message; the Prior's "meaning" in line 317, identical with the hypostatized "meaning" of line 203, is what Lippo has learned to do without. It is in the absence of such a meaning that the "need of art" arises, and the need of an artistic medium capable of keeping time with the different meaning of a developing world.

The Prior's voice "strikes in" where it does, with the regularity of "a bell to chime the hour with," so that Lippo may measure against it the irregular, unpredictable sense of time that his art of temporalized meaning would foster. He claims for art the power of wonder, the power to retard clock time, to stop the mind not with a meaning, but with a meaning deferred.

> The beauty and the wonder and the power,
> The shapes of things, their colours, lights and shades,
> Changes, surprises, — and God made it all!
> — For what? Do you feel thankful, ay or no,
> For this fair town's face, yonder river's line,
> The mountain round it and the sky above,
> Much more the figures of man, woman, child,
> These are the frame to? What's it all about?

204

To be passed over, despised? or dwelt upon,
Wondered at?

                              (283-92)

"God made it all!" "For what?" "What's it all about?" Fra Lippo's questions about the meaning of the phenomena around him receive only the answer with which they have begun, that the creation means intensely. The value and significance of flesh are that flesh has a value and a significance; it is instinct with a purpose transforming physical facts into imaginative figures. The town acquires a "face"; the river determines a "line"; the entire landscape becomes a "frame" for human "figures"; and each of these figurations contributes to the scenic intensity of a meaning everywhere implicit yet nowhere revealed.

Figuration is everywhere in Lippo's monologue, which contains over twenty references to the face or to facial features. What he loves in the face is its infinite suggestiveness, and he returns to the face so often for its restorative power of suggestion, its power to induce "wonder." "Wonder" is Lippo's name here, as it is Browning's elsewhere, for the sense of abeyance, the sense of suspension in a gap of perceptual time between signs and their significance.[22] This gap is not "to be passed over"; such hasty transition is the office of the Prior, who objects to the "wonder at lines, colours, and what not" aroused by Lippo's early paintings (192) and who urges him instead, Lippo says, to paint his subjects "So ill, the eye can't stop there, must go further" (200). But Lippo's purpose as a painter is to stop the eye from passing too quickly, to make it dwell lovingly on "things we have passed / Perhaps a hundred times nor cared to see" (301-2). As Lippo puts it in one of his punning condensations, "The world and life's too big to pass for a dream" (251). The world is not the illusion that the Prior's theology takes it to be; it will not pass for that. Nor will it be bypassed for the sake of the dream of transcendental meaning that theology would erect in its stead. Big with the beauty and the wonder and the power of a perpetually imminent disclosure, Lippo's art refuses to "stop" with the Prior's Giotto (190) and wins him a place at the beginning of art's future.

Fra Lippo ends his monologue with a parable about the difficulty of retaining this place, a cinematic rehearsal of his own appearance in an intended *Coronation of the Virgin*. Lippo emerges "As one by a dark stair into a great light, / Music and talking" (362-63), into his picture of heaven, replete with God, Madonna and child, angels, and saints. The effect upon Lippo of such an orthodox enclosure—from the deity "ringed" by angels (349) and the holy "secured at their devotion" (360), to "my old serge gown and rope that goes all round"

(367)—is understandably to precipitate an attack of claustrophobic anxiety: "I, in this presence, this pure company! / Where's a hole, where's a corner for escape?" (368-69). The episode may be taken as an expression of Lippo's characteristic fear of entrapment in what must be for an artist its least tolerable guise: entrapment by the forms of his own fiction. In its less severe stages, this phobia may make for artistic health by protecting a painter (or poet) from the premature crystallization of creative intention that comes from his believing too simply in the truth of what he has made. On the other hand, the paralysis of Lippo, "mazed, motionless, and moonstruck" (364), suggests that in extreme cases of such phobia, when figuration becomes utterly suspect, an artist's intention may be desiccated and the process of creation inhibited altogether: "Back I shrink" (365).

Lippo's parable tells the story of his salvation from this artistic dilemma, the story of how "all's saved for me" (388) through a restored faith in the difference that distinguishes fictions from facts and lies alike. The agent of Lippo's salvation, an angelic figure of his own creation, checks him from shrinking back too quickly. She extends a helping hand to remind him of the temporal promise of figuration:

> Then steps a sweet angelic slip of a thing
> Forward, puts out a soft palm — "Not so fast!"
> —Addresses the celestial presence, "nay —
> "He made you and devised you, after all,
> "Though he's none of you! Could Saint John there draw —
> "His camel-hair make up a painting-brush?
> "We come to brother Lippo for all that,
> "Iste perfecit opus!"
>
> (370-77)

Lippo's good angel saves him from his claustrophobic fears by openly announcing that she and the pure company of the celestial presence are fictions that Lippo has "made" and "devised" — not naked truths, but not vain shadows either; not facts, not *mere* fictions, but enabling fictions, with powers and privileges of their own to confer. Earlier in the monologue Lippo has argued that the figurations of an intensely meaning world are to be dwelt on and wondered at, and the angelic announcement in these lines claims for artistic figuration a like respect. It is the peculiar privilege of figuration to offer what is neither a certainty nor an absurdity but rather a possibility of meaning. Lippo's good angel invites him to dwell in that possibility when she tells him what imaginative figures always have to tell those who will listen: "Not so fast!"

A provisional trust in the pretense of fiction will let Lippo resume

206

his abandoned authorial intention and proceed towards the moment when he has completed the work, *Iste perfecit opus*. The fiction will be made perfect by taking cognizance of its own fictionality; Lippo's painting himself into the *Coronation of the Virgin* will be an end that crowns the work by violating its heavenly purity and so leaving its meaning open. Only an open meaning will be true to the process whereby Lippo has brought the work into being: a difficult process of opening himself to the independence of the figures he goes on to paint. Lippo's recognition of this difficulty may dictate a textual difficulty in his angel's address. Her paradoxical ascription of priority first to the artist ("He made you and devised you, after all") and then to the fiction ("We come to brother Lippo for all that") traces a genuine paradox of artistic making. Lippo's ultimate awareness that the celestial company are figments devised by his imagination "after all" is one that he must take care to keep ultimate if he is to paint them intensely.[23] He must postpone this awareness to a moment that arrives only "after all"; he must heed the voice that says, "Not so fast!"

Such deliberate suspension is a secret of imaginative capability throughout Browning's poetry. It is the great trick of the poet at once subjective and objective, the most compelling of Victorian dramatic lyricists, to defer to the creations of his own imagination as other, as somehow temporarily real. Blake, who wrote of his own visionary forms dramatic, also wrote in one of the proverbs from *The Marriage of Heaven and Hell* that "the most sublime act is to set another before you." Browning's creative deference to the alien power of his men and women, his setting another before him, sets the scene of his sublimely, grotesquely dramatic writing. The intentional hesitation at the origin of his art of disclosure lets images come to the artist as with a vitality all their own. Hence the happy accuracy of the angel's "We come to brother Lippo for all that." Hence, too, the appearance in Lippo's painting of the otherwise superfluous Job as patron of "painters who need his patience" (359). Job attains heroic stature in his story by virtue of the same ability that makes Lippo a hero in his parable and in Browning's poem: patience, the ability to wait for meaning.

In Lippo's world, however, as in Browning's, patient expectation is less often fulfilled than it is rewarded with a surprise; attendant anxieties give to an artist's patience a creative urgency and edge.[24] The healing address of Lippo's good angel is too "sweet" and "soft" to sharpen this creative edge, and Lippo rebels against her complacency by proceeding to retrieve a necessary measure of the unexpected.

> *So, all smile —*
> *I shuffle sideways with my blushing face*

> *Under the cover of a hundred wings*
> *Thrown like a spread of kirtles when you're gay*
> *And play hot cockles, all the doors being shut,*
> *Till, wholly unexpected, in there pops*
> *The hothead husband!*

(377-83)

With this fetching simile Lippo sidesteps the straight line of orthodox approbation and pops out from under its covering canopy. The figure of the "hothead husband" has the suggestive indeterminacy of similar figures in *Sordello*, but at least one of the things that it may represent here is Lippo's anxious consciousness of artistic tradition. Insofar as he is an heir of that tradition, Lippo performs his work by playing with another artist's muse—Giotto's muse, perhaps, as courted by a century of imitators.

If Lippo is to further the history of art by making paintings that mean in his own different way, he must bear tradition in mind. He must anticipate the tendency of past works suddenly to reappear in works of the present, their tendency in any age to burst into the house of contemporary art, claim a husband's rights, and assert control over works that have aspired to be modern. Otherwise the game will be up; for Lippo to believe in the security of "all the doors being shut" against the incursions of artistic orthodoxy will be to paint himself into a corner of another man's heaven. By fastening the door against tradition and ignoring it, an artist only hastens its return to govern his work in some "wholly unexpected" way that he is powerless to change. In closing his parable, Lippo reintroduces the note of anxiety as a reminder of the vigilant defense, the expectation of the unforeseen, which has motivated his flagrantly improvisatory monologue. When he dismisses the police by saying, "I know my own way back" (391), he means that his own way forward, towards the beginning of a new art, lies through a continuing engagement with the art of the past. Fra Lippo's surest augury of success in this engagement comes with a Paracelsan vision of his successors: "Oh, oh, / It makes me mad to see what men shall do / And we in our graves!" (311-13). He asserts his place in a living tradition by anticipating his future status as a past master, a "hothead husband" of the muse in his own right.

208

CLEON ORDERS HIS URN

Death, death! It is this harping on death
I despise so much, this idle and often
cowardly as well as ignorant harping! Why
should we not change like everything else?
In fiction, in poetry, in so much of both,
French as well as English, and, I am told,
in American art and literature, the shadow
of death — call it what you will, despair,
negation, indifference — is upon us. But what
fools who talk thus! Why, amico mio, *you know*
as well as I that death is life, just as our
daily, our momentarily dying body is none the
less alive and ever recruiting new forces of
existence. Without death, which is our
crapelike churchyardy word for change, for
growth, there could be no prolongation of that
which we call life. Pshaw! it is foolish to
argue upon such a thing even. For myself, I
deny death as an end of everything. Never
say of me that I am dead!

Browning to William Sharp [1]

Browning knew as early as *Pauline* that artistic tradition is a fiction, perhaps an indispensable one, that is constituted and maintained by artists long before it is reconstituted by the custodians of artistic history. The fiction of artistic tradition, like any living fiction, is perennially subject to fresh interpretation. Browning revises Shelley as the Sun-treader, and Fra Lippo Lippi revalues the school of Giotto — each in order to place himself at the beginning

209

of a new chapter in the history of art that he is engaged in writing. In "Cleon," Browning creates an artist who does just the opposite and inscribes himself into what he hopes will be a concluding paragraph: "Live long and happy, and in that thought die: / Glad for what was! Farewell" (336-37). Cleon is finally so "glad for what was," so happy with the task of imposing closure, and so uneasy with anything else, that he may be invited to perform that task here.

According to Cleon's overwhelmingly retrospective view of artistic tradition, he and his multifarious accomplishments in poetry, sculpture, painting, and music, "all my works wherein I prove my worth" (318), are worthy because of their climactic position. The meaning of artistic tradition coalesces in Cleon's sympathetic unification of the works of Homer, Terpander, Phidias, and other precursors, "running these into one soul" (144): "In such a synthesis the labour ends" (94). History stops with Cleon; and he evaluates his achievements by the ahistorical, neo-Aristotelian or proto-Arnoldian criteria of combination (60), composition (65), wholeness (77), and completeness (79). He sees the life of art steadily and sees it whole, because in his deliberate view that life has ceased to grow.[2]

Whether or not Browning had anyone so specific as Arnold in mind for a model, the poem concerns itself less with Cleon's position than with the lyric play between that position and Cleon's motive for taking it up. A central and potent motive is the need to vindicate himself as an important artist. His fiction of artistic tradition satisfies this need by driving competing artists from his field of vision. Cleon's ideal of truncated progress lets him remain glad for what was by accommodating the works of earlier artists as partial achievements that anticipate his consummate integrity. He is a better artist because a later one, "For where had been the progress otherwise?" (91). At the same time, by calling a halt to progress in his entrenched present, he proleptically eliminates his successors from the running. The perfection of his works leaves nothing to be done by future artists: "How shall a certain part, pronounced complete, / Endure effacement by another part? / Was the thing done?—then, what's to do again?" (79-81). Like that other classicist, the Bishop at St. Praxed's (1845), Cleon orders his urn by denying the future; the dying Bishop's inability to recognize and bless his sons bespeaks a less somber version of the isolating impulse within this speaker.

Cleon's fiction of tradition is not the first such consoling fiction that he has made. His letter reveals that a need for artistic vindication has been with him for some time and has at least on one occasion directed his choice of a theme:

> And thus our soul, misknown, cries out to Zeus
> To vindicate his purpose in our life:
> Why stay we on the earth unless to grow?
> Long since, I imaged, wrote the fiction out,
> That he or other god descended here
> And, once for all, showed simultaneously
> What, in its nature, never can be shown,
> Piecemeal or in succession;—showed, I say,
> The worth both absolute and relative
> Of all his children from the birth of time,
> His instruments for all appointed work.

(112-22)

Presumably this "fiction," like Cleon's fiction of tradition, justifies the comprehensiveness of his synthetic labors in "all appointed work." He invokes the descent of his deity in a critical rather than an inspirational capacity for the purpose of conducting a last judgment that includes "all his children from the birth of time." In Browning's poetry the birth of time is a potentially self-renewing process; but Cleon's fiction turns it into a forced march terminating now, "once for all," in the existence of Cleon as the last and most favored of children. Cleon's is a far cry from the cry of Paul at Athens in the verse from which Browning drew his epigraph for the poem: "For in him we live, and move, and have our being; as certain also of your own poets have said, For we are also his offspring" (Acts 17:28). In comparison with Paul's ecumenical life and movement, Cleon's desire for apocalyptic closure seeks fulfillment in what amounts to a curse of sterility banning further offspring.

Yet the fact that as a poet Cleon has to write his fiction out witnesses to the very fertility of time that he is eager to deny. He acknowledges what Sordello has had to acknowledge before him in a seminal passage, which Browning is rewriting here: that the attempt to render "the simultaneous and the sole / By the successive and the many" is doomed by the piecemeal temporality of language (Sordello, II.594-95). Good poems, and good fictions of artistic history for that matter, welcome their temporality and give it play; they owe their success to the use they make of time, to the dramatically unfolding variations and conflicts of which their stories consist. Cleon's reference to writing may remind a reader that this poem, one of Browning's few epistolary monologues, is

211

not a transcription of speech but something originally written out. Despite the local color of its opening paragraphs and occasional later references to place, the poem is highly unlocalized. Its special status as a letter makes its voice more than usually disembodied for a Browning lyric and concentrates attention on the way it lives and moves in time. As Cleon marks the sequence of his letter, from a "first requirement" (42), through a "next" (158), to a "last point" (273), the letter proclaims itself "in its nature" a temporal document that defies his idea of simultaneity.

Organized as it is in time, the entire poem demands to be read against Cleon's overt intention to freeze time. The chilling drama of its local passages arises in his remorseless maneuvering to stabilize temporal energies and to overpower the hapless human yearnings that those energies represent. If Cleon cannot have simultaneity, he can at least have closure as the next-best thing. His cunning rhetoric reflects the closural bias of his view of artistic tradition; the privilege of finality is written into passage after passage in which imaginative possibilities are begotten, allowed brief play, and put to death. The strict will to interpretive closure that oversees Cleon's history of the arts also monitors the little histories constituted in the passages and sentences he writes. His monologue presents a glittering, consistently untrustworthy fabric of reductive self-interpretations; and to read it is to unravel the characteristic dramatic patterns that he knits in time.

Cleon's decidedly undramatic fiction of an aesthetic last judgment, for example, may assume a dramatic interest if one asks what happens in its course to the soulful cry with which it has begun: "Why stay we on the earth unless to grow?" Within a few lines Cleon drafts this disruptive question into the service of a philosophy denying further birth and growth: the passage reinterprets Zeus's "purpose in our life," initially an evolutionary intention, as an absolute goal appointed and achieved. As the passage goes on, Cleon practices further refinements in self-interpretation:

> I now go on to image, — might we hear
> The judgment which should give the due to each,
> Show where the labour lay and where the ease,
> And prove Zeus' self, the latent everywhere!
> This is a dream.

(123-27)

This later fiction irons out what is implicit in its predecessor. All laborers receive their final due; the auditory "hear" of the first line gives place in the third to the visual display of "show"; and a spatially diffused, omnipresent Zeus no longer needs to take the trouble, or

212

the time, to descend. The ultimate perversity of the passage is that Cleon undermines the independence of even so flattened a fiction: "This is a dream." Not content to dismiss his successors to artistic poverty, he dismisses to insignificance his more immediate progeny, his imaginative creations.

Cleon is quite right to hold himself aloof from fictional ways of meaning. He sees, and hates, what Fra Lippo Lippi sees in figuration and loves: its tendency to become a prefiguration intimating the future. Cleon repudiates his own fictions because he recognizes in the process of signification the greatest of threats to his desire for apocalyptic closure, and he measures his own power of finality by his ability to resist the opening power of the sign.

> Is it for Zeus to boast,
> "See, man, how happy I live, and despair—
> "That I may be still happier—for thy use!"
> If this were so, we could not thank our lord,
> As hearts beat on to doing: 't is not so —
> Malice it is not. Is it carelessness?
> Still, no. If care—where is the sign? I ask,
> And get no answer, and agree in sum,
> O king, with thy profound discouragement,
> Who seest the wider but to sigh the more.
> Most progress is most failure: thou sayest well.
>
> (262-72)

To "get no answer," as Browning tells Renan in the "Epilogue" to *Dramatis Personae* and lets Tertium Quid show in *The Ring and the Book*, is to get only too clear and premature an answer. Cleon's letter is formally an answer to Protus's questions and more intimately a succession of answers to his own questions about growth and progress:

> Was the thing done?—then what's to do again?
>
> (81)

> For where had been a progress, otherwise?
>
> (92)

> Why stay we on the earth unless to grow?
>
> (114)

> What, and the soul alone deteriorates?
>
> (138)

> Shall I go on a step, improve on this,
> Do more for visible creatures than is done?
>
> (195-96)

213

Man might live at first
The animal life: but is there nothing more?

(214-15)

All of these lines offer variations upon the fundamentally Browning-esque theme, is there nothing more? Protus may take Cleon's questions at face value, but Browning's reader must know better and must appreciate their function in Cleon's internal bids for power. The more repeatedly and comprehensively Cleon can assert that there is nothing more, the more confidently he will be asserting his own climactic position and saying, "I stand myself" (151). "Most progress is most failure" for Cleon because he defines himself through repeated denials of his own progressive impulses, through carefully staged scenes in which he releases those impulses only to watch them fail.

The greatest show of strength in this passage comes when Cleon denies the significance of the grateful impulse to "thank our lord," which is introduced at line 265. The economic notion of a responsive thanksgiving has the same liberating potential here as in "Fra Lippo Lippi," and Cleon's prospective phrase "as hearts beat on to doing" acknowledges this potential. As Paul's sermon to the Athenians puts it, God has so stationed humankind in time on the face of the earth "that they should seek the Lord, if haply they might feel after him, and find him, though he be not far from every one of us" (Acts 17:27). Paul's emphasis on feeling is shared by Browning, whose psychologized theology would teach that the cordial impulse of gratitude to Zeus is, in fact, the very "sign" of conviction that Cleon professes to be seeking when he asks, "Where is the sign?" But one underestimates both Cleon's ingenuity and Browning's if one fails to distinguish Cleon's professions from his motives. He seeks not the sign, but an invalidation of the sign, a semantic bankruptcy that will let him have the last word.

Cleon recognizes perfectly well that his impulse of gratitude is a sign, but he severely limits the extent of its meaning. He grants it only the negative power of showing that Zeus is not a malicious god; and then, at the precise moment of going further to posit the benevolence of Zeus, he effaces the sign and answers that there is no answer. For Cleon the gratifying theological consequence of this answer is that Zeus becomes neither malicious, nor careless, nor careful, but simply impotent, like Caliban's Setebos. Power devolves instead upon Cleon, who takes his stand on a willed designification of his heart's promptings so that he may enjoy the masterful self-importance of what is a literal disheartening: "profound discouragement." He opens out the vista of a freely responsive exchange between careful creator and thankful creature, only to shut it up in a conclusive response

214

deepening the profundity of one who must preside at a summing up, one who must have all the answers. The penultimate line of the passage is a statement of Cleon's reductive purpose: he sees the wider in order to realize his stubborn intention to sigh the more.

Although for the most part Cleon's interpretive intention operates unobtrusively within his letter, in answering Protus's last point he makes that intention quite explicit. Protus has felicitated him on the superiority of an artist's survival to that of a king: "Thy life stays in the poems men shall sing" (170). Cleon's response to this threat of futurity is to upbraid Protus, twice, for confusing the figurative and literal meanings of "a word":

> *The last point now: — thou dost except a case —*
> *Holding joy not impossible to one*
> *With artist-gifts — to such a man as I*
> *Who leave behind me living works indeed;*
> *For such a poem, such a painting lives.*
> *What? dost thou verily trip upon a word?*
>
> (273-78)

> *"But," sayest thou — (and I marvel, I repeat,*
> *To find thee trip on such a mere word) "what*
> *"Thou writest, paintest, stays; that does not die:*
> *"Sappho survives, because we sing her songs,*
> *"And Æschylus, because we read his plays!"*
>
> (301-5)

The repetition of these defensive disclaimers is significant, as is the ambiguity of Cleon's "word," which may refer to either of two verbs in Protus's letter: "lives" (271) or "stays" (303). With this ambiguity Browning achieves a delicate balance between transcendental and descendental versions of the future: between the prophetic life everlasting preached by Paul as a new way of life in which the redeemed soul lives, and moves, and has its being; and the more literal secular permanence sought by pagan kings and artists, who would stay mutability by living through the works of an Ozymandias, a Protus, or a Cleon. It seems strange that Browning or his readers should expect Cleon to entertain seriously the possibility of accepting Christ. But the force of the poem does not really depend on such an expectation; for Cleon denies not just the future according to Paul, but even the future as offered on venerable pagan grounds. His rejection of Paul's word in the final verse paragraph is an afterthought confirming the reductive impulse behind his entire letter. He rejects the living word in both Christian and pagan senses because what he would purge from the word is its staying power, the elusive life of poetic

215

figuration—the flaw in language upon which the ingenuous Protus has tripped towards the future as happily as the soliloquizing Spanish monk, and with a more naive grace.

Cleon's superbly terminal sophistication depends upon his ability to cover up that flaw, to assert literal over figurative meaning by demonstrating that any sign is "a mere word." He refuses to trip, as he refuses to stoop to Protus's inquiry about the early Christians: "Thou wrongest our philosophy, O king, / In stooping to inquire of such an one, / As if his answer could impose at all!" (346-48). The rival interpreter dismissed in these lines is the apostle Paul, the new master of an expansive, figural hermeneutics. Paul's willingness to begin reinterpreting the poetic word, as expressed in the fragmentary clause that heads this poem, recalls Cleon's chief rival in *Men and Women*, the physician Karshish, who ends his letter in the questioning mode of an interpretation poised on the verge of meaning: "The madman saith He said so: it is strange" ("An Epistle," 312).[3] Cleon must at any cost protect himself against such barbarian beginnings. His philosophy of invincible finality, the temporal equivalent of the utter priority initially claimed by Paracelsus, Sordello, and every lyric speaker in Browning, demands answers that can "impose," answers placing a seal on figuration and suppressing its unruly fertility.

In burying the possibility of the sign, Cleon buries the future. The climactic paragraph of his letter anticipates with grim satisfaction the only future that his strict vision will admit: a literal burial.

> *Thou diest while I survive?*
> *Say rather that my fate is deadlier still,*
> *In this, that every day my sense of joy*
> *Grows more acute, my soul (intensified*
> *In power and insight) more enlarged, more keen;*
> *While every day my hairs fall more and more,*
> *My hand shakes, and the heavy years increase—*
> *The horror quickening still from year to year,*
> *The consummation coming past escape*
> *When I shall know most, and yet least enjoy—*
> *When all my works wherein I prove my worth,*
> *Being present still to mock me in men's mouths,*
> *Alive still, in the praise of such as thou,*
> *I, I the feeling, thinking, acting man,*
> *The man who loved his life so over-much,*
> *Sleep in my urn.*

(308-23)

The swell of a fourteen-line sentence, in which Cleon has opened all the rhetorical stops, is suddenly stopped cold by the curt predicate

216

of this last hemistich. Browning blunted the line both metrically and temporally by revising his 1855 reading, "Shall sleep in my urn." Browning's rhythmic revision enacts the foreshortening of tense whereby Cleon ruthlessly pulls his future, "alive still," into the fatal enclosure of the present.

In the lines that follow, Cleon practices his skill in combination and integration by bringing together the poem's major imaginative possibilities, and he savors his self-directed *Schadenfreude* by rejecting them all in a single, brutal "no!":

> *It is so horrible,*
> *I dare at times imagine to my need*
> *Some future state revealed to us by Zeus,*
> *Unlimited in capability*
> *For joy, as this is in desire for joy,*
> *—To seek which, the joy-hunger forces us:*
> *That, stung by straitness of our life, made strait*
> *On purpose to make prized the life at large—*
> *Freed by the throbbing impulse we call death,*
> *We burst there as the worm into the fly,*
> *Who, while a worm still, wants his wings. But no!*
> *Zeus has not yet revealed it; and alas,*
> *He must have done so, were it possible!*

(323-35)

The creation of an imaginative fiction, the attribution of promising "purpose" to Zeus, the willingness to trust the heart's "throbbing impulse" as a sign transfiguring endings into beginnings—all return from earlier passages in Cleon's letter to be wrought into an eloquent prophecy. But Cleon admits the human need for a future, for an open question, only in order to impose his answer and enjoy its reductive force. Cleon prefers such harsh enjoyment to the "joy" he professes to desire, because he finally prefers the "horrible" to the "possible." He lives to be "stung by straitness of our life," by the astringent exercise of an imaginative asceticism. For Cleon the "need," the "desire," the "joy-hunger," and the "want" all answer to a deeper need: his need to identify power with closure, the "not yet revealed" with the unrevealable, the possible with the present. These necessitarian identities put an end not only to Cleon's imagined "future state," but to any meaningful future whatsoever.

"But no!" The glare of Cleon's defiant retrospect, illuminating the Hellenic tradition in art and his own career as its terminal artist, also lights up the contrasting accomplishments of Browning's early and middle years. Like Cleon, many of Browning's characters are grand refusers; but while Cleon forsakes the future for the present, they do

217

quite the reverse. In *Pauline*, Browning says no to Shelley, and to the ideal of imaginative autonomy that his Shelley represents, for the sake of a future whose significance is at once religious and poetic. In *Paracelsus* and *Sordello*, he dramatizes the transformation of the ideal power of priority into the livelier currency of secondariness and anticipation; Paracelsus's protest against received definitions of the human and Sordello's against the given continuities of the natural order become pledges of definitions and orders yet to be. The apostate Strafford repeatedly denies his early allegiances as a way of establishing a latter beginning. Browning's concentration on the making and marring of images in *Strafford* and other plays suggests that the poet's traffic with images of truth is but a special case of the deferential dynamics whereby all his men and women recreate and maintain their worlds. "Artemis Prologizes" checks a grand refusal comparable to Cleon's by finding new possibilities outside the confines of the funeral pyre—the same pyre that to Cleon means only the dust and ashes of his own incineration, "The consummation coming past escape." And, for Fra Lippo Lippi, Artemis's lesson is second nature: he takes breath and tries to add life's flash, drawing inspiration from his sense of himself as a mutable man in a world poised in intimation. Lippo stands with Browning at the place of meaning, between the present and the future, the carnal and the holy, the secular and the divine.

In contrast to these and other figures, Cleon represents the imagination at once bound by its own grandeur and famished by a sense of insufficiency that can only drive it possessively back upon itself. In this Cleon resembles Browning's Duke; he is, indeed, the ducal reader turned artist and endowed with the greater self-knowledge that distinguishes the artist from the connoisseur. The Duke remains self-possessed by closing up his Duchess, and thus he illustrates the Browningesque paradox that untrammeled self-assertion results in a caricature of the living self. The wages of priority is deathlike entrapment behind a mask that is grotesque, in part, because unwittingly adopted. Cleon is less grotesque than he is horribly great, because he understands the logic of self-possession and pursues that logic to its irresistible conclusion in the vision of his own ashes asleep in their enclosing urn. This vision, the ultimate reduction of human potential, puts "the infinite within the finite" in a sense precisely antithetical to Browning's art. It represents all that his philosophy of the imperfect, and the violent and subtle ploys of his corresponding poetics, endeavor to contest.

Cleon's grand refusal of Browning's religion is also a refusal of Browning's poetry. Its utter negativity provides one of the clearest insights in all Browning's writing into the correlative importance of creativity, possibility, and the sense of the future. The arc of the poet's career traced in the preceding chapters suggests that he found the best resistance to Cleon's will to closure, the best defense of creativity, possibility, and the sense of the future, in the dramatic deference recommended by Fra Lippo's good angel. Against the formidably hard-headed insistence of Cleon's "But no!" Browning worked the angelic countercharm "Not so fast!" He wrote a lifetime of poetry out of the antiphony of these two imperative voices, poetry that survives today because he heeded both voices so persistently, and so inventively orchestrated their discords.

When classifying his dramatic lyrics for republication in 1863, Browning gave "Cleon" pride of place among "Men and Women" after all of the major monologues of the 1840s and 1850s, but he did not let it close the volume. The closing poem bears as its title what seems the inevitable last word for his art of disclosure: "One Word More." It makes little difference to Browning whether poetry is caught up in the radiant gyres of the self-involved sublime or encased within the formalist objectivity of Cleon's well-wrought urn; neither mode, in itself, will sustain the poetry of the future. If every meaning is already present, as the chilling hauteur of "Cleon" shows, there can be no word more and nothing to look forward to. There can be no more to say if all revelation is now.

NOTES

These notes make use of the following abbreviated titles:

BIS	*Browning Institute Studies*
BN	*Browning Newsletter*
BSNotes	*Browning Society Notes*
CE	*College English*
Complete Works	*The Complete Works of Robert Browning with Variant Readings and Annotations*
CPDW	*The Complete Poetic and Dramatic Works of Robert Browning*
JEGP	*Journal of English and Germanic Philology*
MLN	*Modern Language Notes*
MLQ	*Modern Language Quarterly*
MP	*Modern Philology*
N&Q	*Notes and Queries*
PMLA	*Publications of the Modern Language Association of America*
PQ	*Philological Quarterly*
SBHC	*Studies in Browning and His Circle*
SEL	*Studies in English Literature 1500-1900*
SP	*Studies in Philology*
TSLL	*Texas Studies in Literature and Language*
UTQ	*University of Toronto Quarterly*
VN	*Victorian Newsletter*
VP	*Victorian Poetry*
VS	*Victorian Studies*

NOTES

Introduction

1. Letter of 26 November 1866, in *Dearest Isa: Robert Browning's Letters to Isabella Blagden*, ed. Edward C. McAleer (Austin, Texas: University of Texas Press, 1951), p. 251.

2. J. Hillis Miller, *The Disappearance of God: Five Nineteenth-Century Writers* (Cambridge, Mass.: Harvard University Press, 1963), p. 99, refers to "the celebrated philosophy of incompleteness." F. R. G. Duckworth, *Browning: Background and Conflict* (London: Ernest Benn, 1931), p. 151, finds Browning's conception of imperfection and delay "so familiar that one might almost apologize for mentioning it." One of the writers most responsible for familiarizing the philosophy as such, Henry Jones, writes in *Browning as a Philosophical and Religious Teacher*, 2nd ed. (Glasgow: Maclehose, 1892), p. 121: "Morality is the sphere of discrepancy, and the moral life a progressive realization of a good that can never be complete." The philosophy is placed in poetic and cultural contexts by Solomon F. Gingerich, *Wordsworth, Tennyson, and Browning: A Study in Human Freedom* (Ann Arbor, Mich.: George Wahr, 1911), pp. 211 ff.; by Lionel Stevenson, *Darwin among the Poets* (Chicago: University of Chicago Press, 1932), p. 145; and by John Maynard, *Browning's Youth* (Cambridge, Mass., and London: Harvard University Press, 1977), pp. 56-58. Perhaps the clearest of recent expositions, that by Hoxie N. Fairchild, owes its clarity to that author's undisguised difference from Browning's views; see "Browning's Heaven," *Review of Religion*, 14 (1949), 30-37; *Religious Trends in English Poetry*, volume IV (New York: Columbia University Press, 1957), pp. 139-67.

3. Chicago and London: University of Chicago Press, 1968.

4. New York: Oxford University Press, 1973. See also *The Ringers in the Tower: Studies in Romantic Tradition* (Chicago and London: University of Chicago Press, 1971); *A Map of Misreading* (New York: Oxford University Press, 1975); *Poetry and Repression: Revisionism from Blake to Stevens* (New Haven, Conn., and London: Yale University Press, 1976).

5. *CPDW*, p. 1011.

6. *L'écriture et la différence* (Paris: Editions du Seuil, 1967) and *De la grammatologie* (Paris: Editions de Minuit, 1967) are available in English as *Writing and Difference*, trans. Alan Bass (Chicago: University of Chicago Press, 1978), and *Of Grammatology*, trans. Gayatri Chakravorty Spivak (Baltimore: Johns Hopkins University Press, 1976).

7. *Complete Works*, ed. Edmund Gosse and Thomas James Wise, volume XII (London: Heinemann, 1926), p. 146.

8. The complete text is given by David J. DeLaura, "Ruskin and the Brownings: Twenty-five Unpublished Letters," *Bulletin of the John Rylands Library*, 54 (1972), 324-27.

9. Published in *The Works of John Ruskin*, ed. E. T. Cook and Alexander Wedderburn, volume XXXVI (London: Allen, 1909), p. xxxiv. W. O. Raymond, *The Infinite Moment and Other Essays in Robert Browning*, 2nd ed. (Toronto: University of Toronto Press,

1965), p. 10, finds support in this letter for his central argument that "the relation between the form and the content of the poetry of Browning is often a tension rather than a harmony"; that "the crux of the struggle in his life as an artist was the difficulty of bodying forth the content of his imagination and intellect in adequate poetic forms."

10. *Notes on Novelists* (New York: Scribner, 1914), p. 399: "Browning is 'upon' us, straighter upon us always, than anyone else of his race."

11. Letter of 22 August 1846, in *The Letters of Robert Browning and Elizabeth Barrett Barrett 1845-1846*, ed. Elvan Kintner, volume II (Cambridge, Mass.: Harvard University Press, 1969), p. 986. See also the letter of 15 February 1846 in the same edition, volume I, p. 464.

12. Thomas Weiskel, *The Romantic Sublime: Studies in the Structure and Psychology of Transcendence* (Baltimore: Johns Hopkins University Press, 1976), pp. 22-33, connects "the hermeneutic or 'reader's' sublime" with the sense of horizontal endlessness. Although he makes no mention of Browning, readers will recognize the effect Weiskel describes as a characteristic feature of Browning's liminal poetry. On at least two occasions during the 1840's, the poet arrived at demonstrably liminal points in the course of his writing. *The Flight of the Duchess* came to a premature halt in the spring of 1845; when Browning returned to finish the poem at the end of the year, he did so with an image of fresh rupture and belated beginning that represented his own situation as well as that of his Duchess in the new sections of the poem: "Well, early in autumn, at first winter-warning, / When the stag had to break with his foot, of a morning, / A drinking-hole out of the fresh tender ice . . . " (216-18). (For Browning's account of the composition of the poem, see William Clyde DeVane, *A Browning Handbook*, 2nd ed. [New York: Appleton-Century-Crofts, 1955], pp. 171-75.) Similarly, when Browning extended the "Saul" of 1845 into the more prophetic version published ten years later, he overlaid his concerns as stymied poet and David's as arrested singer: "'Saul!' cried I, and stopped" (101). Browning broke out of this prolonged stoppage with the simile of a delayed avalanche; the simile acknowledges both his own delay and subsequent release, and the thunderous anapestic pentameter in which he had newly framed the poem.

13. This discussion appeared in slightly different form under the same title in *SBHC*, 4(2) (fall 1976), 54-70.

14. The Ohio edition misprints "prepare" as "prepared" in line 815.

15. Charles Rivers, "Robert Browning's *Sordello*: An Existential Interpretation," *Northwest Missouri State College Studies*, 31(3) (1970), 11, likens Naddo's advice to that of Pope in the *Essay on Criticism* and sees in Sordello's victory at Mantua the triumph of "romanticism over eighteenth-century neo-classicism." A conflict between classicist and romantic positions persists, of course, in criticism published throughout the early Victorian period. For analyses of the predominantly romantic tendencies of the period, see Alba H. Warren, *English Poetic Theory 1825-1865* (Princeton, N.J.: Princeton University Press, 1950), especially pp. 111-25 on Browning; Lawrence J. Starzyk, *The Imprisoned Splendor: A Study of Early Victorian Critical Theory* (Port Washington, N.Y., and London: Kennikat, 1977). A countermovement, corresponding roughly to the formalist position of Naddo and Eglamor, is surveyed in R. G. Cox, "Victorian Criticism of Poetry: The Minority Tradition," *Scrutiny*, 18 (1951), 2-17.

16. Roma A. King, Jr., *The Focusing Artifice: The Poetry of Robert Browning* (Athens, Ohio: Ohio University Press, 1968), p. 27.

17. On the effect of improvisation in Browning, see John Jay Chapman, *Emerson and Other Essays* (New York: Scribner, 1899), p. 210: "Sometimes his verse fell into coils as it came, but he himself, as he wrote the first line of a poem, never knew in what form of verse the poem would come forth"; Oliver Elton, *A Survey of English Literature, 1780-1880*, volume III (New York: Macmillan, 1920), p. 376, writes of Browning's poems as "never seeming to be thought out beforehand." In a letter of 13 July 1846 to a friend and minor poet, Alfred Domett, Browning relates poetic creativity to a pregnant suspension of the will:

"Endeavour *to think* (the real *thought*), to *imagine*, to *create*, or whatever they call it—as well endeavour to add the cubit to your stature!" (*Robert Browning and Alfred Domett*, ed. Frederic G. Kenyon [New York: Dutton, 1906], p. 127).

18. Park Honan, *Browning's Characters: A Study in Poetic Technique* (New Haven, Conn.: Yale University Press, 1961), p. 13, remarks on the great utility of the dash in Browning's early poetry. Henri Hovelaque, *Browning's English in Sordello* (Paris: Presses Modernes, 1933), p. 69, counts over five hundred dashes in *Sordello* alone. See Duckworth, p. 175: "There is, in Browning, much virtue in a dash."

19. Alexandra Orr, one of the few commentators to have written on these lines, prematurely identifies the secondary spirit with Eglamor but is sensitive to the spirit's "human" appeal. She writes in *A Handbook to the Works of Robert Browning*, 6th ed. (1892; London: Bell, 1937 [reprint]), p. 52, of "the pathos of his modest hopes, and acknowledged, yet scarcely comprehended failure."

20. Compare "Old Pictures in Florence" (1855), in which Browning asks, apropos of Greek "perfection" in art, shall "Man's face, have no more play and action / Than joy which is crystallized for ever, / Or grief, an eternal petrifaction?" (142-44).

21. Classing Browning "with the dithyrambic or daemonic poets," Robert Preyer writes in "Two Styles in the Verse of Robert Browning," *ELH*, 32 (1965), 79: "The poems have the look of constantly being on the point of overleaping their formal structure." According to Miller, p. 149, for Browning, "Art to be authentic must give expressive form to something that denies all form. . . . All Browning's art is based on the paradoxical attempt to give form to the formless." These observations recall Christian N. Wenger's *The Aesthetics of Robert Browning* (New York: Dutton, 1923), p. 163: "For him the truths of art are never represented as though contented and at home in their forms, but rather as though projecting out of, overflowing, and transcending their mediums." See "Rabbi Ben Ezra" (1864): "Thoughts hardly to be packed / Into a narrow act, / Fancies that broke through language and escaped" (145-47). Or see, in a less pontifical vein, *The Inn Album* (1875): "That bard's a Browning; he neglects the form: / But ah, the sense, ye gods, the weighty sense!" (17-18).

22. Robert R. Columbus and Claudette Kemper, "Sordello and the Speaker: A Problem in Identity," *VP*, 2 (1964), 263, note that *Sordello* is a story that was meant to go on and on as though it could never end."

Chapter 1

1. *Complete Works*, volume III, p. 165.

2. DeVane, p. 9. For a lucid and detailed biographical exploration of this paradox, see Maynard, pp. 208-37.

3. Steven J. Fox, "Art and Personality: Browning, Rossetti, Pater, Wilde, and Yeats," Ph.D. dissertation, Yale University, 1972, p. 24. See also Roland A. Duerksen, *Shelleyan Ideas in Victorian Literature* (The Hague: Mouton, 1966), p. 35; Harold Bloom, *The Ringers in the Tower: Studies in Romantic Tradition* (Chicago and London: University of Chicago Press, 1971), p. 149.

4. T. J. Collins objects to Browning's eclecticism in "Shelley and God in Browning's *Pauline*: Unresolved Problems," *VP*, 3 (1965), 151-60, and in *Robert Browning's Moral-Aesthetic Theory 1833-1855* (Lincoln: University of Nebraska Press, 1967), pp. 3-16. Browning's devious will to "lean" is observed by Morse Peckham, "Browning and Romanticism," in *Robert Browning*, ed. Isobel Armstrong (Athens, Ohio: Ohio University Press, 1975), p. 75; and by Samuel Luther Chell, "The Poetry of Duration: A Time-Centered Approach to Browning," Ph.D. dissertation, University of Wisconsin, 1972, p. 60: "The speaker's recurring posture of humility—whether toward Shelley, Pauline, or God—is, in effect, a form of self-enhancement."

5. See Paul A. Cundiff, *Robert Browning: A Shelley Promethean* (St. Petersburg, Florida: Valkyrie Press, 1977), p. 20: "It is most characteristic of him to change paragraph at em-

phatic enunciation, and just as characteristic of him to revert to unfinished thought once he has distracted attention."

6. Loy D. Martin, "Browning: The Activation of Influence," *VN* (53) (spring 1978), p. 6, observes that "even the poem's most Shelleyan moments reveal an organizational logic which renders the text of Shelley a dying, if not already dead, letter." It is possible to profit from this observation without accepting Martin's argument that Browning wishes to *make contact*" (p. 7) and "is trying to make Shelley less distant from him" (p. 8).

7. Richard C. Keenan reads the captive god as Shelley in "Browning and Shelley," *BIS*, 1 (1973), 124.

8. With the exceptions of Frederick A. Pottle, *Shelley and Browning: A Myth and Some Facts* (Chicago: Pembroke Press, 1923), pp. 34-64, and Honan, pp. 11-17, comparatively little close attention has been paid to Browning's concrete revisions of Shelley's poetry, but there exist numerous thematic accounts of the metaphysical revision of Shelleyan romanticism that Browning's poetic technique arguably elaborates. See Edward Dowden, "The Transcendental Movement," *Contemporary Review*, 30 (1877), 317, on Browning's conversion of romantic agony "into an educational instrument, a source of courage and hope, a pledge of futurity"; C. H. Herford, *Robert Browning* (Edinburgh and London: Blackwood, 1905), p. 238. For negative views of this revision, see Duerksen, p. 53; Harold Bloom, *The Anxiety of Influence: A Theory of Poetry* (New York: Oxford University Press, 1973), p. 69. Browning's most explicit critique of the young Shelley's precocious intemperance as a thinker occurs in the *Essay on Shelley*: "He finds himself unawares arrived at the startling conclusion, that all must be changed – or nothing" (*CPDW*, p. 1012). From *Pauline* onward, it is the consistent endeavor of Browning's poetic style, as of his poetic argument, to temporalize such all-or-nothing change and to delay the finality of its "startling conclusion."

9. Browning's image of the narrowing "flag-knots" in lines 776-77 may derive from the following stanza in Shelley's "The Sensitive Plant":

> *Spawn, weeds, and filth, a leprous scum,*
> *Made the running rivulet thick and dumb,*
> *And at its outlet flags huge as stakes*
> *Dammed it up with roots knotted like water-snakes.*
>
> (III.65-69)

While Shelley damns a dam, Browning opens and blesses an outlet, enjoying the grotesque vitality at which Shelley revolts.

10. See *Christmas-Eve* (1850) for a recurrence of this early image:

> *What is left for us, save, in growth*
> *Of soul, to rise up, far past both,*
> *From the gift looking to the giver,*
> *And from the cistern to the river,*
> *And from the finite to infinity,*
> *And from man's dust to God's divinity?*
>
> (1012-17)

11. Charles Du Bos, "*Pauline* de Browning," *Etudes Anglaises*, 7 (1954), 162, understands better than many critics writing in English the buoyant tone of the poem's celebration of difference from Shelley: "Browning précisément découvre qu'il 'n'a rien en commun avec Shelley,' en souffre d'abord comme d'un irrémédiable abaissement, mais bientôt rebondit – rebondit d'autant plus que cette découverte même lui ouvre l'accès à sa vraie nature."

12. Though this "source" is primarily Browning's idealized image of Shelley as a disembodied influence, the passage may also have a concrete textual source in a fluvial image from "Mont Blanc" (123-25): "one majestic River, / The breath and blood of distant lands, for ever / Rolls its loud waters to the ocean waves." Shelley's context recalls both "Tintern

Abbey" and "Kubla Khan" and thus may have instigated Browning's choice of the river as an image for poetic derivation.

13. *Complete Works*, volume I, p. 297. The original reads:

> *Plus ne suis ce que i'ay esté*
> *Et ne le sçaurois iamais estre;*
> *Mon beau printemps & mon esté*
> *Ont faict le sault par la fenestre,*
> *Amour, tu as esté mon maistre*
> *Ie t'ay seruy sur touts les Dieux;*
> *O si ie pouuois deux fois naistre,*
> *Comme ie te seruiroys mieux!*

Maynard, pp. 219-20 and 435-36, finds echoes of Marot's epigram in Byron and discusses the influence of Byron upon Browning in *Pauline*.

14. Mill's entire commentary, along with Browning's responses, may be consulted in William S. Peterson and Fred L. Standley, "The J. S. Mill Marginalia in Robert Browning's *Pauline*: A History and Transcription," *Papers of the Bibliographical Society of America*, 66 (1972), 135-70. Peterson and Standley vigorously dissent from the view of Masao Miyoshi, "Mill and 'Pauline': The Myth and Some Facts," *VS*, 9 (1965), 157, that "the young poet took Mill's comments as encouraging." Still, Browning's reference to the sensitivity of his beloved Shelley as "extraordinary and even morbid," in the *Essay on Shelley* (*CPDW*, p. 1012), lends some weight to Miyoshi's assessment of Browning's response — a response that was after all, and not very surprisingly, an ambivalent one.

15. According to Peckham, in Armstrong, *Robert Browning*, p. 65, the purpose of the confession is "to create an unknown subjective condition."

16. See King, p. 7: "That his final affirmation seems inconclusive (Pauline's comment suggests this) is part of its genuineness. Truth is dynamic, developing; it must not become static. His return is only the beginning." Compare Clyde de L. Ryals, "Browning's *Pauline*: The Question of Genre," *Genre*, 9 (1976), 237-39. See also Stopford A. Brooke's eloquent introduction to *Pauline* in *The Poetry of Robert Browning* (New York: Crowell, 1902), p. 121: "This is the exordium, and it is already full of his theory of life — the soul forced from within to aspire to the perfect whole, the necessary failure, the despair, the new impulse to love arising out of the despair, failure making fresh growth, fresh uncontentment. God has sent a new impulse from without; let me begin again."

17. A note in Browning's copy of *Pauline* identifying this figure as Kean in *Richard III* is quoted in W. Hall Griffin and Harry Christopher Minchin, *The Life of Robert Browning*, 2nd ed. (London: Methuen, 1911), p. 45. See Maynard, pp. 221-27, for persuasive speculation about Kean's role in *Pauline* as bearer of the dramatic vision of Shakespeare.

18. Browning wrote to Elizabeth Barrett on 21 August 1846, in a discussion of Goethe and poetic will, "I should be perhaps more refractory than anybody, if what I cheerfully agree to, as happening to take my fancy, were forced on me, as the only reasonable course" (*Letters of Robert Browning and Elizabeth Barrett Barrett*, volume II, p. 982).

19. "La concentration des idées est due bien plus à leur conception qu'à leur mise en exécution. . . . Chacun une fois obtenu devait former une espèce de plateau d'où l'on pouvait apercevoir d'autres buts, d'autres projets, d'autres jouissances qui, à leur tour, devaient être surmontés." ("The concentration of ideas owes much more to their conception than to their execution. . . . Each [of the soul's possible aims], once attained, should constitute a sort of plateau from which one could glimpse other ends, other projects, other joys to be surmounted in turn.")

20. Browning wrote to Elizabeth Barrett on 11 March 1845, "If there were no life beyond this, I think the hope in one would be an incalculable blessing *for* this life" (*Letters of Robert Browning and Elizabeth Barrett Barrett*, volume I, p. 38). Students of the Victorian

period would do well to resist impulses to read such statements either as conventional expressions of Browning's evangelical piety or as evidence for the metaphysical skepticism of Browning-the-eupeptic-vitalist. Both readings, however convenient, are reductive of his lifelong interest in religious experience and his belief in its human necessity. Passages like this one from *Pauline* can serve as reminders that Browning's was no mere poetry of earth and that from the outset of his career he had made the conventions of evangelical Christianity (to say the least) his own, in part by reconceiving them as *poetic* conventions.

21. As Browning told Mrs. Orr about "the Christian scheme of salvation," "I know all that may be said against it, on the ground of history, of reason, of even moral sense. I grant even that it may be a fiction. But I am none the less convinced that the life and death of Christ, as Christians apprehend them, supply something which their humanity requires, and that it is true for them" (Alexandra Orr, "The Religious Opinions of Robert Browning," *Contemporary Review*, 60 [1891], 879). See also Douglas Bush, *Mythology and the Romantic Tradition in English Poetry* (1937; New York: Pageant, 1957 [reprint]), p. 379: "Browning's God, while welcomed by generations of evangelical readers, is not much more than a pot of gold at the end of the rainbow, a postulated x in the poet's emotional and optimistic algebra."

22. *Poetry and Repression: Revisionism from Blake to Stevens* (New Haven, Conn., and London: Yale University Press, 1976), p. 192.

Chapter 2

1. *Complete Works*, volume III, p. 179.

2. *CPDW*, p. 1010.

3. In a letter of 24 February 1847 to his publisher Edward Moxon, Browning discusses the proposed revisions of 1849 as elaborations of his original intent: "But the point which decided me to wish to get printed over again was the real good I thought I could do to *Paracelsus, Pippa*, and some others; good, not obtained by cutting them up and reconstructing them, but by affording just the proper revisions they ought to have had before they were printed at all" (*Letters of Robert Browning Collected by Thomas J. Wise*, ed. Thurman L. Hood [New Haven, Conn.: Yale University Press, 1933], p. 14).

4. Related themes of tradition, confession, and regeneration reappear as late as Browning's first series of *Dramatic Idyls* (1879) in "Martin Relph" and "Halbert and Hob." Any discussion of these perennial themes in Browning will be indebted, as the present discussion is indebted, to Bloom's readings of " 'Childe Roland to the Dark Tower Came' " (1855), in *The Ringers in the Tower*, pp. 157-67, and in *A Map of Misreading*, pp. 106-22. W. David Shaw, *The Dialectical Temper: The Rhetorical Art of Robert Browning* (Ithaca, N.Y.: Cornell University Press, 1968), p. 124, quotes "Prospice" (1864) to show that "just when Browning isolates himself most thoroughly, he is most completely united, like Childe Roland, with his 'peers, / The heroes of old.' "

5. See Browning's letter of 19 September 1880 to Mrs. Thomas FitzGerald: "Does not all mediocrity (educated mediocrity) come of a beginner's determining to look at nature through the eyes of his predecessors who assuredly began by looking for themselves?" (*Learned Lady: Letters from Robert Browning to Mrs. Thomas FitzGerald 1876-1889*, ed. Edward C. McAleer [Cambridge, Mass.: Harvard University Press, 1966], p. 93). See also Eleanor Cook, *Browning's Lyrics: An Exploration* (Toronto: University of Toronto Press, 1974), p. 20, on "the maddening ambiguity of the song, which reinforces his task at the same time it tempts him to abandon it."

6. See Browning's footnote to the edition of 1835: "He did in effect affirm that he had disputed with Galen in the vestibule of Hell" (*Complete Works*, volume I, p. 233). Browning may have deleted the note in subsequent editions because his textual revisions of 1849 had so emphasized the significance of Paracelsus's dispute with tradition as to render biographical detail superfluous.

7. For a comparison of Zoroaster and Paracelsus, see C. Willard Smith, *Browning's Star-Imagery: The Study of a Detail in Poetic Design* (Princeton, N.J.: Princeton University Press, 1941), p. 36. See also the pertinent observation made by the historical Paracelsus in *Selected Writings*, ed. Jolande Jacobi and trans. Norbert Guterman (New York: Pantheon, 1951), p. 228: "The stars are subject to the philosopher, they must follow him, and not he them. Only the man who is still animal is governed, mastered, compelled, and driven by the stars, so that he has no choice but to follow them. . . . But the reason for all this is that such a man does not know himself and does not know how to use the energies hidden in him, nor does he know that he carries the stars within himself, that he is the microcosm, and thus carries in him the whole firmament with all its influences." It is an entirely characteristic paradox that Browning has his Paracelsus link the thought of freedom from influence with the thought of Zoroaster as an influential predecessor—especially since Browning himself may have been thinking of his predecessor Shelley's allusion to Zoroaster in *Prometheus Unbound*, I. 191 ff.

8. Perhaps the most tireless defenders of Browning against the charge that he espouses a naive optimism are Norton B. Crowell, *The Convex Glass: The Mind of Robert Browning* (Albuquerque, N.M.: University of New Mexico Press, 1968), and Philip Drew, *The Poetry of Browning: A Critical Introduction* (London: Methuen, 1970), pp. 182-98.

9. Browning's vision of judgment in *Easter-Day* (1850) begins with a celestial signature of the divine author: "A fierce vindictive scribble of red / Quick flame" (511-12).

10. These lines may in themselves cast doubt on the statement of Miller, p. 86, that for Browning "the most important experiences are intuitions of indivisible wholes." See also George M. Ridenour's introduction to Browning's *Selected Poetry* (New York and Toronto: New American Library, 1966), p. xi: "Browning's aim, as a poet in the Romantic tradition, is to devise forms in which the elements of reality as he experiences it may be contemplated as unified."

11. *Complete Works*, volume I, p. 276. Cook, p. 270, reads the "gold" primarily as a subterranean mineral; Barbara Melchiori, *Browning's Poetry of Reticence* (New York: Barnes and Noble, 1968), p. 60, interprets it as "the liquid gold of truth" but adds that "truth is something natural, a part of nature herself." The relation of perceiver to perceived, of Paracelsus to the truth he seeks, was even more ambiguous in the editions of 1835 and 1849, in which line 160 read, "A wondrous natural robe in which I went."

12. See F. E. L. Priestley, "The Ironic Pattern of Browning's *Paracelsus*," *UTQ*, 34 (1964), 68-81.

13. Smith, *Browning's Star-Imagery*, p. 30.

14. John T. Nettleship, *Robert Browning: Essays and Thoughts*, 2nd ed. (London: Mathews, 1890), p. 351, expresses the glory of failure in temporal terms of which Browning would have approved: "Faith and progress as Browning presents them are the priceless triumph of man's weakness, the noble prerogative which owes its vitality to his utter ignorance not only of God's purpose in making evil, but of what is going to happen in the next second of time."

15. See Browning's *Essay on Shelley* for an analysis of the poet's ability "out of the calm, purity, and energy of nature to reconstitute and store up, for the forthcoming stage of man's being, a gift in repayment of that former gift in which man's own thought and passion had been lavished by the poet on the else-incompleted magnificence of the sunrise, the else-uninterpreted mystery of the lake" (*CPDW*, p. 1011). See also Alexandra Orr, *Life and Letters of Robert Browning*, volume II (Boston and New York: Houghton Mifflin, 1891), p. 459: "What he loved in nature was essentially its prefiguring of human existence, or its echo of it; and it never appeared, in either his works or his conversation, that he was much impressed by its inanimate forms." Josephine Miles, *Pathetic Fallacy in the Nineteenth Century* (Berkeley and Los Angeles: University of California Press, 1942), pp. 226-28, finds that in *Men and Women* the pathetic fallacy occurs only once in every two hundred eighty lines, far more rarely than in any other poet studied, and twice as rarely as in Tennyson. Perhaps

Browning, having celebrated it so early in his career, came to regard the pathetic fallacy as too facile an assertion of "humanity."

16. Pottle, p. 63, finds in Browning's lines "a clear reminiscence of the vision which came to the hero of *Alastor*; the very words 'sweet human love' are repeated in exactly the same sense." The student of *Pauline* will suspect that the clearer the textual reminiscence of Shelley, the less exact Browning's repetition of Shelley's "sense" is likely to be.

17. At the end of his career, in a letter of 4 March 1887 to F. J. Furnivall, the poet provided a definition that chimes with the early affirmations of *Paracelsus*. Furnivall had asked about the difficult invocation to Browning's "lyric Love" in *The Ring and the Book* (I.1391-1416), and Browning replied, " 'Human'—so as to be *ready*, at the first summons to general service, to drop down &c.; the *readiness* implied as a necessary quality of the humanity" (*Letters of Robert Browning*, p. 262).

18. See in the *Essay on Shelley* Browning's appreciation "of the whole poet's function of beholding with an understanding keenness the universe, nature and man, in their actual state of perfection in imperfection; of the whole poet's virtue of being untempted, by the manifold partial developments of beauty and good on every side, into leaving them the ultimates he found them" (*CPDW*, p. 1010).

19. *Selected Writings of Paracelsus*, p. 183.

Chapter 3

1. *The Divine Order and Other Sermons and Addresses*, ed. Brynmor Jones (London: Isbister, 1884), pp. xi-xii.

2. For recent critical appreciations of Browning's monistic humanism, see Georg Roppen, *Evolution and Poetic Belief: A Study in Some Victorian and Modern Writers* (Oslo: Oslo University Press, 1956), p. 160; Thomas Blackburn, *Robert Browning: A Study of His Poetry* (1967; Totowa, N.J.: Rowman and Littlefield, 1973 [reprint]), p. 50; G. Wilson Knight, *Neglected Powers: Essays on Nineteenth and Twentieth Century Literature* (London: Routledge and Kegan Paul, 1971), pp. 245-46; Bloom, *The Anxiety of Influence*, p. 33; E. LeRoy Lawson, *Very Sure of God: Religious Language in the Poetry of Robert Browning* (Nashville, Tenn.: Vanderbilt University Press, 1974), p. 71; Roger Sharrock, "Browning and History," in Armstrong, *Robert Browning*, p. 90.

3. See Columbus and Kemper, p. 253: "*Sordello* itself as a poem, therefore, appears to be in process, not in stasis." See also Browning's defense of the poem (and incidental use of structural imagery) in a letter of 6 February 1846 to Elizabeth Barrett: "Whatever can be clearly spoken, ought to be: but 'bricks and mortar' is very easily said—and some of the thoughts in 'Sordello' not so readily even if Miss Mitford were to try her hand on them" (*Letters of Robert Browning and Elizabeth Barrett Barrett*, volume I, p. 439). Though Browning may have wavered in his estimation of *Pauline*, he stuck by *Sordello* through all detraction. Even as late as 1872, he could tell his friend Alfred Domett that *Fifine at the Fair* was "the most metaphysical and boldest he had written since *Sordello*" and add that he "was very doubtful as to its reception by the public." (Quoted in Griffin and Minchin, pp. 248-49.)

4. The reader wanting to consult Browning's headnotes as coherent commentary should turn to Ian Jack, *Browning's Major Poetry* (Oxford: Clarendon Press, 1973), pp. 45-54. Jack's decision to reprint the headnotes, sometimes in lieu of critical explication of the text, amply illustrates their unhelpfulness.

5. Isobel Armstrong, "Browning and the 'Grotesque' Style," in *The Major Victorian Poets: Reconsiderations*, ed. Isobel Armstrong (London: Routledge and Kegan Paul, 1969), p. 102, observes of Browning's tactics in *Sordello* that "the grammar, assisted by the breaks in the lines, constantly creates and dispels illusions of meaning and relationship and requires a continuous reorientation and adjustment to its direction." See also Roma A. King, Jr., *The Bow and the Lyre: The Art of Robert Browning* (Ann Arbor, Mich.: University of Michigan Press, 1957), pp. 66-67.

6. For divergent explanations of the two powers in this passage, see Stewart W. Holmes, "Browning's *Sordello* and Jung: Browning's *Sordello* in the Light of Jung's Theory of Types," *PMLA*, 56 (1941), 758-96; Earl Hilton, "Browning's *Sordello* as a Study of the Will," *PMLA*, 69 (1954), 1127-34; Collins, *Robert Browning's Moral-Aesthetic Theory*, p.60; Lawrence Poston, III, "Browning's Career to 1841: The Theme of Time and the Problem of Form," *BIS*, 3 (1975), 79-100; John Grube, "*Sordello*, Browning's Christian Epic," *English Studies in Canada*, 4 (1978), 415. J. W. Harper, " 'Eternity Our Due': Time in the Poetry of Robert Browning," in *Victorian Poetry*, ed. Malcolm Bradbury and David Palmer (London: Arnold, 1972), p. 73, writes that "all of the rest of Browning's work is an elaboration and clarification of this climactic passage in *Sordello*."

7. E. D. H. Johnson, *The Alien Vision of Victorian Poetry: Sources of the Poetic Imagination in Tennyson, Browning, and Arnold* (Princeton, N.J.: Princeton University Press, 1952), p. 77, finds in "the theme of the artist's communicative function" what little unity *Sordello* possesses. For Morse Peckham, *Victorian Revolutionaries: Speculations on Some Heroes of a Culture Crisis* (New York: Braziller, 1970), p. 104, in *Sordello* Browning's theme is "the mask of language."

8. On the fatality of absolute knowledge in Browning, see Norton B. Crowell, *The Triple Soul: Browning's Theory of Knowledge* (Albuquerque, N.M.: University of New Mexico Press, 1963), p. xiv; Peckham, *Victorian Revolutionaries*, p. 114; Sharrock, in Armstrong, *Robert Browning*, p. 93.

9. Quoted in Griffin and Minchin, p. 301.

10. Letter of 5 March 1866: "You are quite right about the classification of *Sordello's* — neither with the first nor the second of those moods of mind: it is the second as 'enervated' and modified by the impulse to 'thrust in time eternity's concern' — that, or nothing. This is just indicated in the passage where these words occur, and the rest of the poem is an example of the same" (*Letters of Robert Browning*, p. 92).

11. See George Santayana's essay "The Poetry of Barbarism," in his *Interpretations of Poetry and Religion* (New York: Scribner, 1905), p. 204: Browning "had no idea of anything eternal." For a restatement of Santayana's position, see Joseph E. Baker, "Religious Implications in Browning's Poetry," *PQ*, 36 (1957), 436-52. See also William James's response to Santayana, quoted in F. O. Matthiessen, *The James Family* (New York: Knopf, 1949), p. 488: "Dramatic unities; laws of versification; ecclesiastical mysteries; scholastic doctrines. Bah! Give me Walt Whitman and Browning ten times over, much as the perverse ugliness of the latter at times irritates me, and intensely as I have enjoyed Santayana's attack. The barbarians are in the line of mental growth, and those who insist that the ideal and the real are dynamically continuous are those by whom the world is to be saved."

12. See in the *Essay on Shelley* the objective poet's function of "getting at new substance by breaking up the assumed wholes into parts of independent and unclassed value, careless of the unknown laws for recombining them (it will be the business of yet another poet to suggest those hereafter)" (*CPDW*, p. 1010).

13. Michael Mason, "The Importance of *Sordello*," in Armstrong, *Major Victorian Poets*, p. 136; Robert Langbaum, "Browning and the Question of Myth," *PMLA*, 81 (1966), 579. Other advocates of "simultaneity" in Browning include Hermann Heuer, "Zum Formproblem in Brownings *Sordello*," *Englische Studien*, 67 (1933), 352 ff.; William Whitla, *The Central Truth: The Incarnation in Robert Browning's Poetry* (Toronto: University of Toronto Press, 1963), p. 151; T. J. Collins, "The Poetry of Robert Browning: A Proposal for Reexamination," *TSLL*, 15 (1972), 325-40; William E. Harrold, *The Variance and the Unity: A Study of the Complementary Poems of Robert Browning* (Athens, Ohio: Ohio University Press, 1973), p. 234; Robert A. Lecker, "The Crisis of Meeting: Mediation and Synthesis in Browning's *Sordello*," *English Studies in Canada*, 3 (1977), 307-25. Harper, in Bradbury and Palmer, p. 64, sees that Browning rejects the possibility of simultaneity as "an intolerable negation of essential human desires." If there be simultaneity in this poem, it is located in

the free indirect discourse that is one of its major narrative modes, the hovering of poetic voice between Sordello's consciousness and Browning's as narrator. But time and again Browning exploits the ironic possibilities of this mode precisely to discredit Sordello's hunger for the perfection and presence that an ideal of simultaneity holds forth.

14. Armstrong, in Armstrong, *Major Victorian Poets*, p. 95. See also Shaw, p. 29, on the purposeful ruptures of Browning's style: "He keeps breaking the rhetorical conventions in order to collapse the wall between subject and object."

15. See Paul de Reul, *L'Art et la pensée de Robert Browning* (Bruxelles: Lamertin, 1929), p. 254: "Précisément parce que l'auteur exige de nous plus d'attention, nous pénétrons dans son esprit plus avant que chez d'autres poètes." Donald S. Hair, *Browning's Experiments with Genre* (Toronto: University of Toronto Press, 1972), p. 31, observes that in *Sordello* "Browning deliberately slows the narrative."

16. For explicit statements of synecdochal deferral as a principle of life as well as letters, see "James Lee's Wife" (1864; line 322): "Now the parts and then the whole!"; "A Death in the Desert" (1864; line 588): "Man partly is and wholly hopes to be."

17. Although the specter of Shelley has been elaborately exorcised just twenty lines back, a ghostly paradigm may underlie Browning's temporal trope; in *Adonais*, 442-43, Shelley describes the "gray walls" of Rome "on which dull Time / Feeds, like slow fire upon a hoary brand."

18. *CPDW*, p. 1009.

19. See Elissa Schagrin Guralnick, "Browning's Transcendental Platan: *Sordello* Reconsidered," Ph.D. dissertation, Yale University, 1973, p. 103: "We are made to feel throughout the poem a continuous tension of possibility in the moment which is present."

20. When referring in the *Essay on Shelley* to Shelley's "complete enginery of a poet," Browning may have thought of this passage—and of his own more prospective incompleteness (*CPDW*, p. 1010).

21. William Irvine and Park Honan, *The Book, the Ring, and the Poet: A Biography of Robert Browning* (New York: McGraw-Hill, 1974), p. 86.

22. Mark D. Hawthorne, "Browning, *Sordello*, and Don Quixote," *MLN*, 92 (1977), 1033-37, traces the allusion to Cervantes in this passage and offers pertinent remarks on Browning's sense of his fiction, his audience, and his protagonist.

23. See Herford, p. 252: Browning " 'welcomes the rebuff' of every jagged excrescence or ragged fray, of every sudden and abrupt breach of continuity." Elton, volume III, p. 393, offers observations on Browning's temporal strategy in the late *Parleyings* (1887) that also hold true for *Sordello*, with its effect "of an interrupted stumbling gallop, of a concision that causes delay."

24. Browning wrote to Elizabeth Barrett on 17 May 1846, "The cant is, that 'an age of transition' is the melancholy thing to contemplate and delineate—whereas the worst things of all to look back on are times of comparative standing still, rounded in their impotent completeness" (*Letters of Robert Browning and Elizabeth Barrett Barrett*, volume II, p. 710). See Brooke, p. 305, on the poet's love for the early Renaissance, "a period which was shaking off the past, living intensely in the present, and prophesying the future"; Lawrence Poston, III, "Browning's Political Skepticism: *Sordello* and the Plays," *PMLA*, 88 (1973), 264, on Browning's ability to "anticipate the imaginative force behind the Renaissance."

25. For brief studies of Browning's relation to Dante, see Ruth Elizabeth Sullivan, "Browning's 'Childe Roland' and Dante's 'Inferno,' " *VP*, 5 (1967), 296-302; Cook, p. 298.

26. See the note to this passage in *Complete Works*, volume II, p. 418.

27. For the two readings compare Reul, p. 163, and Rivers, p. 6. For the more accurate view that Browning's classification of poets may be ultimately untenable, see Charles Carroll Everett, "Sordello: The Hero as Poet," *Poet-lore*, 8 (1896), 252; Michael G. Yetman, "Exorcising Shelley Out of Browning: *Sordello* and the Problem of Poetic Identity," *VP*, 13 (1975), 88. See also Browning's interesting vacillation in his letter to Dowden of 5 March 1866, quoted above (*Letters of Robert Browning*, p. 92). A similar vacillation between the

categories of "objective" and "subjective" poets in the *Essay on Shelley* was identified as early as 1891 by Orr, *Life and Letters*, volume I, p. 272: the distinction is "one which tends more and more to efface itself in the sphere of the higher creative imagination."

28. For cheerful and bleak interpretations of this moment of failure, compare William John Alexander, *An Introduction to the Poetry of Robert Browning* (Boston: Ginn, 1889), p. 176, and John Lucas, "Politics and the Poet's Role," in *Literature and Politics in the Nineteenth Century*, ed. John Lucas (London: Methuen, 1971), p. 27. See the impromptu translation of *Purgatorio*, V. 53-57, that Browning offered to Elizabeth Barrett as "just my Sordello's story" in a letter of 21 December 1845 (*Letters of Robert Browning and Elizabeth Barrett Barrett*, volume I, p. 336):

> *And sinners were we to the extreme hour;*
> *Then, light from heaven fell, making us aware,*
> *So that, repenting us and pardoned, out*
> *Of life we passed to God, at peace with Him*
> *Who fills the heart with yearning Him to see.*

Chapter 4

1. Letter of 16 November 1845 (*Letters of Robert Browning and Elizabeth Barrett Barrett*, volume I, p. 270).

2. Browning makes this distinction in the original preface to *Strafford* (*Complete Works*, volume II, p. 9). The consistency of Browning's thinking about the drama appears in the similarity between this preface and his remarks in a letter of 11 January 1846 sent to Elizabeth Barrett with the manuscript of *Luria*, the last full-length play he wrote: "It is all in long speeches – the *action, proper*, is in them – there are no descriptions, or amplifications – but here. .in a drama of this kind, all the *events*, (and interest), take place in the *minds* of the actors. .somewhat like Paracelsus in that respect" (*Letters of Robert Browning and Elizabeth Barrett Barrett*, volume I, p. 381).

3. Irvine and Honan, p. 71, epitomize a critical consensus that "Browning was fascinated by motives, but seemed scarcely interested in how motives produced action or how one action must be linked logically and psychologically with another." See Bernard Bosanquet, *A History of Aesthetic* (London: Swan Sonnenschein, 1892), p. 74; Henry Jones, "Browning as a Dramatic Poet," *Poet-lore*, 6 (1894), 27; Reul, pp. 296-97. J. M. Cohen, *Robert Browning* (London: Longmans, 1952), p. 22, writes, "Dramatic development is almost entirely lacking. So static is *The Return of the Druses*, indeed, that it is possible to read act five immediately after act one without missing anything of importance." Rare dissenting voices have expressed a willingness to take Browning's plays on his own terms. See Charles Carroll Everett, "The Tragic Motif in Browning's Dramas," *Andover Review*, 11 (1889), 116, on the imaginative autonomy of Browning's dramatic world; Caroline L. Sparrow, "Browning's Dramas," *MLN*, 22 (1907), 103, for emphasis on "the mood and its impulse"; C. E. Vaughan, *Types of Tragic Drama* (London: Macmillan, 1908), p. 252, for an appreciation of "inwardness" and "swift play"; Percy Lubbock, "Robert Browning," *Quarterly Review*, 217 (1912), 446, for "the pleasure of watching moment break in on moment" and for "the agile interlacing of action and reaction." Patricia Ball, *The Central Self: A Study in Romantic and Victorian Imagination* (London: Athlone Press, 1968), p. 58, views "event" in romantic drama as a revelation of character and romantic drama as an anticipation of Browning; Terry Otten, *The Deserted Stage: The Search for Dramatic Form in Nineteenth-Century England* (Athens, Ohio: Ohio University Press, 1972), p. 109, suggests that Browning "was groping toward a modern concept of drama in which dramatic action is centered in the individual character as an autonomous being who creates his own sense of order and meaning."

4. Noblesse oblige is a well-worn interpretive key in Orr, *Handbook*, p. 75; James W. Tupper, "*A Soul's Tragedy*: A Defense of Chiappino," *Englische Studien*, 44 (1912), 361-74; Frances Theresa Russell, "Browning's Account with Tragedy," *Sewanee Review*, 31

(1923), 97; Ioan M. Williams, *Browning* (London: Evans, 1967), p. 60. Almost every critic has followed Elizabeth Barrett in finding Luria "noble" (letter of 16 April 1846, in *Letters of Robert Browning and Elizabeth Barrett Barrett*, volume II, p. 628); see M. K. Hill, "*Luria*: A Study," *Temple Bar*, 126 (1902), 49-56; Smith, *Browning's Star-Imagery*, p. 130; Hair, p. 67. Dale Kramer, "Character and Theme in *Pippa Passes*," *VP*, 2 (1964), 244-45, sees Browning's characters "performing deeds which seem to abnegate self, but which are on the whole egoistic." For Kramer such egoism is a blot on the drama; but for Marvin P. Garrett, "Language and Design in *Pippa Passes*," *VP*, 13 (1975), 47-60, selfishness rightly understood is the salvation of Browning's characters.

5. Critics who have invoked an economic model to describe Browning's poetic attitudes have generally done so in order to disparage them; compare Henry Charles Duffin, *Amphibian: A Reconsideration of Browning* (London: Bowes, 1956), p. 213; Baker, p. 441; Irvine and Honan, p. 97. See also an essay on debt attributed to Browning, "Some Strictures on a Late Article in the 'Trifler,' " *Trifler*, February 1835, p. 18: "Wilt thou not rather submit with docile alacrity to the manifest necessity which hedges thee round and hems thee in, and, conforming thyself to a debtor's estate, make it thine only business to contrive how best co-operating with the design of thy being, thou mayst *owe* more and more?" (The attribution to Browning first appears in Orr, *Life and Letters*, volume I, p. 94; Maynard, pp. 109-10, discusses the essay and reprints it in full, pp. 380-82.)

6. See James Patton McCormick, "Robert Browning and the Experimental Drama," *PMLA*, 68 (1953), 982-91.

7. Carol T. Christ, *The Finer Optic: The Aesthetic of Particularity in Victorian Poetry* (New Haven and London: Yale University Press, 1975), p. 87. See also Williams, p. 85: "*Pippa Passes* does support the conclusion of Pippa herself, but it is merely *her* conclusion, and the meaning which is conveyed in the action is of wider reference." E. Warwick Slinn, " 'God a Tame Confederate': The Reader's Dual Vision in *Pippa Passes*," *UTQ*, 45 (1976), 169, shows how each character "is the victim of his illusions and the puppet of his own desires" and how Browning finds his theme "in the ironies of the egotistical sublime." The present reading contends that the burden of Browning's irony weighs on the reductive simplicity of such self-sublimating egos.

8. William Sharp, *Life of Robert Browning* (London: Scott, 1890), p. 100, asks of Pippa's hymn, "From the dramatist's point of view, could anything be more shaped for disaster?" Jones, *Browning as a Philosophical and Religious Teacher*, p. 104, points out the consequences of ascribing Pippa's perspective to Browning: "For if *all*, as he says, is for the best, there seems to be no room left for the differences apparent in the world, and the variety which gives it beauty and worth." See King, *The Focusing Artifice*, p. 54, on the "repetitious" and "anticlimactic" structure of the play; for an opposing view compare Harrold, p. 35.

9. As Ruskin complained in his letter to Browning of 2 December 1855, "Every now and then poor Pippa herself shall speak a long piece of Robert Browning." Edmund Clarence Stedman, *Victorian Poets*, rev. ed. (Boston: Houghton Mifflin, 1889), p. 318, observes of Pippa's songs, "If they have the wilding flavor, they have more than need be of specks and gnarledness." For a humanized Pippa, see Betty Cobey Senescu, "Another Pippa," *VN* (33) (spring 1968), 8-12.

10. In the text of 1841, before Pippa begins her song the Monsignor gives an ambiguous response to the Intendant's offer: "Why, if she sings, one might. . . ."

11. As Miller (p. 145) writes of a similar image at the close of the parleying with "Bernard de Mandeville" (1887), "For Browning the sun in the burning-glass is precisely *not* the true sun, but only another expression of the infinite distance of man from the deity." The myth of Perseus, which figures prominently in Browning's works from *Pauline* through *The Ring and the Book* and beyond, might be approached afresh as a romance of representation by focusing on the reflecting shield that empowers Perseus-Browning to overcome his enemies, notably the petrifying Gorgon of closure. As he wrote on 14 June 1845 to his own

Andromeda, Elizabeth Barrett, " 'Reflection' is exactly what it names itself – a *re*presentation, in scattered rays from every angle of incidence, of what first of all became present in a great light, a whole one. So tell me how these lights are born if you can!" (*Letters of Robert Browning and Elizabeth Barrett Barrett*, volume I, p. 95).

12. Miller, pp. 130-31, observes that "the plays study the question of *power*, political rather than magical or poetical power, but still power." It should be added that in Browning political power may be taken as a figuration of poetic power. The poet's oration in Book V of *Sordello*, as discussed in chapter 3, intertwines themes of poetic and political power. See also Balaustion's assertions that "poetry is power" in *Balaustion's Adventure* (1871; line 236) and in *Aristophanes' Apology* (1875; line 5582) – two poems with incidental political themes.

13. "Browning's Use of Historical Sources in *Strafford*," in *Six Studies of Nineteenth-Century English Literature and Thought*, ed. Harold Orel and George J. Worth, University of Kansas Humanistic Studies, no. 35 (Lawrence: University of Kansas Publications, 1962), pp. 34-35. Mary Rose Sullivan, "Browning's Plays: Prologue to *Men and Women*," *BIS*, 3 (1975), 18, follows the problem of illusion from *Strafford* into Browning's subsequent dramas: "His protagonists invariably *refuse* to accept the fact of betrayal: blinding themselves to the irrefutable evidence, they cling stubbornly to the idol, rather than admit his human imperfection."

14. Browning was well acquainted with, if indeed he did not write, these passages from John Forster's 1836 biography of Strafford: "Strange that, at such a moment, Lord Strafford should have recalled the memory of the virtuous and indomitable Eliot! He was soon to know on whose shoulders the mantle of Buckingham's great opponent had fallen"; and later, "Suddenly upon the sight of Strafford broke the vision of the long unseen assembly of the people, with the old chiefs and the old ceremonies, only more august and more fatal." Quoted from John Forster, *The Statesmen of the Commonwealth*, ed. John Overton Choules (New York: Harper, 1846), pp. 227 and 241. For a discussion of Browning's role in the writing of the biography, see DeVane, pp. 62-63; William S. Peterson, "A Re-Examination of Robert Browning's Prose Life of Strafford," *BN* (3) (fall 1969), 12-22; Michael Hancher, "Note on the Prose Life of Strafford," *BN* (4) (spring 1970), 42-45; Bruce S. Busby, "A Note to the Editor of *Thomas Wentworth, Earl of Strafford*," *SBHC*, 5 (2) (fall 1977), 65-70.

15. Emily H. Hickey's annotations in *Strafford: A Tragedy*, ed. Emily H. Hickey, 2nd ed. (London: Bell, 1891), p. 84, state that the star represents Strafford's "love for Charles." Smith, *Browning's Star-Imagery*, p. 45, identifies the star as Strafford without hesitation – apparently on the slender evidence of Lady Carlisle's speech at II.ii.267-68 – and without considering the implications of Strafford's thus becoming his own "guide." Walter Federle, *Robert Brownings dramatisches Experiment*, Ph.D. dissertation, University of Zürich, 1954 (Pfäffikon-Zürich: Schellenberg, 1954), p. 58, quotes from a manuscript "acting-copy" in the British Museum a version of the passage that expresses more frantically Strafford's confusion about his images of himself and of Charles. Who is guiding whom here?

> Oh, let me bear him safe
> Thro' the great warfare – calm thro' the drear sea
> Of blood – with one supremest star to guide –
> One face as of an angel bright on me!

16. Browning complained in a letter of 19 March 1864 to Isa Blagden that a recent tragedy "was just the usual failure . . . the ways & phrase are conventionally the old Elizabethan, and one knows there is no truth nor life in it all" (*Dearest Isa*, p. 188).

17. It seems likely that in writing this passage Browning had in mind the song of Shelley's spirits:

> Like veiled lightning asleep,
> Like the spark nursed in embers,

> *The last look Love remembers,*
> *Like a diamond, which shines*
> *On the dark wealth of mines,*
> *A spell is treasured but for thee alone.*
> *Down, down!*
>
> *We have bound thee, we guide thee;*
> *Down, down!*
> *With the bright form beside thee;*
> *Resist not the weakness,*
> *Such strength is in meekness. . . .*
> *(Prometheus Unbound,* II.iii.83-94)

The image of a central, veiled image is itself central to Shelley, and the image of the "diamond," in close conjunction with the ideas of love, of a treasuring up, and of an exalted weakness, makes this passage especially plausible as a source. Yet despite numerous correspondences between these lines and those spoken by Lady Carlisle, Browning's use of the Shelleyan passage seems less a borrowing than a reversal. She and all of his characters sustain their precious "weakness" not through hypnotic relaxation, but through active resistance to their own strength.

18. Browning's association of futurity with such an emblem of flawed perfection found confirmation in the "pretty phaenomenon" of which he wrote to Elizabeth Barrett on 5 August 1846: "Our Druids used to make balls for divining out of such *all-but-solid* gems with the central weakness—I have had them in my hand" (*Letters of Robert Browning and Elizabeth Barrett Barrett*, volume II, p. 933). Browning's letter redoubles the poetic associations already present in his allusion to the bardic Druids by quoting the poet Claudian's use of the image; he returns to it himself in section CII of *Fifine at the Fair.*

19. Orel, in Orel and Worth, p. 36. See the perplexity of an anonymous reviewer at the "starts and jerks" of the play, in "Browning's *Strafford;* a Tragedy," *Edinburgh Review,* 65 (July 1837), 144; Robert Brainard Pearsall, *Robert Browning* (New York: Twayne, 1974), p. 38, on *Strafford'*s "broken syntax and skewed semantics."

20. Hair, pp. 43-72, and Poston, "Browning's Political Skepticism," pp. 65-70, stress irony in the dramas, following the lead of Arthur E. DuBois, "Robert Browning, Dramatist," *SP,* 33 (1936), 626-55. DuBois's analysis of the ironic suspension that concludes *In a Balcony* shows how the poet as ironist "distrusts absolutes" (p. 644).

21. Quoted in Maisie Ward, *Robert Browning and His World: Two Robert Brownings?* (New York: Holt, Rinehart and Winston, 1969), p. 205. See Browning's own comment on *Luria* in a letter of 22 January 1846 to Elizabeth Barrett: "Whatever comes of it, the 'aside,' the bye-play, the digression, will be the best, and the only true business of the piece" (*Letters of Robert Browning and Elizabeth Barrett Barrett*, volume I, p. 411). Philip Hobsbaum, "The Rise of the Dramatic Monologue," *Hudson Review,* 28 (1975), 227-45, derives Browning's most distinctive genre from the increasing elaboration of the soliloquy and monologue in post-Shakespearean drama.

22. Melchiori seeks the reticence rather in the poet than in his characters. Dorothy M. Mermin, "Speaker and Auditor in Browning's Dramatic Monologues," *UTQ,* 45 (1976), 139, observes of the characters in the plays, "Their obsessive concern with what they have or haven't said, will or won't say, generally retards the action and is often the centre of the plot."

23. One of the "inscriptions" Browning was clearing up in this play may have been Shelley's unfinished drama *Charles the First.* While *Strafford* is remarkably free of allusions to Shelley's play, Browning would have noticed in the fragmentary text published with the *Posthumous Poems* of 1824 that his hero is introduced there as "the apostate Strafford."

24. Hickey, p. 91.

25. Charles, "pour ne point effaroucher l'ombrageuse ambition de son père, s'efforça de dissimuler les talents qu'il avait reçus de la nature" (*Biographie universelle ancienne et moderne* [Paris: Desplaces, 1854-1865], volume VII, p. 586). Compare Vasari, an important source later in Browning's career, on "a certain timidity of mind, a sort of diffidence and want of force" in Andrea del Sarto (quoted in DeVane, p. 246).

26. Katherine Florence Gleason, *The Dramatic Art of Robert Browning* (Boston: Badger, 1927), p. 27, observes that the improbable ending of *King Victor and King Charles* is unhistorical as well. From this observation one may conclude that Browning makes his "statement" on the power of imagination in this play by mastering and characteristically "restating" the historical facts. Isobel Armstrong notes during a review article in *BSNotes*, 3(1) (1973), 31, that for Browning history "is always framed with the ironic, multiple qualifications of the present" and that "the discovery of the past is nothing more (or less) than the creation of the imagination." Recent criticism, especially of *The Ring and the Book*, gives ample support to this view. See Morse Peckham, "Historiography and *The Ring and the Book*," *VP*, 6 (1968), 243-57; Jacob Korg, "The Music of Lost Dynasties: Browning, Pound, and History," *ELH*, 39 (1972), 420-40. But this view of history has yet to be extensively applied to personal history, to those creations or revisions of the past that are the province of autobiography—and of the form of fictive autobiography that is Browning's most celebrated achievement, the dramatic lyric. John King McComb, "The Ever-Present Past in Robert Browning's Poetry," Ph.D. Dissertation, Johns Hopkins University, 1972, p. 121, presents a brief discussion of the importance of revisionary memory in Browning's dramatic art.

27. Ida M. Street's description of the poet's progress "from institutionalism to individualism" in "A Study of Browning's Dramas," *New Englander and Yale Review*, 55 (1891), 212, puts the matter in the most optimistic of lights; an unidentified contributor notes less leniently in "Robert Browning," *N&Q*, 11th Ser., 5 (1912), 342, that Browning's individuals are "all solitary at the core, and egoistic—self-explaining, self-admiring, self-pitying"; DuBois, p. 634, witnesses "vast vistas of emptiness of heart" in Browning's dramatic vision. Orr, "Religious Opinions," pp. 887-88, records more neutrally from conversations with the poet "an impression, to which he was subject, that all reality centred in himself; that the world he lived in was an illusion of his own mind."

Chapter 5

1. An abbreviated version of this chapter appears under the title "Browning's Lyric Intentions" in the winter 1980 issue of *Critical Inquiry*.

2. See a letter of 10 August 1846 to Elizabeth Barrett: "Will the deeds suffice?—not in their own value, no!—but in their plain, certain intention,—as a clear advance beyond mere words?" (*Letters of Robert Browning and Elizabeth Barrett Barrett*, volume II, 950). See also *Red Cotton Night-Cap Country* (1873): "Who is a poet needs must apprehend / Alike both speech and thoughts which prompt to speak" (3281-82).

3. On the plurality of the self in Browning's speakers see S. S. Curry, *Browning and the Dramatic Monologue* (Boston: Expression Company, 1927), p. 58; Christian N. Wenger, "The Masquerade in Browning's Dramatic Monologues," *CE*, 3 (1941), 235; Isobel Armstrong, "Browning and Victorian Poetry of Sexual Love," in Armstrong, *Robert Browning*, p. 283; Harold Bloom, *A Map of Misreading* (New York: Oxford University Press, 1975), p. 86. Miller suggests that many of Browning's dramatic monologues "are really internal dialogues" that "juxtapose or intermingle contradictory points of view" (p. 87) and points to the poet's own "indeterminacy of selfhood" and "wavering inner fluidity" (p. 104). Christopher Ricks speculates in his anthology *The Brownings: Letters and Poetry* (Garden City, N.Y.: Doubleday, 1970), p. 26, that Browning's "fascinated loathing of mesmerism and spiritualism may be not just a fear of having his self discovered, but of having his lack of a self discovered."

4. Orr, *Life and Letters*, volume II, p. 495, observes of the *Dramatic Idyls* of 1879 and 1880, "In them the act and the motive are not yet finally identified with each other. We see the act still palpitating with the motive; the motive dimly striving to recognize or disclaim itself in the act." J. A. Boulton, "Browning: A Potential Revolutionary," *Essays in Criticism*, 3 (1953), 168, mentions "the mingled process of confession, excuse, and justification" in the dramatic lyrics; Miller, p. 85, traces a process of "crystallization leading to discovery of its inadequacy and a return to chaos"; George M. Ridenour, "Browning's Music Poems: Fancy and Fact," *PMLA*, 78 (1963), 376, notes "the lyric and discursive poles that Browning constantly manipulates." Peckham, *Victorian Revolutionaries*, p. 91, defines a "feedback phenomenon" in Browning: "The flow of utterance becomes part of and changes the situation." Compare Harper, in Bradbury and Palmer, p. 77, on the "desperate dissatisfaction" of the monologists; David Sonstroem, "On Resisting Brother Lippo," *TSLL*, 15 (1974), 722-23, on the importance to Browning of "unresolved differences" that elicit "a vibration of attitudes."

5. See letters to Elizabeth Barrett of 17 January and 29 March 1846: "I should say, no words, no *feelings* even, do justice to the whole conviction and *religion* of my soul — and tho' they may be suffered to represent some one minute's phase of it, yet, in their very fulness and passion they do injustice to the *unrepresented, other minute's*, depth and breadth of love"; "The little I *have* written, has been an inconscious scrawling with the mind fixed somewhere else: the subject of the scrawl may have previously been the real object of the mind on some occasion, — the very thing which *then* to miss, (finding in its place *such another* result of a still prior fancy-fit) — which then to see escape, or find escaped, was the vexation of the time!" (*Letters of Robert Browning and Elizabeth Barrett Barrett*, volume I, pp. 396, 568).

6. For Browning's remarks on the dramatic principle in *Pauline*, see DeVane, p. 41; Michael A. Burr, "Browning's Note to Forster," *VP*, 12 (1974), 343-49. See also Michael Hancher, "The Dramatic Situation in Browning's *Pauline*," *Yearbook of English Studies*, 1 (1971), 149-59; Philip Drew, "Facts and Fancies," *BIS*, 3 (1975), 144.

7. Robert Langbaum, *The Poetry of Experience: The Dramatic Monologue in Modern Literary Tradition* (1957; New York: Norton, 1963 [reprint]), p. 152.

8. See Arnold Williams, "Browning's 'Great Text in Galatians,' " *MLQ*, 10 (1949), 89-90; Gordon Pitts, "Browning's 'Soliloquy of the Spanish Cloister': 'Hy, Zy, Hine,' " *N&Q*, 211 (1966), 339-40; James F. Loucks, " 'Hy, Zy, Hine' and Peter of Abano," *VP*, 12 (1974), 165-69.

9. See Langbaum, *Poetry of Experience*, pp. 109-36; E. D. H. Johnson, "Robert Browning's Pluralistic Universe," *UTQ*, 31 (1961), 20-41.

10. G. K. Chesterton writes in *Robert Browning* (1903; London: Macmillan, 1925 [reprint]), p. 38: "*Sordello* was the most glorious compliment that has ever been paid to the average man." Compare George Eliot's confession in an unsigned review of *Men and Women* in *The Westminster Review*, 65 (January 1856), 291, that "what we took for obscurity in him was superficiality in ourselves"; the appreciation of Browning's speed in Swinburne's 1875 essay on Chapman, reprinted in Swinburne's *Complete Works*, volume XII, p. 145: "He is something too much the reverse of obscure; he is too brilliant and subtle for the ready reader of a ready writer to follow with any certainty the track of an intelligence which moves with such incessant rapidity"; George Saintsbury's more specialized interest in Browning's prosodic "breathlessness," in *A History of English Prosody*, volume III (London: Macmillan, 1910), p. 218.

11. See lines 1389 and 1436 of *Hippolytus*, trans. David Grene, in *Greek Tragedies*, ed. David Grene and Richmond Lattimore (Chicago and London: University of Chicago Press, 1960), I, 290.

12. For Browning's attitudes toward Hellenism, see two discussions by W. C. DeVane: *Browning's Parleyings: The Autobiography of a Mind* (New Haven, Conn.: Yale University Press, 1927), pp. 238-40; and "Browning and the Spirit of Greece," in *Nineteenth-Century*

Studies, ed. Herbert Davis, William C. DeVane and R. C. Bald (Ithaca, N.Y.: Cornell University Press, 1940), pp. 179-98. See also Kenneth L. Knickerbocker, "Greek Wisdom and Browning: A Reply," *Classical Journal*, 50 (1950), 393-94.

13. Letter of 9 February 1858 to Madame du Quaire, in *Letters of Matthew Arnold 1848-88*, ed. George W. E. Russell (London: Macmillan, 1895), volume I, p. 61.

14. Browning rekindled this fire when breaking away from the somber shades of *La Saisiaz* in the opening stanzas of its companion poem, *The Two Poets of Croisic* (1878).

15. The standard indentation marking Browning's quatrains in "Pictor Ignotus" is here retained. (The Ohio edition, and no other, justifies the left margin of the poem.)

16. See Michael H. Bright, "Browning's 'Pictor Ignotus': An Interpretation," *SBHC*, 4 (1) (spring 1976), 58-59.

17. Hair, p. 107, observes that "the specks give the water whatever taste it has." Walter Bagehot's 1864 essay on "Wordsworth, Tennyson, and Browning; or Pure, Ornate, and Grotesque Art in English Poetry," reprinted in his *Collected Works*, ed. Norman St. John-Stevas (Cambridge, Mass.: Harvard University Press, 1965), volume II, p. 353, identifies a struggle with imperfection as the hallmark of Browning's "grotesque" art: "It takes the type, so to say, *in difficulties*. It gives a representation of it in its minimum development, amid the circumstances least favorable to it, just while it is struggling with obstacles, just where it is encumbered with incongruities."

18. In 1836 Browning included in a headnote a citation from Defoe's 1704 *Dictionary of All Religions*, defining the sect allegedly founded by Johannes Agricola: "Antinomians, so denominated for rejecting the Law as a thing of no use under the Gospel dispensation" (*Complete Works*, volume III, p. 242).

19. See Harper, in Bradbury and Palmer, p. 61, on Johannes's "manipulation of tense sequence" as revealing "a particular theory of time, the necessitarianism which results from inability to reconcile human freedom and divine omniscience."

20. Quoted in DeVane, *Handbook*, p. 124. For details on Johannes's dispute with Luther in 1537, see *Complete Works*, volume III, p. 383-84.

21. *On Sublimity*, trans. D. A. Russell (Oxford: Clarendon Press, 1965), p. 12.

22. Compare the ironic response of the first voice of *Easter-Day* to the naive optimism the second voice espouses: "I see! / You would grow as a natural tree, / Stand as a rock, soar up like fire" (93-95).

23. W. David Shaw, "Browning's Duke as Theatrical Producer," *VN* (29) (spring 1966), p. 21, links rhetoric and psychology by finding in the Duke a classic case of obsessional neurosis, marked by "ceremonial compulsions." See also the brief but incisive reading of "the Duke's desperate attempt at rhetorical control" by Sanford Pinsker, " 'As If She Were Alive': Rhetorical Anguish in 'My Last Duchess,' " *Concerning Poetry*, 9 (2) (fall 1976), 71-73.

24. For the different view that this passage represents the Duke's reduction of his Duchess to mechanical monotony, see Shaw, "Browning's Duke," pp. 19-20. Robert A. Greenberg, "Ruskin, Pugin, and the Contemporary Context of 'The Bishop Orders His Tomb,' " *PMLA*, 84 (1969), 1592-93, investigates the Browningesque clash of conflicting eras and finds in this passage "a throwback to an earlier value structure."

25. See George Monteiro, "Browning's 'My Last Duchess,' " *VP*, 1 (1963), 237.

26. Quoted in Hiram Corson, *An Introduction to the Study of Robert Browning's Poetry* (Boston: Heath, 1889), p. viii.

27. Louis S. Friedland, "Ferrara and 'My Last Duchess,' " *SP*, 33 (1936), 656-84. See Browning's allegorization of Euripides' *Helena*, in a letter of 2 September 1864 to Julia Wedgwood: "Does this mean, a good poem suffering from the world's misconception of it?" (*Robert Browning and Julia Wedgwood: A Broken Friendship as Revealed by Their Letters*, ed. Richard Curle [New York: Stokes, 1937], p. 61). See also Browning's preface to his translation *The Agamemnon of Aeschylus* (1877), in which he refuses to exercise "the scholar's privilege of trying his fancy upon each obstacle whenever he comes to a stoppage, and effectually clearing the way by suppressing what seems to lie in it."

Chapter 6

1. Letter of 25 June 1864, quoted in Curle, p. 29.
2. Quoted in DeVane, *Handbook*, p. 207, from a letter of 24 February 1853 to Joseph Milsand.
3. Clyde de L. Ryals, *Browning's Later Poetry 1871-1889* (Ithaca, N.Y.: Cornell University Press, 1975), p. 243, writes: "The universe of Browning's late poetry is very nearly one of absurdity, where man is depicted dealing with fictions in order to reach the 'Truth,' which in itself may be only the supreme fiction." Although the fictionality of meaning is rarely made explicit in earlier Browning, it remains a pervasive theme. Ryals's insight is too central to be confined to the later works alone.
4. Quoted in Orr, "Religious Opinions," p. 880.
5. Orr reports that Browning's religious belief "held a saving clause, which removed it from all dogmatic, hence all admissible grounds of controversy; the more definite or concrete conceptions of which it consists possessed no finality for even his own mind; they represented for him an absolute truth in contingent relations to it" (*Life and Letters*, volume II, p. 630). In the *Essay on Shelley* Browning attributes much the same quality of belief to his romantic precursor, who "would have finally ranged himself with the Christians": "I find him everywhere taking for granted some of the capital dogmas of Christianity, while most vehemently denying their historical basement" (*CPDW*, p. 1013). On the role of "representation" in Browning's Christianity, see C. R. Tracy, "Browning's Heresies," *SP*, 33 (1936), 620; Shaw, *Dialectical Temper*, p. 302; Roma A. King, Jr., "The Necessary Surmise: The Shaping Spirit of Robert Browning's Poetry," in *Romantic and Victorian: Studies in Memory of William H. Marshall*, ed. W. Paul Elledge and Richard L. Hoffman (Rutherford, N.J.: Farleigh Dickinson University Press, 1971), p. 349; Elizabeth Bieman, "The Ongoing Testament in Browning's 'Saul,' " *UTQ*, 43 (1974), 160. Elinor Shaffer, "Browning's St. John: The Casuistry of the Higher Criticism," *VS*, 16 (1972), 213, provides an admirable reading of "A Death in the Desert," which places the poet's beliefs in their Victorian (and romantic) contexts: "Coleridge's late perception that Christian European civilization rests upon a lie is never far from Browning; and both poets learned this from the higher criticism, and learned too how to transform it into something like a virtue, indeed, into a philosophical method."
6. Yeats's 1890 essay is reprinted in *Letters to the New Island* (Cambridge, Mass.: Harvard University Press, 1934), p. 97. Compare Pater's 1887 review article on Browning, reprinted in his *Essays from "The Guardian"* (London: Macmillan, 1920), p. 43: "The world and all its action, as a show of thought, that is the scope of his work." Browning receives a more brisk salute in Pound's "Mesmerism": "Thought's in your verse-barrel!" (*Personae* [New York: New Directions, 1926], p. 13). See also Lascelles Abercrombie, "Robert Browning," in *The Great Victorians*, ed. H. J. Massingham and Hugh Massingham (Garden City, N.Y.: Doubleday, 1932), pp. 81-82; André Gide, *Journal* (Paris: Gallimard, 1951), volume I, p. 1306.
7. Hoxie N. Fairchild, "Browning the Simple-Hearted Casuist," *UTQ*, 18 (1949), 234-40, advances the objection that Browning's conclusions are often "giveaways" of his meaning. For two answers to this objection, see Rupert E. Palmer, Jr., "The Uses of Character in 'Bishop Blougram's Apology,' " *MP*, 58 (1960), 108-18; David R. Ewbank, "Bishop Blougram's Argument," *VP*, 10 (1972), 257-63. Browning's emphasis on means rather than ends is discussed in more general terms by Peckham, *Victorian Revolutionaries*, p. 96; Christ, p. 112.
8. Compare the assessment of the relations between music and meaning, and between composer and performer-auditor, in section XC of *Fifine at the Fair* (1565-88). While Don Juan turns to the past master Schumann for authoritative "truth," "knowledge," "certitude," and "assurance," he seeks corroboration not of a proposition, but of a feeling. Since "no speech may evince / Feeling like music," Don Juan prizes the ability of the composer,

"feeling once what I feel now," to "*record* what other men / Feel only to forget!" Browning twice italicizes *record* — "I strike the key, I bid *record* / The instrument — thanks greet the veritable word!" — in order to stress the emotional force at the root of *recordari*: to lay to heart moments that may move and hearten others. Both composer and performer "record" an experience shared across the years through a creative, secondary recovery analogous to the jeweler's "repristination" at the beginning of *The Ring and the Book*. Though modern phonographic technology has greatly increased the distance between the composer and most auditors (and has incidentally given quite a different sense to "record" as a musical term), to remember that both Don Juan and Browning's 1855 speaker are performing the music they hear is to redouble one's focus on the ways in which they are themselves passionately generating the meanings they find in Schumann and Galuppi.

9. See the influential second chapter of Langbaum's *Poetry of Experience*, pp. 75-108.

10. See Ridenour, "Browning's Music Poems," p. 373: "The two parts comment on each other. Neither, however, annihilates the other, nor is there genuine synthesis, outside the imaginative force that lets us consider them together."

11. Edgar F. Harden, "A New Reading of Browning's 'A Toccata of Galuppi's,' " *VP*, 11 (1973), 333, observes of the lovers, "What they try, as the speaker only partly understands, is to live in the whirl and flow of the process, to extend the past into the future, living the moment so intensely that satiation can never come."

12. See Dougald B. MacEachen, "Browning's Use of His Sources in 'Andrea del Sarto,' " *VP*, 8 (1970), 61-64.

13. Betty Miller, *Robert Browning: A Portrait* (New York: Scribner, 1952), p. 187.

14. Honan, p. 213, writes that "Andrea's repetition suggests spiritual as well as physical debility."

15. See Margaret Willy, *A Critical Commentary on Browning's "Men and Women"* (London: Macmillan, 1968), pp. 23-24; Elizabeth Bieman, "An Eros *Manqué*: Browning's 'Andrea del Sarto,' " *SEL*, 10 (1970), 668.

16. Knight, p. 247.

17. See Glen Omans, "Browning's 'Fra Lippo Lippi': A Transcendentalist Monk," *VP*, 7 (1969), 141: "Browning was certainly using Fra Lippo to express to his own age his own theory of poetic technique." King, *The Bow and the Lyre*, pp. 32-51, describes the growth of Lippo's understanding during the monologue.

18. Susan Hardy Aiken, "Patterns of Imagery in 'Fra Lippo Lippi,' " *SBHC*, 3 (1) (spring 1975), 61-75, follows the imagistic ascent of the poem toward a blasphemous equation of Lippo's creativity with God's.

19. For "fat and lean" Browning originally wrote "good and bad"; the revision — from signifieds, as it were, to signifiers — bespeaks the saving of appearances and the deferral of meaning that inform Lippo's evolving thinking about representation. Variant readings may be consulted in William S. Peterson, "The Proofs of Browning's *Men and Women*," *SBHC*, 3 (2) (fall 1975), 23-39.

20. On fidelity to "the observed fact," see Johnson, *Alien Vision*, pp. 116-17; also see Richard Benvenuto, "Lippo and Andrea: The Pro and Contra of Browning's Realism," *SEL*, 13 (1973), 643-52.

21. Compare two passages from the *Essay on Shelley*. The objective poet endeavors "to reproduce things external (whether the phenomena of the scenic universe, or the manifested action of the human heart and brain), with an immediate reference, in every case, to the common eye and apprehension of his fellow-men, assumed capable of receiving and profiting by this reproduction"; the subjective poet endeavors "to lift his fellows, with their half-apprehensions, up to his own sphere, by intensifying the import of details and rounding the universal meaning" (*CPDW*, pp. 1008-9). Fra Lippo's temporalization of meaning lets art perform both objective and subjective functions.

22. Sonstroem, p. 734, complains that "Lippo mistakes phenomena for significance." For a better view of the process of signification celebrated here and elsewhere in Browning,

see Mark Siegchrist, "Browning's *Red Cotton Night-Cap Country*: The Process of Imagination," *VP*, 12 (1974), 137, on "a gap between the perceiver and his subject, the crossing of which provides a measure of the imaginative power capable of performing such a feat."

23. See Henry James, *William Wetmore Story and His Friends* (Boston: Houghton Mifflin, 1903), volume II, pp. 216-27, for successive analyses of Story and of Browning as artists. Story's failure is attributed to a lack of "intensity" and "insistence" — the qualities in Browning's art that so intrigued James that he turned them into a tale in "The Private Life" (1909).

24. Compare a letter of 3 September 1882 to Mrs. FitzGerald in which Browning describes a dream work typical of the operation of his poetic works as well: "By a law of the association of ideas — *contraries* come into the mind as often as *similarities* — and the peace and solitude readily called up the notion of what would most jar with them" (*Learned Lady*, p. 152).

Epilogue

1. Quoted in Sharp, pp. 195-96.

2. For discussions of the poem as a response to Arnold, see A. W. Crawford, "Browning's 'Cleon,' " *JEGP*, 26 (1927), 485-90; Bloom, *Poetry and Repression*, p. 177. Adrienne Munich, "Emblems of Temporality in Browning's 'Cleon,' " *BIS*, 6 (1978), 117-36, offers suggestive parallels with poems on Hellenic themes by Arnold and Tennyson. Putting Cleon's "joy-hunger" in the broad context of British romanticism, she finds "the identification of Browning with his creation, Cleon, to be quite close" (p. 136).

3. Wilfred L. Guerin, "Irony and Tension in Browning's 'Karshish,' " *VP*, 1 (1963), 138, notes the importance of delay in that poem. See also Richard D. Altick, "Browning's 'Karshish' and St. Paul," *MLN*, 72 (1957), 494-96; William Irvine, "Four Monologues in Browning's *Men and Women*," *VP*, 2 (1964), 161. For Browning's use of typology, see Ward Hellstrom, "Time and Type in Browning's *Saul*," *ELH*, 33 (1966), 370-89.

SELECTED BIBLIOGRAPHY

SELECTED BIBLIOGRAPHY

BROWNING'S PUBLISHED WRITINGS

The Complete Poetic and Dramatic Works of Robert Browning, ed. Horace E. Scudder. Boston and New York: Houghton Mifflin, 1895.

The Complete Works of Robert Browning with Variant Readings and Annotations, ed. Roma A. King, Jr., et al., 4 volumes to date. Athens, Ohio: Ohio University Press, 1969 -   .

"Introduction." *The Divine Order and Other Sermons* by Thomas Jones, ed. Brynmor Jones, pp. xi-xiii. London: Isbister, 1884.

"Some Strictures on a Late Article in the 'Trifler.'" *Trifler* (February 1835), pp. 16-19.

The Works of Robert Browning, ed. F. G. Kenyon, 10 volumes. London: Smith, Elder, 1912.

BROWNING'S LETTERS

Dearest Isa: Robert Browning's Letters to Isabella Blagden, ed. Edward C. McAleer. Austin: University of Texas Press, 1951.

Learned Lady: Letters from Robert Browning to Mrs. Thomas FitzGerald 1876-1889, ed. Edward C. McAleer. Cambridge, Mass.: Harvard University Press, 1966.

The Letters of Robert Browning and Elizabeth Barrett Barrett 1845-1846, ed. Elvan Kintner, 2 volumes. Cambridge, Mass.: Harvard University Press, 1969.

Letters of Robert Browning Collected by Thomas J. Wise, ed. Thurman L. Hood. New Haven, Conn.: Yale University Press, 1933.

Robert Browning and Alfred Domett, ed. F. G. Kenyon. New York: Dutton, 1906.

Robert Browning and Julia Wedgwood: A Broken Friendship as Revealed by Their Letters, ed. Richard Curle. New York: Stokes, 1937.

BOOKS AND ESSAYS ABOUT BROWNING

Armstrong, Isobel. "Browning and the 'Grotesque' Style." *The Major Victorian Poets: Reconsiderations*, ed. Isobel Armstrong, pp. 93-123. London: Routledge and Kegan Paul, 1969.

Bagehot, Walter. "Wordsworth, Tennyson, and Browning; or Pure, Ornate, and Grotesque Art in English Poetry." *The Collected Works of Walter Bagehot: The Literary Essays*, ed. Norman St. John-Stevas, volume II, pp. 321-66. Cambridge, Mass.: Harvard University Press, 1965.

Ball, Patricia. "Browning's Godot." *Victorian Poetry*, 3 (1965), 245-53.

———. *The Central Self: A Study in Romantic and Victorian Imagination*. London: Athlone Press, 1968.

Benvenuto, Richard. "Lippo and Andrea: The Pro and Contra of Browning's Realism." *Studies in English Literature 1500-1900*, 13 (1973), 643-52.

Bloom, Harold. *The Anxiety of Influence: A Theory of Poetry*. New York: Oxford University Press, 1973.

———. *A Map of Misreading*. New York: Oxford University Press, 1975.

———. *Poetry and Repression: Revisionism from Blake to Stevens*. New Haven, Conn., and London: Yale University Press, 1976.

———. *The Ringers in the Tower: Studies in Romantic Tradition*. Chicago and London: University of Chicago Press, 1971.

Brooke, Stopford A. *The Poetry of Robert Browning*. New York: Crowell, 1902.

Chesterton, G. K. *Robert Browning*. 1903 (reprinted in London: Macmillan, 1925).

Christ, Carol T. *The Finer Optic: The Aesthetic of Particularity in Victorian Poetry*. New Haven, Conn., and London: Yale University Press, 1975.

Cook, Eleanor. *Browning's Lyrics: An Exploration*. Toronto and Buffalo: University of Toronto Press, 1974.

DeVane, William Clyde, Jr. *A Browning Handbook*, 2nd ed. New York: Appleton, 1955.

DuBois, Arthur E. "Robert Browning, Dramatist." *Studies in Philology*, 33 (1936), 626-55.

Du Bos, Charles. "*Pauline* de Browning." *Etudes Anglaises*, 7 (1954), 161-64.

Hair, Donald S. *Browning's Experiments with Genre*. Toronto and Buffalo: University of Toronto Press, 1972.

Harper, J. W. " 'Eternity Our Due': Time in the Poetry of Robert Browning." *Victorian Poetry*, ed. Malcolm Bradbury and David Palmer, pp. 59-87. London: Arnold, 1972.

Herford, C. H. *Robert Browning*. Edinburgh and London: Blackwood, 1905.

Honan, Park. *Browning's Characters: A Study in Poetic Technique*. New Haven, Conn.: Yale University Press, 1961.

Irvine, William, and Park Honan. *The Book, the Ring, and the Poet: A Biography of Robert Browning*. New York: McGraw-Hill, 1974.

James, Henry. "The Novel in 'The Ring and the Book.' " *Notes on Novelists*, pp. 385-411. New York: Scribner, 1914.

Johnson, E. D. H. *The Alien Vision of Victorian Poetry: Sources of the Poetic Imagination in Tennyson, Browning, and Arnold*. Princeton, N. J.: Princeton University Press, 1952.

———. "Robert Browning's Pluralistic Universe." *University of Toronto Quarterly*, 31 (1961), 20-41.

Korg, Jacob. "The Music of Lost Dynasties: Browning, Pound and History." *ELH*, 39 (1972), 420-40.

Langbaum, Robert. "Browning and the Question of Myth." *PMLA*, 81 (1966), 575-84).

———. *The Poetry of Experience: The Dramatic Monologue in Modern Literary Tradition*. 1957 (reprinted in New York: Norton, 1963).

Lubbock, Percy. "Robert Browning." *Quarterly Review*, 217 (1912) 437-57.

Martin, Loy D. "Browning: The Activation of Influence." *Victorian Newsletter* (53) (spring 1978), pp. 4-9.

Mason, Michael. "The Importance of *Sordello*." *The Major Victorian Poets: Reconsiderations*, ed. Isobel Armstrong, pp. 125-51. London: Routledge and Kegan Paul, 1969.

Maynard, John. *Browning's Youth*. Cambridge, Mass., and London: Harvard University Press, 1977.

Miller, Betty. *Robert Browning: A Portrait*. New York: Scribner, 1952.

Miller, J. Hillis. *The Disappearance of God: Five Nineteenth-Century Writers*. Cambridge, Mass.: Harvard University Press, 1963.

Munich, Adrienne. "Emblems of Temporality in Browning's 'Cleon.' " *Browning Institute Studies*, 6 (1978), 117-36.

Orr, Alexandra (Mrs. Sutherland). *A Handbook to the Works of Robert Browning*, 6th ed. 1892 (reprinted in London: Bell, 1937).

———. *Life and Letters of Robert Browning*, 2 vols. Boston and New York: Houghton Mifflin, 1891.

———. "The Religious Opinions of Robert Browning." *Contemporary Review*, 60 (1891), 876-91.

Peckham, Morse. "Historiography and *The Ring and the Book*." *Victorian Poetry*, 6 (1968), 243-57.

———. *Victorian Revolutionaries: Speculations on Some Heroes of a Culture Crisis*. New York: Braziller, 1970.

Pottle, Frederick A. *Shelley and Browning: A Myth and Some Facts*. Chicago: Pembroke Press, 1923.

Preyer, Robert. "Two Styles in the Verse of Robert Browning." *ELH*, 32 (1965), 62-84.

Priestley, F. E. L. "The Ironic Pattern of Browning's *Paracelsus*." *University of Toronto Quarterly*, 34 (1964), 68-81.

Raymond, W. O. *The Infinite Moment and Other Essays in Robert Browning*, 2nd ed. Toronto: University of Toronto Press, 1965.

Ridenour, George M. "Browning's Music Poems: Fancy and Fact." *PMLA*, 78 (1963), 369-77.

Robert Browning, ed. Isobel Armstrong. Athens, Ohio: Ohio University Press, 1975.

Ryals, Clyde de L. *Browning's Later Poetry 1871-1889*. Ithaca, N.Y., and London: Cornell University Press, 1975.

Santayana, George. "The Poetry of Barbarism." *Interpretations of Poetry and Religion*, pp. 166-216. New York: Scribner, 1905.

Shaffer, Elinor. "Browning's St. John: The Casuistry of the Higher Criticism." *Victorian Studies*, 16 (1972), 205-21.

Shaw, W. David. *The Dialectical Temper: The Rhetorical Art of Robert Browning*. Ithaca, N.Y.: Cornell University Press, 1968.

Smith, C. Willard. *Browning's Star-Imagery: The Study of a Detail in Poetic Design*. Princeton, N.J.: Princeton University Press, 1941.

Swinburne, Algernon Charles. "George Chapman." *The Complete Works of Algernon Charles Swinburne*, ed. Edmund Gosse and Thomas James Wise, volume XII, pp. 143-55. London: Heinemann, 1925-1927.

Yetman, Michael G. "Exorcising Shelley Out of Browning: *Sordello* and the Problem of Poetic Identity." *Victorian Poetry*, 13 (1975), 79-98.

INDEX

INDEX

Discussions of Browning's poems and prose writings are indexed by title, references to his letters by correspondent. The notes are indexed only selectively.

"Old Pictures in Florence," 158, 225
"One Word More," 188, 219
Optimism, 64-65, 73, 76, 187, 239n22. *See also* Innocence
Orel, Harold, 132-33
Origination, 4, 31-32, 57, 60, 96-101, 108, 117-19, 126-27, 128-30, 134, 136-37, 170-71, 202. *See also* Discontinuity; Election; Protest
Orr, Alexandra, 186, 225, 228, 229, 234, 237, 238, 240
Ottima, in *Pippa Passes*, 122, 125, 127, 130-31

Palma, in *Sordello*, 90, 108, 112, 113
Paracelsus, 27-28, 36, 48, 51, 53-83, 84-85, 87, 88, 89, 90, 92, 93, 94, 99, 103, 109, 118, 129, 142, 150, 151, 183, 218, 228-30
Paracelsus, in *Paracelsus*, 53-83, 84, 87, 89, 92, 94, 124, 134, 151, 160, 208, 216, 218
Parleyings with Certain People of Importance in Their Day: "Charles Avison," 12; "Gerard de Lairesse," 12, 158; "Bernard de Mandeville," 234; mentioned, 232n23
Pater, Walter, 240
Pathetic fallacy, 79, 229-30
Paul, the apostle, 155-56, 211, 214, 215, 216
Pauline, 9, 12, 27, 30-52, 53, 54, 55, 58, 59, 61, 62, 65, 66, 67, 69, 72, 89, 90, 92, 94, 100, 109, 111, 118, 121, 130, 150, 152-53, 160, 209, 218, 225-28, 230, 234, 238
Pauline, in *Pauline*, 41, 42, 46, 47, 49, 50
Peckham, Morse, 227, 231, 237, 238, 240
Perception, 94-95, 97. *See also* Interpretation
Perseus, 45, 234-35
"Pheidippides," 12
Phidias, 210
"Pictor Ignotus," 165-71, 195-96
"A Pillar at Sebzevar," 182
Pippa, in *Pippa Passes*, 122-31, 134, 143, 147, 196, 234
Pippa Passes, 46, 122-31, 133, 134, 145, 196, 228, 234
Plot, 5, 62-67, 120-26, 131, 142, 233. *See also* Digression; Narrative
Pluralism, 157
Politics, 14, 28, 99, 102, 110, 127, 132, 137, 144, 232, 235, 237

Polyxena, in *King Victor and King Charles*, 144, 146-47
Pope, Alexander, 224
"Popularity," 11, 15, 149, 171
Possession, 137-38, 184, 218
Possibility, 5, 10, 118, 158, 217, 218-19
Pottle, Frederick, 226, 230
Pound, Ezra, 4, 240
Presence, 4-5, 21, 33, 45-46, 65-67, 123-25, 128-29, 133-34, 141-42, 164, 186. *See also* God; Simultaneity; Space and time
Prince Hohenstiel-Schwangau, 154
Priority. *See* Autonomy
"Prologue" to *Asolando*, 13, 168, 174
Prophecy, 170, 198-200, 224, 236
Prosody, 3, 7, 75, 102, 103, 190, 191-92, 216-17, 224, 238
"Prospice," 228
Protest, 78-79, 81, 97-101. *See also* Discontinuity; Origination
Psychology and temporality linked, 96-97, 132-33, 190, 198
Punctuation, 24, 86-87, 97, 100, 105, 110, 225
Puns, 22, 55, 78, 91, 163, 205. *See also* Ambiguity
Pym, in *Strafford*, 133, 136

"Rabbi Ben Ezra," 161, 225
Rafael, 197, 201
Raymond, W. O., 223-24
Realism, 201, 203
Red Cotton Night-Cap Country, 127, 150, 237
Relativism, 157
Religion. *See* Faith
Renaissance, 110-11, 165, 232
Renan, Ernest, 185-87
Repetition, 22, 42-43, 44, 46, 48, 69, 85, 105, 115, 124, 162-64, 180, 194-95, 199-200, 202-3, 215
Representation, 8-9, 27, 84-85, 95, 103, 116, 128-31, 137, 139-40, 143-47, 180-81, 182-83, 187-88, 201-5, 234-35, 238, 240, 241n19, 241-42. *See also* Figuration; Form and content; Memory; Rhetoric
The Return of the Druses, 129, 132, 145, 147, 233
Revision. *See* Browning, Robert: revisions of his works
Rhetoric, 7, 62, 101-3, 129-30, 178, 194-95, 212, 216-17, 239n23. *See also* Figura-

"'Transcendentalism: A Poem in Twelve Books,'" 15, 187, 188-89
Triumph, 5, 24, 25, 44-45, 66, 67, 76, 112, 192. *See also* Autonomy
The Two Poets of Croisic, 161, 239n14

Vane, in *Strafford*, 134-35
Vasari, Giorgio, 194, 237
Verb tenses, 23, 33, 165, 167, 173, 186, 217
Victor, in *King Victor and King Charles*, 144-47, 151, 152
Victorian literary criticism, 224. *See also* Browning, Robert: relation to public
Victorian religious crisis, 5-6, 8, 185-87. *See also* Browning, Robert: Christianity; Faith
Virgil, 110

Wedgwood, Julia, 184, 239n27
Weiskel, Thomas, 224
Whitman, Walt, 15, 231
"Women and Roses," 162
Wonder, 15, 20, 27, 43, 69-70, 188, 204-5
Wordsworth, William: Browning's attitudes toward, 13-14, 175; "Intimations Ode," 13; *The Prelude*, 14-15; "Tintern Abbey," 46, 226-27
"The Worst of It," 149

Yeats, W. B., 3, 187, 188

Zeus, 210, 212, 213, 214, 217. *See also* Jupiter
Zoroaster, 62, 63, 229